the successful gardener guide

North Carolina

Rhododendron
Garden

the successful gardener guide

North Carolina

Leah Chester-Davis and Toby Bost

John F. Blair, Publisher  Winston-Salem, North Carolina

1406 Plaza Drive
Winston-Salem, North Carolina 27103
www.blairpub.com

Manufactured in South Korea

Cover Image - *Iris prismatica*, by Robert E. Lyons

pages ii - iii   Hostas and caladiums, by Connie Little
page v   Bengal tiger canna, by Robert E. Lyons
page vi   Hybrid rhododendron, by Robert E. Lyons
page viii   Lenten rose, by Robert E. Lyons
page x   Butterfly, by Robert E. Lyons
page xiv   Plum, by Michael Parker
page 1   Crape myrtle, by Robert E. Lyons
page 2   Cutting garden, by Toby Bost
page 6   Tulips, by Dennis J. Werner
page 67, top   Woody plants, by Robert E. Lyons
page 67, bottom   Herbaceous plants, by Robert E. Lyons
page 68   Weeping blue atlas cedar, by Robert E. Lyons
page 117   Seasonal gardening, by Robert E. Lyons
page 118   Spring water feature, by Robert E. Lyons
page 143   Green roof with sedum, by Robert E. Lyons
page 144   Tree sanctuary, courtesy J. C. Raulston Arboretum
page 169   Vegetables protected by deer-proof enclosure, by Toby Bost
page 170   Creeping raspberry serving as a groundcover accent, by Connie Little
page 191   Oakleaf hydrangea, by Robert E. Lyons
page 192   Invincibelle Spirit® hydrangea, by Thomas G. Ranney

Authors' caution: It is a violation of state and federal laws to use any pesticide in a manner inconsistent with the label. Products mentioned in this book are used for the sole purpose of education and do not imply an endorsement.

Library of Congress Cataloging-in-Publication Data

The Successful Gardener guide / edited by Leah Chester-Davis and Toby Bost.
p. cm.
Successful Gardener guide
Includes index.
Summary: A compilation of material from 10 years of research for the North Carolina Cooperative Extension's Successful Gardener (registered trademark) newsletter.
ISBN 978-0-89587-515-0 (alk. paper)—ISBN 978-0-89587-516-7 (ebook) 1. Landscape plants—North Carolina. 2. Landscape gardening—North Carolina. 3. Gardening—North Carolina. I. Chester-Davis, Leah. II. Bost, Toby. III. North Carolina Cooperative Extension Service. IV. Title: Successful Gardener guide.
SB407.S83 2011
635.09756—dc22

2010043096

Design by Debra Long Hampton

Dedication

To Jeff Davis, who always listens and keeps me laughing. And to Virgil and Shirley Chester, who grew both kids and gardens on our Arkansas family farm.

Leah Chester-Davis

To my loving wife, Becky, for always being there. You are a true writer's angel.

Toby Bost

Contents

Foreword

By Bryce Lane, host of
In the Garden *on UNC-TV and member*
of the Department of Horticultural Science
faculty at North Carolina State University

Being an avid home gardener, I am always looking for reliable gardening information. I am also a "plant geek" who has created a plant collector's garden of sorts. My plants don't have to be new and improved, just worthy of my limited space. I have journeyed through the art and science of gardening on the same site for 27 years and still seek out the latest and greatest tips. As a college teacher and as host of *In the Garden*, I am also committed to sharing the best, most up-to-date gardening information I can with my students and viewers. When it comes to gardening, trial-and-error is still my friend, and so are the expert North Carolina Cooperative Extension horticulture agents from across the state, who provide the latest, most accurate information to North Carolina gardeners.

I always look forward to another edition of the *Extension's Successful Gardener®* newsletter, a great, timely publication that provides me with tips, plant suggestions, and seasonal information. I really appreciate the efforts of our Cooperative Extension agents as they put together an excellent resource. Imagine my excitement when I found out that a book—*The Successful Gardener Guide*—would feature the best of the newsletter. If you're like me, you probably haven't saved all the newsletters in a notebook but wished you had. Now, readers have at their fingertips a book that highlights the very best information provided to North Carolina gardeners.

The book is organized in a way that is easy to follow and enjoy. The extensive "Gardening Features" and "70 Top Plant Choices" chapters will help gardeners plan for the best possible home landscapes, whether they are starting new garden areas or renovating existing spaces. All too often, gardeners worry about what they should be doing at specific times of the year and in certain regions of North Carolina. Be sure to check out the "Seasonal Gardening Calendar" chapter to schedule gardening activities. The "Enviro-Tips" chapter features water-wise gardening, weed control, rain gardens, and other valuable information and technologies to help readers garden in a sustainable, environmentally friendly way. If you're like me, it's always helpful to read about challenges other gardeners have with insects, diseases, weeds, and other landscape problems. The "Q&A" chapter will help solve many such garden problems. Round it out with a chapter about "Tried-and-True and Hot New Plants for Carolina Gardens" and you have a much-needed resource of gardening information!

Many thanks to all our hardworking North Carolina Cooperative Extension agents for tirelessly bringing the latest research-based horticultural information to so many gardeners in the Southeast. Thanks also to Toby Bost and Leah Chester-Davis for having the vision and energy to put a book like this together. I appreciate their efforts and wholeheartedly recommend making *The Successful Gardener Guide* a part of your gardening library!

Preface

By Toby Bost

Gardening is America's top hobby, and no wonder. It beautifies homes and communities, relieves stress, offers enjoyment, improves the environment, and adds economic value to homes and neighborhoods. Through the years as a horticultural agent with North Carolina Cooperative Extension, I've met and worked with some of the state's finest gardeners, as well as novices who wanted to know more. I've also met many newcomers to our great state who found that they needed to learn about cultural practices and plants best suited to our environment. The *Extension's Successful Gardener®* newsletter was born out of the need to help steer North Carolinians in the right direction in gardening decisions. This book, *The Successful Gardener Guide*, brings together a selection of noteworthy articles from 10 years of the newsletter. While the information throughout is research based and timeless, we made sure to select plants that are excellent choices for today's gardeners. I believe both well-seasoned gardeners and newcomers will find sage advice from outstanding gardening professionals.

My coeditor, Leah Chester-Davis, a marketing communications specialist with North Carolina State University and North Carolina Cooperative Extension, is the creator and founding editor of the *Extension's Successful Gardener®* newsletter and served for 10 years as team leader of the statewide horticultural program of the same name. She will be the first to tell you that North Carolina Cooperative Extension has an amazing cadre of knowledgeable horticultural agents based in counties across the state, many of whom have a strong volunteer corps known as "Extension's Master Gardeners."

Extension's Successful Gardener® was started to help address the demand for sound, research-based horticultural information across the state. Now, *The Successful Gardener Guide* is more than a gardening book replete with beautiful plant pictures and gardening vignettes. It includes what people most want to know from county Cooperative Extension Centers throughout the state.

The "Gardening Features" chapter addresses a plethora of horticultural topics apropos to landscape gardening in all hardiness zones of the Carolinas. Want to learn more about the planting and care of a fescue lawn? Need money-saving tips when selecting perennial flowers or planting a vegetable garden? Want to know how to manage fruit trees after establishing a backyard orchard? These and other topics are covered by Cooperative Extension agents as they address common gardening concerns and recommend ecologically sound principles for pest and garden management.

What gardening book would be complete without coverage of the special plants native to or generally well suited to its area's climatic conditions? Found in this book's second chapter are 70 species of amazing plants, many gleaned from trials in the renowned J. C. Raulston Arboretum at North Carolina State University. The plant descriptions offer suggestions on how to use each plant most effectively in the landscape. They also include advice on the best cultivars available in the market. These selections and many more wonderful taxa can be observed on a plant excursion to the award-winning public garden in Raleigh.

Gardening in the South can be challenging due to weather extremes, humidity, and poorly drained, acidic soils. The "Seasonal Gardening Calendar" chapter will prove useful in properly caring for plants. Readers will find that some gardening practices are unique to particular geographic regions of North Carolina. The chapter includes tips for the mountains, Piedmont, and coast. While one gardener "limes the soil," another incorporates sulfur to increase the acidity for better flower color or food production.

More than ever, people are conscious about where their dollars go. *The Successful Gardener Guide* offers practical ways to manage landscape investment while minimizing carbon footprint. The "Enviro-Tips" chapter will prove invaluable in understanding the principles of sustainability as they relate to maintaining a landscape investment.

Cooperative Extension agents have a rich history of assisting the gardening public and farmers alike with myriad pest problems and plant-growing concerns. The answers to gardeners' most perplexing questions may be only a telephone call away. Some of the most frequently asked questions are included in the "Q&A" chapter. Plant problem diagnostics is a fee-based service handled by agents. Telephone numbers for the 101 North Carolina Cooperative Extension Centers are listed in the appendix.

The nursery industry brings gardeners new introductions on a regular basis. Some of the best and most exciting varieties offered across the state are listed in the "Tried-and-True and Hot New Plants for Carolina Gardens" chapter. Maybe you have just the right spot for something new in your landscape.

Finally, it has been said that gardening has the ability to transform not only space but culture as well. Gardeners are an amazingly resourceful lot, and much of what they know is shared in friendly over-the-fence conversations with their neighbors. As free advice goes, it can be useful, though often not as scientific as it should be with regard to maintaining the significant investments people have in their personal gardens. Readers can depend on the information in *The Successful Gardener Guide* to be scientifically accurate and written for gardens in their region. Clearly, it isn't necessary to be a Master Gardener to benefit from the information that thousands of North Carolina residents have come to depend on from their Cooperative Extension agents.

Acknowledgments

By Leah Chester-Davis

When I had the opportunity to start the *Extension's Successful Gardener®* newsletter more than 10 years ago, a core group of North Carolina Cooperative Extension horticulture agents rallied to help bring the project to fruition and to grow it through the years. The effort expanded to Successful Gardener® Learning Centers at home-and-garden shows across the state, monthly gardening e-tips, a website, and numerous workshops and other activities. The *Extension's Successful Gardener®* newsletter and program have won numerous awards through the years. I am particularly proud of a Garden Writers Association award, which reflects the outstanding work of our talented team.

Early on, a few Cooperative Extension agents, county directors, and district directors made all the difference in the world. Stephen Greer, then with Gaston County and now with Forsyth, and John MacNair of Mecklenburg County worked with me to raise funds from sponsors, write grant proposals, recruit our team of horticulturists, and pull together the early issues. Karen Neill of Guilford County served as assistant editor for nearly seven years. Toby Bost, coeditor of this book, then served as assistant editor for about a year until his retirement. Though both Karen and Toby had the title of assistant editor, they indeed were the gardening experts on the editorial staff. I thank Toby in particular for helping me compile and expand the best of the newsletter into this book. Emily Revels of Mecklenburg County was critical to the project's success, as were the North Carolina Cooperative Extension staff members in Mecklenburg and their interim county director, Marilyn Gore, when I started the newsletter. I thank county Cooperative Extension directors Martha Burris, Cheryl Lloyd, and Debbie Bost, as well as all the county directors who have agents represented in this book. Special thanks go to district director Deborah Crandall for her strong endorsement and support of this effort.

The staff at the J. C. Raulston Arboretum (JCRA) and the faculty of the North Carolina State University Horticultural Science Department were extremely helpful. Robert E. Lyons, as director of JCRA, reviewed numerous plant features and provided lovely photography for nearly 10 years, which made my role as editor much easier and made the newsletter both educational and beautiful. I owe thanks as well to Dennis J. Werner, who provided assistance with articles and photography when he became director of JCRA. Both Bob and Denny provided valuable assistance with this book. My thanks also go to Christopher Glenn with JCRA, Bryce Lane of the North Carolina State Horticultural Science Department, and Thomas G. Ranney at the Mountain Horticultural Crops Research and Extension Center.

Of course, none of this would have happened without the core group of knowledgeable horticulture agents, who worked together to deliver an award-winning newsletter chock-full of sound advice. Along with Master Gardeners, the agents also staff Successful Gardener Learning Centers at home-and-garden shows across the

state. Anyone who wants to learn more about gardening can't have a better resource than these experts.

My appreciation goes to the core team and other contributors: Amy-Lynn Albertson, Davidson County; Nancy Anderson and Shauna Haslem, Cumberland County; Master Gardener Ann Armstrong, Scott Ewers, Aaron Lancaster, John MacNair, Jim Monroe, and Emily Revels, Mecklenburg County; Shawn Banks and Cathy Kloetzli, Johnston County; David Barkley, Brunswick County; Darrell Blackwelder, Rowan County; Mark Blevins, Peggy Drechsler, Ben Dungan, and Julie Flowers, Gaston County; Linda Blue, Buncombe County; Toby Bost and Craig Mauney, Forsyth County; Lucy Bradley, Art Bruneau, Bill Cline, Becky Kirkland, Adonna Mann, Jonathan Nyberg, Michael Parker, and Sheri Thomas, North Carolina State University; Donald Breedlove, Iredell County; Allen Caldwell, Caldwell County; Tim Clune and Crystal Paul, Currituck County; Al Cooke, Chatham County; Mark Danieley, Mary Helen Ferguson, and Kimberly Johnson, Randolph County; Viv Finklestein, JCRA volunteer; Terry Garwood, Surry County; Charlotte Glen, Pender and New Hanover counties; David Goforth, Cabarrus County; Stephen Greer, Forsyth and Gaston counties; Kelly Groves, Franklin and Catawba counties; Royce Hardin, Orange County; Craven Hudson and Taylor Williams, Moore County; Sarah Lane Ivy, Lee County; Cyndi Lauderdale, Wilson County; Danny Lauderdale, Pitt County; James Lee, Paul McKenzie, and Michelle Wallace, Durham County; Heather Lifsey, Northampton County; Carl Matyac, Orange and Wake counties; Jan McGuinn, Rutherford County; Fred Miller, Catawba County; Charles Mitchell, Franklin County; David Nash, New Hanover County; Karen Neill, Guilford County; Master Gardener Carol Norden and Mitch Woodward, Wake County; Richard T. Olsen, North Carolina State University and the National Arboretum; Jeff Rieves and Willie Earl Wilson, Union County; Lenny Rogers, Alexander County; Miranda Shearer and Kevin Starr, Lincoln County; Daniel Shires, Cleveland County; Bill Skelton, Haywood and Henderson counties; Will Strader, Caswell, Rockingham, and Franklin counties; Donna Teasley, Burke County; Diane Turner, Henderson County; John Vining, Polk County; and Mike Wilder, Nash County.

My thanks also go to the North Carolina Cooperative Extension administration, Jon Ort and Joe Zublena in particular.

Special thanks go to our funding sponsors through the years: the North Carolina Association of Nurserymen; the North Carolina Division of Forest Resources and the United States Forest Service; Duke Energy; WTVI in Charlotte; North Carolina State University Extension; Mecklenburg County Park and Recreation; Greensboro Parks and Recreation; North Carolina Green Industry Council; Ironite; Wyatt-Quarles; Black Kow; CORTAID; and the North Carolina Agricultural Foundation, Inc.

I also offer special thanks to the numerous garden centers, nurseries, lawn maintenance companies, and public gardens that shared the newsletter with their customers and visitors. Among the numerous home-and-garden shows across the state, I'd particularly like to thank Robert, Joan, and David Zimmerman of Southern Shows and their outstanding garden-show staff, particularly Debbie Ball.

I appreciate the support of the North Carolina State University College of Agriculture and Life Sciences, Department of Communication Services. In particular, I thank Mike Gray, Rhonda Green, Charlotte Simpson, Barbara Scott, Erin McCrary, and Mark Dearmon. Shane Sellers and Martin Rose of ABZ Design always proved helpful. And student intern Colleen McEnaney provided valuable assistance as this book was being pulled together.

At John F. Blair, Publisher, my thanks go to Carolyn Sakowski, Steve Kirk, and Debbie Hampton in particular.

I've learned a tremendous amount from North Carolina Cooperative Extension horticultural agents through the years. This book represents just the tip of the iceberg in terms of all the knowledge they have to share. Happy Successful Gardening!

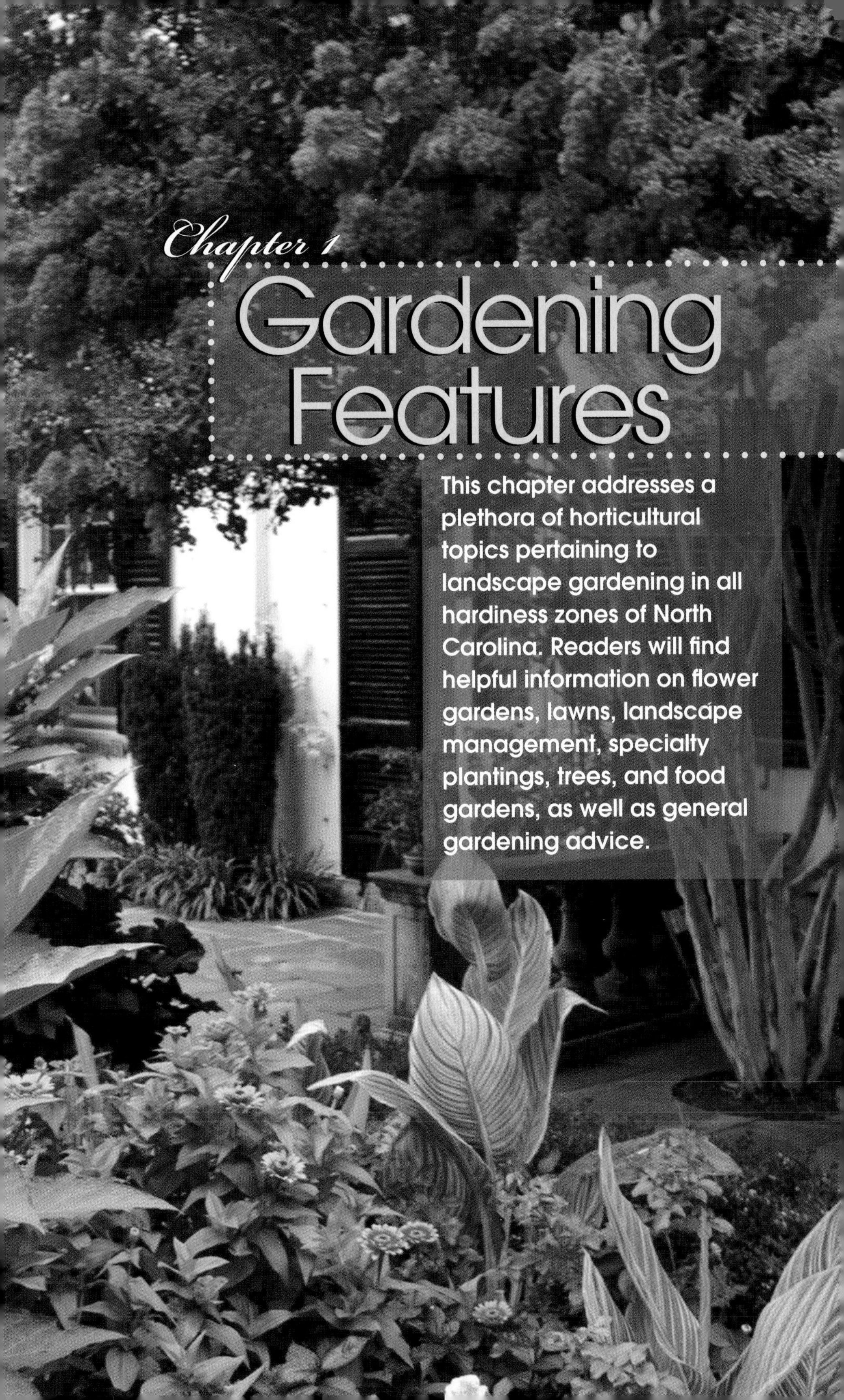

Chapter 1

Gardening Features

This chapter addresses a plethora of horticultural topics pertaining to landscape gardening in all hardiness zones of North Carolina. Readers will find helpful information on flower gardens, lawns, landscape management, specialty plantings, trees, and food gardens, as well as general gardening advice.

OUTER BANKS

Gardentalk:

"Any garden demands as much of its maker as he has to give. But I do not need to tell you, if you are a gardener, that no other undertaking will give as great a return for the amount of effort you put into it."

Elizabeth Lawrence

Flower Gardens

Conserve Water with Drought-Tolerant Annuals

By Karen Neill, Guilford County

Warm-weather annuals are durable plants that continue to bloom for months in heat that drives most people indoors. A few perform well even in dry conditions. These are the annuals to consider if you wish to conserve water or have little time for watering. Besides selecting drought-tolerant plants, consider the soil. Conditioning the soil with organic matter helps to retain moisture. All of the following drought-tolerant annuals will require water initially to establish good root systems. Once established, however, they require little watering. All perform best in full sun.

- *Gomphrena globosa*, globe amaranth, is available in purple, white, or red. This heat- and drought-tolerant selection is ideal for Southern gardens. *G. globosa* has ½-inch cloverlike flowers that bloom from June through September. The plant matures at a height of 18 inches to three feet, with a two-foot spread. The globe amaranth is excellent for mid-border or mass planting in a bed. Enjoy the blooms as fresh-cut or dried flowers.

- *Portulaca grandiflora*, rose moss, is a low-growing, drought-tolerant annual often called moss rose. Its flowers range from white, pink, and yellow to red and purple and are found on the terminals. These plants, which bloom all summer, are suitable for dry banks, rock gardens, and containers.

- A third heat-tolerant annual to consider is *Zinnia angustifolia*, narrow-leaf zinnia. This plant blooms consistently through the heat of summer and has a yellow-orange daisylike flower with a similar-colored center. The narrow-leaf zinnia is ideal for a bed or mass planting because it spreads to fill in the growing space quite well. The plant reaches a height of 18 to 36 inches, with an 18-inch spread.

Drought-tolerant plants
Robert E. Lyons

- *Tithonia rotundifolia*, Mexican sunflower, has large daisylike flowers resembling zinnias. The flowers are up to three inches across. Standing four to five feet in height, this makes a nice background plant. Native to Mexico and Central America, it is one of the most heat-resistant flowers.

- *Gaillardia pulchella* is the annual gaillardia that's known for its low-growing, warm-colored flowers that appear fringed. Also known as Indian blanket, this annual bears flowers with yellow or yellow-and-red centers and petals that are solid yellow, solid red, or red at the base and yellow at the tip.

- *Verbena × hybrida*, clump verbena, is a superb groundcover and a good choice in baskets or beds. It has a multistemmed, weeping growth habit with red, pink, or white flowers. It can be cut back to stimulate additional growth if it becomes too long or leggy. It is more heat tolerant and has fewer problems than many of the verbena hybrids.

- *Melampodium paludosum* has an abundance of small, yellow daisylike flowers that it retains throughout the summer and well into fall.

- Let's not forget dusty miller, *Senecio cineraria*, an attractive foliage plant that works well in the foreground. Its gray foliage makes it a good choice for bringing other plants together.

- A plant that already has been adopted because of its performance under heat and drought conditions is *Catharanthus roseus*, the Madagascar periwinkle or annual vinca. The newer cultivars of the annual vinca have become quite popular, since they bloom well under the heat and drought conditions of the South. These vincas come in a variety of colors, including pinks, purples, and white.

Plant these annuals and enjoy their beauty late in summer, when the heat and drought are taking a toll on other plants. For more plant ideas, visit www.ces.ncsu.edu/depts/hort/consumer/factsheets/annuals/annual_index.htm.

Container gardening
Robert E. Lyons

Design a Container Garden

By Amy-Lynn Albertson, Davidson County

Limited space and time need not keep you from enjoying a garden. Container gardening is an easy way to have a garden on a smaller scale. These gardens can make a big color statement in a small place.

The container you select impacts your plant selection. Anything from barrels and wooden boxes to beautiful Mexican or North Carolina pottery can be used for a container. The most important thing to look for in your container is a drainage hole. If it does not have a drainage hole, drill one or place another container with a drainage hole inside the decorative container that doesn't have one. A drainage hole gives excess water somewhere to go, allows for air movement in the root system, and helps ensure success.

When choosing the soil, make sure the mixture allows for good drainage. For the best results, choose a quality potting soil, preferably one designed for container use. A good container mix drains well and quickly, holds air and water, and is light enough for roots to penetrate. Annual or perennial, the plants in container gardens have the same needs: food, water, and a little light housekeeping. Because a planter is limited in space and soil, you must water and feed frequently. By mixing a slow-release fertilizer in with your potting mix, you will provide your plants with enough feed for the season. If growing sun-loving plants in pots, water them every day. Never let the container become totally dry. Light housekeeping involves pulling out the odd weed and deadheading to remove faded blooms as they die.

As in cut-flower arranging, container gardens have design principles to follow. But these are just guidelines, not unbreakable rules.

Plant Selection

When choosing for a container, it's important to select plants that have the same or similar requirements when it comes to water, sun, and temperature. Plant form is another important principle to keep in mind. It's good to pair or balance one type of plant with another. A tall species like dracaena spike, phormium, agastache, or any ornamental grass adds height to your container. A mounded species like geranium, begonia, or helichrysum adds mass to the design. Low-growing plants like calibrachoa, wave petunia, alyssum, bacopa, or bidens add depth and soften the edges of a container. Texture is another principle that has an effect on design. Balance coarse-textured foliage like coleus with light, fine textures such as asparagus fern.

A Focal Point with Balance

Balance is another important principle in container gardening. Symmetrical balance is formal and geometric. To create a symmetrically balanced design, use equal, almost identical elements on each side of a central axis with the highest point over the center of the container. Asymmetrical balance is informal, relaxing, and somewhat abstract. In an asymmetrical design, the two sides of the central axis should not be mirror images but should have the same visual weight.

Focus is the point or area the eye is drawn to first. Large-leafed or coarse-textured plants or vibrantly colored flowers or foliage serve as focal points for a container garden. Place the focal plant below the tallest point in the container garden to achieve balance. Develop focus by making it appear as though all the plant material is radiating out from the center of the container garden like fronds on a fern.

Keeping the size and quantity of the plants in proportion to the pot is another design principle. The height of the tallest plant should not exceed one to two times the height of a tall container or the width of a low bowl. Rhythm gives a design flow and harmony. Use repetition and gradation of plant form, texture, and color to develop rhythm in your design.

The Color Punch

Color is one of the most important aspects of design. Pastel tints set a mood of tranquility. They look best when viewed up close and can appear washed out in bright midday sun. Bright colors invigorate and energize a container garden. They hold up well to brilliant sunshine and attract the eye, even from a distance. Colors that are opposite one another on the wheel—yellow and violet, orange and blue, green and red—are considered complementary colors. Their high contrast brings energy and vitality to the container garden. Harmonious colors are next to each other on the wheel—blue and violet, orange and red, orange and yellow. These combinations are gentler on the eye than complementary colors. A harmonious color scheme unifies a design while allowing enough range of color to not become monotonous. In a monochromatic container garden, you can create interest by using plants with different sizes and shapes of flowers of the same color. You might also highlight foliage with interesting textures and colors.

Fall for Spring Bulbs

By Toby Bost, Forsyth County

Fall is the best time to plant bulbs to create a kaleidoscope of color next spring. Thousands of tulips and daffodils find their way into Tar Heel gardens each year. Bulbs are planted in the fall in order to develop root systems and to satisfy the cold requirement necessary for the robust, colorful flower buds. It is best to wait until the ground has cooled to below 60° F before planting. For most of North Carolina, that is October or November.

Soil Preparation

Good soil drainage is essential for spring-flowering bulbs. Poorly aerated soil is probably the biggest factor in bulbs that fail to naturalize and return year after year. If the soil is mostly clay, mix in an organic amendment such as compost or aged pine bark, 25 percent or more by volume. Or plant in raised beds that are well prepared. If the soil is sandy, add an organic amendment to increase water- and nutrient-holding capacity.

Crocus
Dennis J. Werner

Soil pH is another critical issue for the longevity of bulb plantings. The pH of the planting area should be in the 6 to 7 range. Frequently, both limestone and phosphorus fertilizer are deficient in new planting beds. One of the myths about bulb planting is that bonemeal gives better results. Studies at North Carolina State University indicate that commercial bulb fertilizer is the preferred method of supplying nutrients. If you need assistance in this area, contact your county Cooperative Extension Center for a soil test kit.

Where to Plant

Use spring-flowering bulbs in borders with annuals or perennials, groundcovers, rock gardens, and wooded areas. They do best in areas that receive light shade during midday, especially in hotter zone 8 gardens. Some bulb types such as crocus, muscari, and allium can be interplanted in the same area based on time of flowering and plant heights.

In established bulb beds, summer is a good time to divide old plantings to ensure continuous flowering and bulb health. Before replanting, excavate new beds to as much as a one-foot depth. This improves aeration and drainage for the roots.

Space and Plant Bulbs According to Size

Plant bulbs to the proper depth. Measure from the base of the bulb to soil level.

- Plant small-sized bulbs (one inch in height) three to five inches deep. Space small bulbs (crocus and snowdrop) one to two inches apart.

- Plant large-sized bulbs (two or more inches in height) five to eight inches deep. Space large bulbs (tulips and daffodils) three to six inches apart.

These planting depths will help protect the bulbs against frost, animals, and physical damage due to hoeing or other gardening chores. Be certain to thoroughly loosen the soil under the bulbs.

Plant dozens of bulbs in an area to create a more effective flower display. After covering the bulbs with soil, water thoroughly. Cover beds with two to three inches of mulch. Most bulbs are sensitive to preemergent herbicides, so restrict weed control to hand-weeding, mulch, and grass weed killers. If fall conditions are dry, water as needed.

Bulb Fertilization

Fertilization improves bulb performance. In addition, it encourages bulbs to naturalize. Two fertilizing methods are available for spring-flowering bulbs. The first system calls for a single fall application at planting, using a slow-release bulb fertilizer. The fertilizer should be incorporated into the rooting area. The second system uses 10-10-10 in the fall, followed by a repeat application of the same fertilizer as soon as new shoots break through the ground in late winter.

Bulb Pests

When attempting to grow bulbs, gardeners complain most about the wildlife they encounter. Though squirrels will leave poisonous daffodil bulbs alone, they may nibble a tulip flower. The real menace for lily growers is the presence of pine mice, also known as voles. Fortunately, there are legal ways to control voles, including snaptraps and rodenticides. For the average homeowner in suburbia, a good cat will go a long way, as will amending the soil with gravel or Voleblock™.

Not Just for Spring Anymore

Bulbs are not just for spring flowers. In the Carolinas, bulbs encompassing a mix of species can bloom throughout the year.

Indulge yourself with the wonderful woodland varieties like magic lilies, autumn crocus, and rain lilies. For vertical accents, scatter a few gladiolus and crocosmia bulbs in a sunny perennial border. Oriental lilies produce large, exquisite, picture-perfect blooms for cutting, while their smaller Asiatic cousins are made for color beds.

Inspiration from the Roadsides

By Mike Wilder, Nash County

Wildflowers create dazzling bursts of color along our highways, add pleasure to our travels, make us smile, and help relieve the worries of highway driving. The North Carolina Department of Transportation (DOT) Wildflower Program began small in 1985. Today, more than 3,000 acres of wildflower beds across the state are planted and maintained by the DOT's roadside environmental personnel.

Mixed species of annuals and perennials are planted to achieve several flowerings each growing season. Some of the more popular mixes include *Papaver rhoeas*, red

Wildflowers
Robert E. Lyons

corn poppy; *Chrysanthemum leucanthemum*, oxeye daisy; *Hesperis matronalis*, dame's rocket; and *Coreopsis lanceolata*, lanceleaf coreopsis. Native wildflowers such as *Bidens aristosa*, bur marigold; *Helianthus angustifolius*, narrow-leaf or swamp sunflower; and *H. annuus*, common sunflower, are planted for their beauty and to preserve the diversity of natural vegetation.

To bring the beauty of these roadside gardens to your own landscape, the DOT recommends the following tips.

- Select a well-drained, visible, sunny site.
- Take a soil sample to determine plant nutrient requirements.
- Remove unwanted weeds with a nonselective herbicide containing glyphosate.
- Add plant nutrients and lime according to soil test results. General recommendations require three to five pounds of 10-10-10 fertilizer and 25 to 70 pounds of lime per 1,000 square feet.
- Plow or rototill the site to a depth of three to five inches. Incorporate well-composted organic matter to improve soil quality.
- Plant wildflower seed according to the optimum date for the species you select, usually between September 1 and April 30.
- Broadcast seed evenly over the area as you would in planting a lawn.
- Rake very lightly to barely cover the seed with soil to a depth of 1⁄16 inch.
- Mulch lightly with a weed-free mulch such as pine straw or coastal Bermuda hay. Allow 25 percent of the soil surface to be visible after mulching.
- Water the area to keep the soil moist for adequate germination.

You will enjoy watching your wildflowers grow in a few weeks. Keep in mind that no magic wildflower mixes exist. A successful planting requires sound agronomic practices and maintenance. Remember to remove weeds, to topdress with fertilizer, and to water as needed.

To learn more about wildflowers, visit www.ncstate-plants.net, then click on "Plant Factsheets." You can find out more about DOT's Wildflower Program and other roadside environmental beautification programs at www.ncdot.org/~beautification.

Ginger lily
Toby Bost

Bring an Exotic Touch to Your Garden

By Carl Matyac, Orange and Wake Counties

Ah, the tropics—vibrant colors, bold foliage, exotic blooms, warm breezes, and easy, relaxed living. The image may have you wanting a tropical garden of your own. The question is, Is it possible? The tropics are the zones close to the equator, and we're several zones away. Our temperatures drop below 40° F, which they never do in tropical zones.

Thousands of strange and wonderful species of plants and flowers grow in the humid and warm-to-hot climate of the tropics and subtropics. The tropical rain forests of Central and South America have the greatest variety of tropical flowers. Other species of flowering tropical plants are native to Hawaii, the southern regions of China, South Africa, and even southern Florida. Many of these plants are stunning, but are they the ones to grow in North Carolina? Many dedicated gardeners grow tropical species in the summer months and drag them indoors or into greenhouses in the winter. How many of us have the time, energy, and space for tropical container gardens?

The good news is that some alternate plant choices look like the exotics in the tropics but are hardy here in North Carolina. This is a journey that can go as far as your imagination will take you. Imagine a four-foot ginger lily with four-inch fragrant flowers accented by six-foot elephant ear plants swaying in a sea of feather reed grass under the shade of a beautiful yucca.

Let's take a look at planting such a garden, step by step.

1. Start with your choice of a flowering perennial or woody plant that has some spunk. Consider the ginger lily, *Hedychium* sp.; a butterfly bush, *Buddleia* sp.; one of the standard purple coneflowers, *Echinacea purpurea*; or rose mallow, *Hibiscus mutabilis*. Or go way out and try a voodoo lily, *Amorphophallus* sp.

2. Next, behind the flowering centerpiece, add the big, bold foliage of elephant ears, either the old-fashioned *Colocasia* sp. or the newly introduced *Alocasia* sp.; the straplike foliage of cast iron plant, *Aspidistra*; or one of those big, fat hostas like 'Sum and Substance'. Other choices might include Canna lilies or *Fatsia japonica*, with its shiny green palmate leaves that look like a supersized schefflera. If you are willing to provide a little winter protection, go ahead with a banana plant from the genera *Musa* or *Musella*.

3. Add to the background with a mass planting of feather reed grass, *Calamagrostis* sp., *Miscanthus sinensis* 'Morning Light', or the lovely fountain grasses, *Pennisetum* sp. You can achieve the same effect with mass plantings of dwarf pampas grass, *Cortaderia*, or even seeding love grass, *Eragrostis*.

4. The final cap might be a specimen yucca or agave (century plant). Agaves are delightful but antisocial tropical plants native to the Southwest. These spiny, beautiful plants are great in rock gardens or otherwise sited in hot, sunny areas. If you like the idea of a tropical garden, this might be just the plant to add as a finishing touch.

Lawns

Plan Now for Fall Lawn Care

By Toby Bost, Forsyth County

Summer's heat and dry weather take their toll on turfgrasses that normally prefer lower temperatures and moist soil. Fortunately, a lush green lawn doesn't have to be just a dream.

A beautiful lawn in springtime begins in the fall. Start by evaluating your ground. Take the time to test the soil if you have neglected applying limestone for a few years. A soil report will recommend the fertilizer needed for a healthy lawn.

Clay soils are often compacted due to foot traffic and mowing equipment. If you plan to renovate an existing lawn, consider aerification before overseeding. The benefits of aerification include improved water penetration into the soil, increased oxygen levels for the roots, and better root development. The best aerating equipment removes cores or plugs of soil, increasing the germination of seed while improving soil

Lawn renovation
Connie Little

structure. Well-aerated soil helps the grass roots go deeper and enables the lawn to better survive droughts.

Some people prefer to hire professionals to aerate their lawns, since it can be physically challenging. Do-it-yourselfers can contact rental companies to learn the availability of equipment.

When the aerification step is complete, remove excess thatch. You will now have a good environment in which to broadcast seeds. Many of the seeds will fall into the holes and sprout promptly after a couple weeks of daily irrigation. Below are more details on renovation.

Renovating a Tall-Fescue Lawn

- Early fall is the best time to renovate fescue lawns.

- If applying an herbicide, remember to use postemergent chemicals four to six weeks before overseeding. If you use a nonselective herbicide such as

Photograph by Toby Bos

Roundup®, do so seven to 10 days prior to renovation.

- Mow grass at the lowest setting and collect the clippings. If needed, use a dethatcher at this time to collect thatch in the grass. Next, core aerate to provide good seed-to-soil contact.

- Apply a starter fertilizer according to directions over the prepared lawn area.

- Apply grass seed at the rate of at least three pounds per 1,000 square feet.

- Keep the renovated area moist with light sprinklings of water twice daily. As the seed germinates, reduce the frequency of watering but increase the duration.

- Mow the renovated lawn at a height of 2½ to 3½ inches.

Caring for an Established Lawn

- If you have not had a soil test, use a complete fertilizer with a ratio of 4-1-2 or 3-1-3 (N-P-K, or nitrogen, phosphorus, potassium) in lieu of a soil test. Fertilize fescue lawns in September, November, and March using one pound of nitrogen per 1,000 square feet of lawn.

- Continue to water in the fall, applying one inch of water per week early in the morning.

- For weed problems, spot-treat with a broad-leaf herbicide in the fall. Be sure to follow the label directions.

- Core aerate compacted lawns to move air and water down to the roots, then seed if necessary. If your lawn is well established, do not overseed.

- Continue to mow fescue grass during the fall months at a height of 2½ to 3½ inches.

Establishing a New Lawn

- When planting a new lawn, put the emphasis on soil preparation. Have the soil tested. Based on the results, apply the needed lime and fertilizer, mixing them into the top six to eight inches of soil.

- For seeding fescue lawns, the rule of thumb is to apply six pounds per 1,000 square feet.

- Mulch the newly seeded lawn lightly with straw to reduce erosion and to keep moisture around the seed.

- Keep the seed moist with light waterings two to three times per day.
- As the seed begins to germinate, water for longer periods less frequently.
- Begin mowing when grass is about four inches high.

Turfgrasses for Shade

By David Goforth, Cabarrus County

Trying to grow grass in areas with less than 50 percent sunlight or less than four hours of full sun each day is a losing battle. Many plants will grow in those conditions, including some that look like grasses. But turfgrasses simply will not. Most prefer full sun but will grow moderately well in about 60 percent sunlight. Only certain shade-tolerant turfgrass cultivars will grow in those areas.

Turfgrass and shade
Toby Bost

The region where you garden will determine which turfgrass works best in low-light conditions. In the coastal plain, St. Augustine grass will tolerate more shade than Bermuda grass. In the Piedmont and mountains, mixtures of tall fescue and shade-tolerant cultivars of Kentucky bluegrass (80 percent and 20 percent by weight, respectively) will work, particularly when the lawn is fertilized properly. The addition of a fine fescue—specifically, cultivars of hard fescue—is beneficial in lawns with less maintenance. A mixture of 80 percent tall fescue, 10 percent Kentucky bluegrass, and 10 percent hard fescue by weight seeded at six pounds per 1,000 square feet is recommended.

Other fine fescues, such as certain cultivars of creeping red and chewing fescues, perform well under low light in other states but are thinned by disease in North Carolina. Perennial ryegrass and Sabre rough bluegrass have also performed poorly in shade trials in North Carolina.

Choosing the correct species and cultivar of turfgrass is only the first step. As they grow, trees constantly increase the amount of shade they cast. A partially shaded area is just a few growing seasons from becoming fully shaded. Removing trees and limbs will help reduce the amount of shade. The trees' crowns should be raised to at least six feet and preferably more.

Mowing at the correct height will help grass collect more sunlight. Tall fescue and bluegrass blends should be cut at four inches and St. Augustine grass at three inches.

Finally, woodchip and bark mulches don't mind shade. Increasing the mulched area around a tree will typically cover the worst-performing part of the lawn. This also offers the satisfaction of working with nature, instead of against it.

For more information about growing turfgrasses, visit North Carolina State's turfgrass website, www.turffiles.ncsu.edu.

Select the Best Grass for Your Region

By Carl Matyac, Orange and Wake Counties

Lawn care can easily become a burden in terms of the time required to maintain that beautiful green around your house. However, you can reap the rewards of a handsome lawn by taking care in selecting the type of grass you wish to grow. With proper choices, a durable lawn will grow with minimal maintenance and pesticide use.

What to plant? No one type of grass is best suited to all situations. You'll need to consider a number of factors before deciding which grass to plant. Base your decision on region, climate, intended use or wear at the site, and desired appearance. Both cool-season and warm-season grasses are grown in North Carolina. Here is a highlight of the choices for our state's regions.

Cool-Season Grasses

Cool-season grasses—including turf-type tall fescue, Kentucky bluegrass, and fine fescue—grow best in the Piedmont and western regions of the state. It's best to grow a combination of these as a blended mix. For example, Kentucky bluegrass grows well in other parts of the country but doesn't perform well in our heat. It's best used as part of a blend that includes several cultivars of tall fescue.

Cool-season grasses look their best in the spring and fall. They stay reasonably green in the winter but will go dormant in summer if they aren't watered. Nevertheless, green color remains in the lawn practically all year long. Tall fescue blends are moderate- to coarse-bladed, heavy-duty grasses that tolerate clay soils and have better shade tolerance than most other turf. Tall fescue has few serious pest problems but is subject to brown patch disease under warm, wet conditions. It is a bunchgrass that does not recover well from injury and thus must be reseeded if bare areas appear. Reseeding is best done in the fall.

Cool-season grass
Robert E. Lyons

Zoysia grass
Toby Bost

Warm-Season Grasses

If you live in the coastal plain, have sandy soil, or do not wish to irrigate, you may find that a warm-season grass such as centipede, Bermuda grass, or zoysia grass may best suit your needs. Warm-season grasses are slow to green up in the spring, grow best in the summer, then turn brown and go dormant after the first heavy frost. Once these grasses are established, they are extremely drought tolerant and thus will save money on irrigation and reseeding.

Centipede grass is a slow-growing, apple green, coarse-leafed, warm-season turfgrass that is adapted for use as a low-maintenance, general-purpose turf. It requires little fertilizer and infrequent mowing and grows well in full sun to moderate shade. It does not tolerate traffic, compaction, or heavy shade.

Zoysia grass is a very low, slow-growing grass that makes a dense, wear-resistant lawn. This type of turf forms the most luxurious type of grass that money can buy. Zoysia grass grows well in full sun or partial shade. It is slow to establish when plugged and slow to recover from injury. Zoysia is well adapted to the Piedmont and coastal plain and is usually vegetatively planted, although procedures are now available for seeding common zoysia grass.

Bermuda grass varieties are typically fine in texture and grow low and dense. They are drought tolerant, require full sunlight, and grow well on all but poorly drained soils. Bermudas withstand wear and traffic, establish quickly, and recover rapidly from injury. This grass can invade flower beds and other areas where it is not wanted because it has a strong above- and below-ground stem system.

For more information, visit www.turffiles.ncsu.edu.

Control Brown Patch

By Donna Teasley, Burke County

Brown patch, a common disease of both warm- and cool-season grasses, often can be controlled by avoiding excessive amounts of nitrogen during conditions that are favorable to the development of the disease.

Cool-season lawns should receive limited applications of nitrogen in the late spring and little or no nitrogen during the summer. The majority of fertilizers should be applied in the fall at the time when most root development is occurring. Never apply more than one pound of nitrogen per 1,000 square feet at any one time. Avoid watering late in the day, as this promotes disease development. Make sure mower blades are sharp to avoid wounding turf. Never mow a wet lawn, and always mow high. Fungicide applications are only marginally helpful when applied to home lawns.

Warm-season lawns are susceptible to brown patch during periods of cool, wet weather in the spring and fall. As with cool-season grasses, late-day watering, dull mower blades, lack of sufficient drainage, and lack of air movement can increase the likelihood of brown patch occurrence. Avoid high nitrogen fertilizer when conditions are suitable for the development of brown patch. Adequate levels of phosphorous and potassium are necessary in both cool- and warm-season turfgrasses. Use a soil test to determine the levels needed. No fungicides are labeled for the effective control of brown patch in warm-season grasses.

Growing Warm-Season Grasses

By David Barkley, Brunswick County

Following a basic care guide for warm-season grasses will help you grow a beautiful lawn. The first step is to know what kind of grass you have. Warm-season grasses include Bermuda, centipede, St. Augustine, and zoysia. They are used widely in coastal areas and, unlike cool-season grasses, need to be fertilized through the summer.

Maintenance of warm-season grass begins in May, which is the time to seed, sprig, plug, or sod, since later plantings may not have enough time to establish properly before cold weather returns in the fall. Other maintenance tasks such as fertilizing, watering, and mowing should be conducted according to the various plant needs. Follow the guidelines for warm-season grass care below.

Bermuda Grass

- Mow lawn at ¾ to 1 inch.

- Apply one pound of nitrogen per 1,000 square feet every four to six weeks. In the absence of a soil test, apply a complete nitrogen, phosphorus, and potassium (N-P-K) turf-grade fertilizer with a 3-1-2 or 4-1-2 ratio, such as 12-4-8 or 16-4-8.

- Water to a soil depth of 4 to 6 inches. Apply about 1 to 1¼ inches of water weekly. Sandy soils will require more frequent watering—for example, ½ inch of water every third day.

- Check for white grubs and control if necessary.

Centipede Grass

- Mow lawn at one inch.

- Apply ½ pound of fertilizer per 1,000 square feet in mid-June. Use a high-potassium fertilizer such as 5-5-15, 6-6-12, or 8-8-24.

- Water to prevent drought stress, about ½ inch every third day in sandy soils.

- Apply postemergent herbicides as needed to control summer annual and perennial broadleaf weeds.

St. Augustine Grass

- Mow lawn at 2½ inches.

- Fertilize with ½ pound of nitrogen per 1,000 square feet in June and August and 1 pound in July. In the absence of a soil test, use a complete nitrogen, phosphorus, and potassium (N-P-K) fertilizer with a 3-1-2 or 4-1-2 ratio—for example, 12-4-8 or 16-4-8.

- Water to prevent drought stress. Sandy soils often require frequent watering.

- Check for chinch bug activity in sunny locations when yellow to brownish spots or drought symptoms appear.

Zoysia Grass

- Mow lawn at ¾ to 1 inch.

- Fertilize with ½ pound of nitrogen per 1,000 square feet in late June or early July and repeat in mid-August, using a complete N-P-K, turf-grade fertilizer with a 3-1-2 or 4-1-2 ratio.

- Water to a soil depth of 4 to 6 inches. Zoysia needs a weekly application of 1 to 1¼ inches. On sandy soils, apply ½ inch of water every third day.

- Apply postemergent herbicides if needed. Control grubs in August when they are small and close to the soil surface.

Additional guidelines for both warm- and cool-season grasses are available at www.turffiles.ncsu.edu. This excellent resource based on research at North Carolina State University is also available at your county Cooperative Extension Center.

Each grass has advantages and disadvantages. Try to select the grass you are most capable of dealing with, and redesign your lawn if necessary. Since water restrictions are becoming more common, consider enlarging flower beds, incorporating groundcovers, and mulching shady spots. A completely mulched area usually won't look right unless it is under tree canopy, with plenty of understory plantings and groundcovers.

Most landscaping problems can be solved with a compromise. Turfgrasses can be used for erosion control, to create a cooling effect, for wear tolerance, and, most importantly, for the unifying effect on the total landscape, making the house and all the other construction hardscape fit together.

Front-yard garden
Robert E. Lyons

Landscape Management

Front-Yard Gardens Maximize Space

By Mark Blevins, Gaston County

Neighbors used to gather on each other's front porches to exchange neighborhood news, to enjoy a rest stop while walking the dog, or perhaps to enjoy a refreshing glass of iced tea. Today, many front porches are still surrounded by large green lawns. But during the last few decades, Americans have turned their lifestyles completely around, choosing the backyard over the front for friendly gatherings and personal relaxation. Many landscapes suffer from this conversion. Backyards are only so big and can soon run out of room. Meanwhile, front lawns go unnoticed, unused, or neglected.

Gardening in the front yard may be the cure for space limitations in a postage-stamp-sized yard. Front-yard gardens can add to the experiences you enjoy inside and out as you expand your garden territory.

Grass has great benefits for the environment, recreation, and aesthetics around a home, but consider the time, materials, and equipment required to keep it looking its best. If well designed, front-yard gardens also offer many benefits and can require less maintenance, depending on the plants chosen. You have many plants to select from

Photograph by Robert E. Lyons

that will provide interest to your landscape and remain attractive year-round with minimal maintenance.

Birds and wildlife will benefit from native plants that provide flowers, berries, and nuts year-round. A cutting garden can be incorporated into the front yard, particularly for those who long to fill vases with homegrown flowers. But keep in mind that this type of garden may require high maintenance to keep it looking its best.

Tropical plants can make stepping out the front door feel like an exotic vacation. Colorful herbs and vegetables can mingle with annuals planted along the front walk.

A welcoming entry to a home adds personality to the entire neighborhood and departs from the old standard of a lawn, shrubs against the house, and a tree or two. You can have fun expanding your living space into the front yard. You can create a spot to have a late Saturday breakfast, to grow herbs for Sunday dinner, and to greet friends and relatives who will remember the home you've made outside your house.

While most contemporary houses may not be conducive to front-yard gardens, small beds can be created to enhance the entrance garden. Get started by mapping out areas of your front landscape you would like to change, such as those with thin turf, overgrown hedges, or poor views from inside the house. On your map, include the things you won't change this time—the driveway, utility fixtures, sunny and shady areas, sidewalks, and other features. You may need to call your utility companies to determine the location of underground pipes and cables.

Think about uses and themes for your front yard, starting with public areas including the entryway, the front walk, and places to gather with friends. Semiprivate areas for reading a book or relaxing may need to be shielded by a hedge or nestled into a corner of the yard. You can also add a water feature or a birdbath. You can scatter flowers, herbs, vegetables, or wildlife plants throughout the whole plan or just in spaces designed for those elements. You may still need some turf out front for a game of croquet or to clear the view to a beautiful tree. Consider leaving some existing plants to make the transition from lawn to garden a little easier.

Before installing any additional plants, get your soil tested. Contact your county Cooperative Extension Center for a free soil test kit. Visit www.ces.ncsu.edu and click on "County Centers" in the left-hand column. A soil report will provide recommendations on the type of fertilizer and the amount of lime that will best balance the needs of your future plants with the nutrition in your soil. You can match plants for your landscape plan with the helpful lists in the "Lawn & Garden" section of the Cooperative Extension website. Native and well-adapted plants have defenses for pests and thrive in our climate, so they will require less maintenance overall. Take advantage of the many learning opportunities offered by Cooperative Extension, including the *In the Garden with Bryce Lane* and *Almanac Gardener* shows on the UNC-TV network.

Involve your friends and family and maybe even your neighbors in the planting process to share the fun of gardening. Then enjoy using this new portion of your landscape for more than lawn mower practice. Share some time and maybe a handful of flowers or herbs from your new front-yard garden with someone special.

These Annuals and Perennials Accent Fall Color Show

By Amy-Lynn Albertson, Davidson County

Fall for many North Carolinians is one of the great highlights of the gardening year. After a hot, humid summer, the air feels crisp and the temperature is tolerable. Many of us are rejuvenated and ready to enjoy our gardens again. A world of color bursts from our deciduous trees, and our annuals and perennials have a lot to offer, too. Although pansies and mums are great old standbys, you'll also find many other flowers out there to try.

In the perennial garden, you can complement the brilliant red, scarlet, orange, and yellow of fall trees with a mix of lilac, violet, and blue. *Sedum* 'Autumn Joy' and *S.* 'Vera Jameson' have beautiful cotton-candy pink flowers. *Boltonia latisquama* 'Masbolimket' is a complement to yellow colors with its lavender blooms and yellow centers, offset by dark green foliage. *Solidago* species add bright yellow flames to the garden; their height and upright blooms make a nice contrast with the mounded forms of mums. Japanese anemones bloom from late summer into fall, their gorgeous white and pink

Fall garden
Robert E. Lyons

blooms held gracefully on branching stems arising from handsome green foliage. Calendula, also known as pot marigold, prefers full sun and comes in orange, reddish orange, and yellow. Dianthus hybrids, or China pinks, prefer full sun to partial shade and come in white, pink, red, and violet. Dianthus hybrids will overwinter and perform with your pansies for early-spring color. They are also more heat tolerant than pansies.

Don't overlook foliage in the fall garden. The foliage of many peony cultivars turns bronze or wine red, and some *Heuchera* species develop red patterns on their foliage. Ornamental grasses can be the star of any fall garden; many bear great flower heads that remain showy well into winter. Grasses also add structure to the garden, in contrast to the compact mounded forms of many of the perennials.

If mum is the word for your fall garden, try some of the newer Belgian varieties. Regular garden mums come in many different flower types. Cushion mums have small, tight flowers about the size of cotton balls and offer the longest bloom time. Petal blooms are between cushion and daisy types and offer beautiful blooms and long-lasting color. Daisy blooms are open petals with small cushion centers. They offer lots of color, including two-tone blooms. The Belgian varieties have the same flower types, but the plants are a little smaller and have three to four times the number of blooms as other varieties, in an array of colors. When choosing mums at a garden center, keep in mind that the inexpensive mums in small containers can be as big as the larger ones soon after they are planted. Some are in full bloom, while others may not be. The ones in full bloom will give you instant color, but those just opening will last longer into the season.

Don't forget annuals in the flower mix. Change out some of the faded summer-blooming annuals in your container gardens for new fall-blooming annuals from Proven Winners. Osteospermums provide great color contrast and add depth to many containers. Agryanthemums, or Marguerite daisies, have delicate foliage and cute daisy flowers in an array of colors. Diacias and nemesias make lovely hanging baskets or edging for the garden. Hardy to zone 8, these delicate flowers may overwinter in the coastal plain. Dusty miller is an excellent source of cool-season color and overwinters in many parts of the state. Coleus can add diversity to your fall foliage, too. Those in the warmer parts of North Carolina might try violas or Johnny-jump-ups instead of pansies. Violas look like smaller versions of pansies with a lot more blooms. They are much more heat tolerant, giving you more bloom for your buck. If you absolutely need pansies for that cool-season color, look at the Magnum series. This pansy stands up to heat better than most, resisting the urge to get leggy as temperatures rise. Like other pansies, the Magnum series can take cold temperatures and will flower in partial shade as well as full sun.

Some new favorites for fall gardens are edible ornamental peppers. The show comes from the brightly colored fruit that covers the top of the plant. If you get tired of looking at them, you can harvest the peppers and add them to a favorite recipe. Some other treats for the eye are ornamental cabbages and kales. Redbor kale is a large selection producing wavy, deep burgundy leaves. Some of the ornamental kales can get as large as three feet by two feet, so think big when placing these plants in the garden. Red Giant mustard produces burgundy-and-green foliage that is beautiful and edible. Other greens like mustard, tatsoi, and arugula make nice foliage additions to your fall garden and your salad.

Shade plants
Robert E. Lyons

A Landscape Made in the Shade

By Fred Miller, Catawba County

Those wonderful trees that offer shady relief from the harsh summer sun also create a challenge for gardeners. Keeping other ornamental plants alive in areas where thirsty trees and shrubs compete for moisture and nutrients and block the sunlight necessary for photosynthesis can be difficult. Follow these simple steps to increase your plants' chances for survival.

Defining Shade

Dappled, dense, and *partial* describe shade in terms of the relative amount of sunlight available for plant growth. Other adjectives such as *damp* and *dry* may further define shady areas. While it is difficult to quantify shade, it is important to attempt to grasp the basic differences in order to make appropriate plant selections.

Pruning to Increase Available Light

Where shade is too dense, remove the lower limbs of trees to let in more sunlight. By "raising the canopy," you will allow additional morning and afternoon sunlight for plant growth. Most evergreens and deciduous trees will tolerate removal of as much as 20 percent of their foliage, if done properly. Shade density varies depending on the species of tree. Consider choosing trees such as 'Heritage' river birch or honey locust, which offer all-day dappled shade.

Preparing Soil and Beds

Remove weeds prior to planting to reduce competition with your ornamentals. Hand-digging or pulling the offensive weeds may be necessary to lessen damage to tree roots. This will also give you a better feel for locations where root competition will be minimized, resulting in better plant survival. In dry weather, irrigate the area a day or so in advance to facilitate the digging process. As a last resort, apply a nonselective

'Annabelle' hydrangea / *Toby Bost*

herbicide with a wick or sponge applicator, but use extreme caution. Trees may be susceptible to the herbicide and could be damaged if it is not applied according to the label.

Avoid large-scale mechanical tillage to minimize root damage to existing shade trees.

Watering New Plants

Water new plants until established. All plants will benefit from irrigation during extended dry periods. Root competition is intense beneath shade trees. Small understory plants are at a disadvantage when competing with large shade trees for water. Use mini sprinklers and drip irrigation to direct water where it is most needed and to minimize water waste and potential disease problems. Add a three- to four-inch layer of an organic mulch such as pine needles or bark to help hold moisture.

Selecting Plants for Shade

Choose plants that perform well in the shade. Because of the limited palette of summer-blooming plants, successful shade gardeners tend to rely on plants that bloom in the spring, prior to full development of the shade canopy. Plants that have interesting and persistent foliage are also good choices.

Consider your personal goals for your shade garden when choosing plant materials. If your goal is to "lighten up" a shady area, many shade-tolerant plants from shrubs such as privet and azalea to herbaceous perennials and annuals come with foliage variegated with whites and yellows that provide visual interest. Keep in mind that some shrubs tend to lose their variegation in all but light shade, so check with your local garden center.

The hosta is the undisputed star of the shade garden, thanks to its variety of greens and golds and its many variegated patterns. Impatiens, another old favorite, adds a splash of bright color among hostas and other perennials.

If you are shooting for a low-maintenance landscape, consider the variegated groundcovers. When well established, the low-growing evergreen varieties of periwinkle, *Vinca minor*, offer a reliable year-round foliage carpet. Among the most popular is the white-margined 'Ralph Shugert'. This plant has small-leaved foliage and large blue blossoms in the spring. If you take care because of potential invasiveness, the lighter variegated silver ajugas and the tricolored 'Burgundy Glow' cultivar offer beautiful year-round color.

Letting Mother Nature Do It

Natural areas can be the perfect solution for problem areas under trees where soil is depleted and tilling is dangerous to tree health. Mother Nature is the most economical mulcher and the most efficient rebuilder of topsoil. Help her out by leaving evergreen needles and leaves where they fall. Over time, they will decay and begin to form new topsoil. Natural wooded areas can have a surprising visual appeal of their own, but they also can be dressed up with woodland favorites such as hellebores and the spectacular Asian woodland lilies.

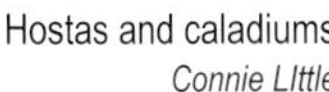
Hostas and caladiums
Connie LIttle

Perennials for Dry Shade Areas

By Donald Breedlove, Iredell County

Dry shade conditions can provide a challenge when it comes to selecting plants. Here are some examples of dry shade conditions:

- Sandy soil with overshadowing tree canopies
- Clay or loamy soil on high ridges
- Soil confined to planters or raised beds
- Perennials on a northern exposure
- Plants under an overhanging roof without regular irrigation or rain
- Native plant areas where trees and ornamentals and their roots create competition for light and moisture

Perennials that will perform best in these areas of dry shade to partial dry shade are toad lily, astilbe, spiderwort, woodland phlox, pachysandra, Lenten rose, coralbells, hardy ferns, Japanese forest grass, and liriope. Other flowers for specific uses can be found at www.ces.ncsu.edu/depts/hort/hil/hil-552.

Shaded sites pose additional problems if tree roots are nearby. Maples and other shallow-rooted trees present constant root growth, even in the most well-prepared sites. A barrier can be constructed between the perennial bed and tree roots. Arborists suggest copper flashing between the two, as roots will not encroach beyond copper. Furthermore, there is no danger that this technique will kill the tree.

Preparing the Site

With regard to site and soil preparation, perennials are no different from other plants, although using a rototiller within the drip line of an established tree can be fatal. A soil test is recommended for checking and adjusting the site's pH with lime and fertilizer. Soil pH requirements vary among perennials, but most prefer a range between 5.5 and 6.5. Apply lime to select groups of plants needing a higher pH. Apply fertilizer in accordance with soil tests and incorporate it into the top five to six inches before planting. Test the soil every three years. The North Carolina Department of Agriculture's Agronomic Division provides routine analysis for lime and fertilizer at no cost. You can pick up soil sample boxes at your county Cooperative Extension Center.

On new sites, the area should be as weed free as possible. Control weeds—nutsedge and Bermuda grass in particular—before beginning soil preparation. This may take six months to a year.

Selecting Plants

Select perennials for a specific purpose such as edging, accenting evergreens, adding masses of color, or providing specimens for rock gardens. If possible, buy named varieties of plants for their known characteristics of disease resistance, growth habit, temperature tolerance, and color. When these plants are in the flowering stage, planting or transplanting is not highly recommended. If you are relocating perennials by transplanting, try to take a large enough root ball to reduce shock and reduce the time of site acclimation. The new location should be two to three times the diameter of the root core from the old location. Many perennials left in the same place for more than three years are likely to become overcrowded and will need dividing. The best time to divide most plants is from late winter through early spring, when the new shoots are two to three inches, or in the fall, when the foliage starts to die back. Some perennials, however, are best left in place and not divided. This is true of baby's breath, wild indigo, gas plant, goat's beard, globe thistle, peony, and sea holly.

Mulching, Fertilizing, Deadheading

A mulched area has an orderly look, requires little weeding, and maintains uniform soil moisture. Apply mulches after plants are well established or up and starting to grow. A maximum of three inches of pine bark, pine needles, or shredded leaves over the area works well. Perennials have an advantage over bedding plants in that more preemergent herbicides are available to manage weeds in perennial beds.

Fertilization, deadhead pinching, and occasional staking are part of the maintenance involved. Most plants are light feeders and generally require an application of fertilizer as they start to grow in the spring and a second dose in midsummer. After the flowers are spent, remove them so the plants won't waste energy producing seeds. This will help extend blooming. On shady and windy sites, staking is often necessary to prevent top-heavy plants from falling over.

Set in Stone

By David Goforth, Cabarrus County

Stones suggest permanence and reliability. In the landscape, they can provide a natural beauty and a functional solution to problems. Stones and concrete pavers that resemble stones are quite beautiful for walkways, patios, curbs, and low retaining walls.

When using stone, avoid the mistake many novice gardeners make in inadequately preparing the site. Just as in planting a garden, preparing the site will yield better results. Dig about 12 inches into the subgrade to develop a stable base. Cover the area with a geotextile fabric, then add a base. On clay soils, an eight-inch layer of crusher run gravel will make a suitable base. Add the gravel in two-inch layers and compact between layers. In well-drained sandy soils, you can get by with four to six inches of this material.

On top of the base, add a one-inch layer of sand to form a setting bed for the pavers. Use an iron pipe one inch in diameter as a screed rail to level and smooth the sand. Do not compact the sand before setting the pavers. An edge restraint of some type is necessary. If the edge restraint is not enough to keep the sand under the pavers, use additional geotextile fabric. For best results, establish a 90-degree angle as a starting point. Mark the sand with a chalk line. Otherwise, use lines suspended over the bed to lay the pavers in a straight line. Joint sand has a structural function; don't subject the pavers to any traffic before adding the joint sand.

In addition to their use in walkways and other hardscaping, stones and pavers can be striking in other ways. Large stones in the landscape help create an informal focal point. The most common mistakes with large stones are allowing them to sit too high and using same-sized stones. Position the stones so that their bases are four to six inches into the ground, and mix up the sizes to make the composition more interesting. Choose the stones that work best for your landscape, whether flagstone, weathered sandstone, decorative gravel, boulders, or one of the many other options available.

Landscaping with stone
Connie Little

Set in stone
Connie Little

If used properly, stone adds to the aesthetics of the landscape. Gardeners can soften the hardness of stone and pull it into the overall design with delicate, colorful, or fine-textured plants.

Soil testing
Connie Little

Soil Testing Saves Time and Resources

By Amy-Lynn Albertson, Davidson County

Soil testing by the North Carolina Department of Agriculture and Consumer Services is one of the best services our state tax dollars provide. In other states, similar soil tests cost as much as $50. Here, we pay only for the postage to mail a test to the Raleigh lab. The Agronomic Division analyzes soil for its nutrient content and other properties that affect plant growth, such as cation exchange capacity (CEC) and pH. This test is much more accurate and complete than any home-test kit available for purchase at a garden center.

Your soil test report will provide recommendations for lime and fertilizer. Using only as much fertilizer as needed minimizes nutrient runoff and saves money, time, and natural resources.

A soil test is only as good as the sample you send. Be sure the sample represents the garden area. Take a sample a few months before planting a new lawn or starting a new flower or vegetable garden. If your test results recommend lime, you will have enough time to apply it and adjust the soil pH before planting. Sample the soil in an established landscape or garden once every three or four years.

You can take a soil sample any time of the year with a garden trowel, spade, or shovel. Do not use brass, bronze, or galvanized tools, which can contaminate the sample with copper and zinc.

Take separate samples for your vegetable garden, lawn, and flower garden. Take at least six to eight cores of soil from an area and combine them to make one sample. Mix soil cores for each sample in a clean plastic bucket. If the bucket has been used for fertilizer or other chemicals, make sure you wash it before using it for soil samples.

Soil samples for lawns should be taken at a depth of four inches and should not include any turf thatch. For vegetable and shrubbery beds, sample four to six inches deep.

After mixing all the cores of each sample together, fill a soil test box to the line indicated on the side. Boxes and forms are available at your Cooperative Extension Center and many garden centers, as well as from regional agronomists and the Agronomic Division laboratory in Raleigh. Use permanent ink or pencil to fill out forms and label boxes.

Give each sample a unique code that combines up to five letters, numbers, or both. Put this code on the form and the sample box. Use a code that will help you remember the area the sample corresponds to, such as FYARD, ROSES, VEGIS, or GRASS. Be sure to list the plants you will grow in the area by selecting a crop code for each sample. The codes are listed on the back of the form.

Package your soil samples properly. Do not tape the box or put soil in a plastic bag. If you are sending the samples in the mail, pack them carefully in a sturdy container. Soil samples are usually analyzed within a week. From late fall through early spring, processing may take several weeks due to the sample influx from farmers.

When your test is complete, a report will be mailed to you and posted at www.agr.state.nc.us/agronomi/uyrst.htm. A cover sheet and a crop-specific note will be sent with your report. If you need help interpreting your soil test report, contact your local Cooperative Extension Center.

Make Your Landscape Water Wise

By Carl Matyac, Orange and Wake Counties

In North Carolina, we are fortunate to have lakes, streams, rivers, and coastal waters that contribute to the quality of life, making this a great place to live. In order to conserve and protect these resources, make your landscape water wise.

Analyze Your Soil

Get your hands dirty. In order to select the right fertilizers, additives, and amendments, learn the characteristics of your soil. Soil testing by the North Carolina Department of Agriculture and Consumer Services is a great place to start. The lab report will tell you about lime and nutrient deficiencies.

Improve the structure of your soil. Never work soil when it is wet. This destroys soil structure and leads to compaction. Take a small handful of soil and make it into a ball. If you drop this ball and it stays intact, then the soil is probably too wet.

Till the soil as deeply as possible when installing new plants. This reduces compaction, allows oxygen to get deep into the soil, and facilitates new plant establishment.

Amend your soil with compost. This is magic stuff. Compost holds enough moisture for water-needy plants and at the same time improves soil structure and allows excess water to drain. Don't just add organic amendments to the planting hole. Apply three or four inches of compost to the surface and incorporate it into the soil.

You can always buy your way to success. Topsoil from a reputable soil contractor

Water-wise landscaping
Toby Bost

is a wonderful thing. Use this new soil to raise the grade of existing beds by 10 or 12 inches.

Study the drainage characteristics of the site. Few landscapes are perfectly flat. This means that water flows over the surface when heavy rains occur. Know the location of the hot, dry areas as well as the wet, shady spots. Take notes. All of this information will be important in locating plants in the landscape.

Limit Fertilizer Use

Apply full rates of fertilizer to plants you want to grow larger. Mature plants need only occasional fertilization in order to maintain health.

Minimize Turf Areas

Match the landscape features to your family needs. Be realistic. If you use your lawn for parties, soccer, or chipping practice, then keep the turf. Otherwise, transform that sea of green into landscape beds that are natural areas or into low-maintenance groundcovers, perennials, shrubs, or ornamental grasses. If you have tons of turf, consider a drought-tolerant species such as Bermuda, centipede, or zoysia. Turf requires significant amounts of water, fertilizer, and time.

Choose Low-Maintenance, Drought-Tolerant Plants

To learn about plants that are well adapted to your local climate, visit public gardens, your county Cooperative Extension Center, or garden centers. Acquiring knowledge can be fun. Join a garden club or volunteer as one of "Extension's Master Gardeners." You will find that gardening brings out the best in all of us.

For a complete list of tough plants, visit www.ces.ncsu.edu. Click on "Extension Departments." Go to "Horticultural Science" and then "Consumer/ Home Horticulture."

Mulch, Mulch, Mulch

Spreading organic mulches on top of landscape beds conserves moisture and moderates soil temperature, allowing for rapid root development. Mulches also prevent the crusting of the surface, allowing rainfall to penetrate the soil and reducing the need for irrigation.

Sweep Fertilizer from Driveways and Sidewalks

Nitrogen and phosphorus in fertilizers swept into gutters and storm drains go directly into our rivers. No treatment plant cleans this water. In addition, never dump oil, paint, or solvents into the gutter.

Use Pervious Surfaces When Possible

Impervious surfaces such as concrete and asphalt do not allow water infiltration. This causes rapid runoff and greater stormwater management problems. Gravel and paver products such as turfstone slow runoff, allow for water infiltration, and thus feed our groundwater supplies.

Learn More

A number of research-based publications such as *Fertilizer Recommendations to Maintain and Protect Water Quality, Managing Lawns and Gardens to Protect Water Quality*, and *Wise Water Use in Landscaping* are available at your county Cooperative Extension Center or by visiting www.ces.ncsu.edu/depts/hort/consumer/ag_publications.html.

Specialty Plantings

Creative Companion Plantings for Your Garden Canvas

By Emily Revels, Cumberland and Mecklenburg Counties

Companion planting is the technique of creating "buddy" plants that grow well together. These combined plants benefit from each other's characteristics.

Native Americans developed one of the first examples of companion planting. Called "Three Sisters," it involved planting corn, beans, and squash together in a hill. The cornstalks provided support for the climbing beans, and the squash growing at the base of the corn shaded out weeds.

One effect sought through companion planting is reduced insect pests. Companion plants may be used to hide, repel, or trap pests. For example, Japanese beetles and spider mites do not like garlic, so this is a good companion for roses. Onions, garlic, and chives may help block ants, aphids, and flea beetles. Mint may keep cabbage loopers off cabbage plants, while basil can discourage tomato hornworms. Companion plants such as numerous perennials, asters, calendulas, and cosmos add

White garden
Connie Little

welcome color in the garden and attract a variety of beneficial insects.

Companion planting in its simplest form can be the combining of plants for no purpose other than visual effect. Gardeners can combine plants to extend the flowering period in a planting bed, to create a focal point, or to provide a backdrop for flowers. Combining annuals, perennials, ornamental grasses, vines, and herbs can provide a spectacular flower show in both garden beds and containers.

Be creative and experiment with what works well for your garden. Sometimes companion-planting "accidents" result in better combinations of colors and textures than do carefully laid plans.

Remember these basic tips. Do not plant sun-loving plants with shade-loving plants because some of the plants will not be happy. Do not put plants that prefer to stay moist with plants that do not like "wet feet." Also consider the combinations of flower colors and the colors and textures of the leaves.

The J. C. Raulston Arboretum at North Carolina State University offers the following recommendations:

- The scarlet flower of the *Crocosmia × crocosmiiflora* 'Lucifer' blooming in the middle of yellow daylilies, *Hemerocallis* hybrid, during July

- A red cardinal flower, *Lobelia cardinalis*, coming out of the green-and-white foliage of the *Miscanthus sinensis* 'Variegatus' ornamental grass

- A beautiful bleeding heart, *Dicentra eximia* 'Luxuriant', blooming deep pink as new, young hosta leaves are growing. The fringe foliage of the *Dicentra* intertwined in the hosta leaves adds interest.

- *Zinnia angustifolia* 'Star White' with *Gaillardia pulchella* 'Red Plume'

- *Rudbeckia hirta* 'Indian Summer' with *Zinnia angustifolia* 'Crystal White'

- Ice plant, *Delosperma cooperi*, with *Sedum album* 'Murale'

- Fountain grass, *Pennisetum alopecuroides*, with *Iris × germanica*, bearded iris
- Fountain grass, *Pennisetum setaceum* 'Rubrum', with *Verbena bonariensis*
- *Impatiens walleriana* with Hakone grass, *Hakonechloa macra* 'Aureola'
- Pulmonarias with heucheras
- *Lantana camara* with duckfoot coleus

Become a garden artist and paint your canvas with companion plants.

Herbs
Connie Little

Plant Herbs for Landscape and Culinary Flair

By Donna Teasley, Burke County

Americans are learning to cook with a new attitude these days. The shift toward healthier lifestyles has brought about a new interest in an old method of cooking. Culinary herbs have been used for centuries to flavor everything from salads and fish to soups and stews. Because of the concern about high amounts of salt, fat, and sugar in the foods we eat, herbs are being used in increasing amounts as a healthier way to flavor our meals.

Many herbs are easy to grow. Herbs can be grown in containers, tucked in and around other plants, or star in a garden devoted just to them. They are quite versatile, both for the landscape and for culinary creations.

Some easy selections to start with are basil, chives, oregano, parsley, sage, rosemary, and thyme. Although they may sound rather ordinary, their addition to many dishes makes a striking difference in the taste. The proper use of these easy-to-grow herbs can turn a plain meal into a gourmet experience.

Most culinary herbs grow best in sunny, well-drained areas where the soil is deep and loose. Choose a site that receives at least six hours of direct sun each day. Water should be plentiful, but the soil should not be wet. Compensate for poor drainage with raised beds amended with compost. Apply balanced fertilizers sparingly to leafy, fast-growing herbs. Heavy applications of fertilizer, especially those containing large amounts of nitrogen, will decrease the concentration of essential oils in the lush green growth. Herbs rarely suffer severe disease or insect damage.

Flavor is usually best when herbs are picked during the leaf-growing stage. When the plants start to flower, the leaves often get a bitter taste. Picking the leaves and stems is often the best way to keep the plants from blooming, and it also keeps them actively growing.

Some herbs are perennials, which means they will come back each year. Many herbs are winter hardy in all or parts of North Carolina and can be left in the garden. Some can be brought indoors to overwinter. Other herbs are annuals, meaning they die at the end of the season. Some herbs are biennials, which means they die after two years. Use caution when planting some perennial herbs, as they can be quite aggressive and can quickly take over a garden. Grow aggressive herbs such as mint in clay pots planted in the garden, so as to keep the roots from spreading. When more herbs are in the garden than can be used, continue to harvest on a regular basis to prevent the plants from going to seed.

Most herbs can be used either fresh or dried. Some can even be frozen for later use. With fresh herbs, a general rule is to use three times more than the dried amount. Always pick herbs in the morning after the dew has dried. Cut the stems on a diagonal and stand them upright in a glass or jar of water, cover loosely with a plastic bag, and store in the refrigerator. They will remain fresh for at least a week if the water is changed every day.

What herbs go with what foods? This question often stumps would-be herb users. Websites and books match herbs with the most appropriate foods. Containers of dried herbs list foods that will benefit from those particular herbs. Many recipes include the proper herbs and correct amounts to use. And it never hurts to experiment on your own. Try small amounts at first and gradually branch out as your confidence grows.

For a chart that matches herbs and foods, visit www.culinaryherbguide.com. You can learn more about growing, harvesting, preserving, and winterizing herbs at www.ncstate-plants.net.

Ornamental Grasses Add Color, Texture, and Variety to the Landscape

By Willie Earl Wilson, Union County

Ornamental grasses are quite popular for North Carolina landscapes. Their striking array of textures, forms, sizes, and colors offers multiseason interest with unique appeal for designers and gardeners. The term *ornamental grass* describes all grasslike plants, including sedges, reeds, rushes, and a wide host of others.

The leaves and flowers of grasses have distinct ranges of color. Spring and sum-

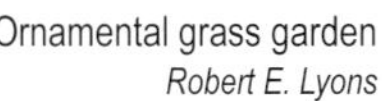
Ornamental grass garden
Robert E. Lyons

Annual flower and ornamental grass garden
Connie Little

mer foliage colors include myriad greens, from dark forest to lime and gray-green to blue-green, as well as powder blue, red, and bright yellow. Variegated foliage adds cream white and snow white to the choice, as well as occasional suffusions of rose pink during cool days at the beginning and end of the growing season.

The foliage colors of grasses have a long-lasting presence in the garden, remaining as various flowers come and go. The spring foliage of golden millet, *Milium effusum* 'Aureum', is vivid chartreuse, which can match the color strength of May flowers in the landscape garden. The rich sea-blue fescue, *Festuca glauca* 'Meerblau', will continue long after the surrounding heaths and heathers have ceased blooming.

Following are a few grasses with brief descriptions of form, habit, and color.

Weeping lovegrass, *Eragrostis curvula*, is a favorite for eastern North Carolina on slopes or eroded areas. It is hardy in zones 6 to 10. *Pennisetum alopecuroides* 'Hameln' is a dwarf fountain grass that is great in masses and works well in small gardens. It grows to two feet with plumes and is hardy in zones 5 to 9. Quaking grass, *Briza media*, is a cool-season perennial that grows best in full sun. Used in rock gardens and dried arrangements, it is hardy in zones 4 to 7. Northern sea oats, *Chasmanthium latifolium*, are an excellent grass to use in a mass planting or as a specimen plant. Northern sea oats spread by underground creeping rhizomes, grow two to five feet, and are green during spring and summer before turning a beautiful tan in late fall. *Imperata cylindrica* 'Red Baron', Japanese blood grass, grows 12 to 18 inches tall and exhibits beautiful cranberry-colored foliage in summer and fall. It is hardy to zone 7.

The *Carex* genus includes over 3,000 species whose popularity in the landscape has increased tremendously in the past few years. *C. comans* 'Bronze', a New Zealand hair sedge, has long, thin, arching, and trailing foliage with bronze color. Its unique shape makes it an excellent specimen plant. It is hardy in zones 7 to 9. *C. albula* 'Frosty Curls' is a versatile plant. It does well in full sun to partial shade and is drought tolerant. Its light green, thin leaves cascade down and almost lie on the ground. 'Frosty Curls' is a great container plant that sometimes appears silvery in shade gardens. It is hardy in zones 7 to 9.

Ornamental grasses are highly resistant to insect and disease problems, are tolerant of heat and drought, and require little or no pruning. Two important requirements are full sun and well-drained soil. The grasses noted above have specific hardiness limitations and should not be used beyond the recommended zones.

Prune back ornamental grasses in spring to eliminate any overwintering insects or diseases. This is best accomplished with pruning shears or electric hedge clippers. New growth will begin to appear in late spring when it is time to apply fertilizer. General recommendations include 8-8-8 or 10-10-10 fertilizer. For clump-type grasses, use 1 to 1½ cups per established plant. For groundcover-type plantings, use two to three pounds of a complete fertilizer per 100 square feet of bed area.

Rain Gardens Help the Environment

By Craven Moore, Gaston County, and Mitch Woodward, Wake County

Rain gardens are depressions created in the landscape that work by capturing water runoff and holding it a couple of days, allowing it to slowly drain into the soil. They are usually sized to capture the "first flush" of runoff from storms. This runoff contains most of the pollutants.

Rain gardens are a relatively new concept. They are designed to be small, yet effective. The retained water percolates down through the soil, trapping sediment and allowing nutrients to be used by plants in the rain garden. During rains, more runoff can come into the garden than it can hold, so it is important to give the excess water a place to go. For this reason, it's best not to place a rain garden near a well or septic system.

Some yards—especially properties located in environmentally sensitive areas, such as those adjacent to streams or lakes—provide ideal situations for rain gardens. For example, when it rains, runoff from a road may wash fertilizer and soil across a lawn and down a sloped driveway before it then pools in a low spot by a stream. During larger storm events, the runoff may wash directly into the stream—not the best scenario for the landscape or for water quality.

Getting Started

The first steps in installing a rain garden are to watch where the water flows during rains and to prepare the site properly. Low areas where water pools often are the best locations for rain gardens, but there are exceptions to this rule. Remember, the purpose of the rain garden is to treat water runoff during storms. Sufficient water and room are necessary to make the rain garden a success. If there is enough water but the low area is not a suitable site, landscape drainage pipes can be installed to carry water to the rain garden.

Before removing the first shovelful of earth, perform a simple but effective test of soil permeability. Check soil drainage by digging a small hole about the width of a shovel and one foot deep, then fill it with water. If the water drains quickly and disap-

Rain garden
Toby Bost

pears within 24 hours, that's a good sign. If water remains longer than three to four days, subsurface drainage likely will be required. For a rain garden to work, it needs to be moist but not waterlogged. Standing water lasting more than four to five days under normal conditions indicates a drainage problem that will likely turn your rain garden into a wetland and might possibly create mosquito problems.

If your site passes the drainage test, remove the sod and dig out the chosen area, excavating to a depth of one foot. To properly size a rain garden, a good rule of thumb is that it should be about 5 to 7 percent of the size of the area draining to it. This calculation should take into account driveways, rooftops, patios, and any other areas where rainfall is not absorbed directly into the soil. For instance, if the impervious surfaces add up to a 2,000-square-foot area providing water to the rain garden, then a 10-by-10-foot garden (100 square feet) is adequate.

When the digging is complete, it is time to install plants. Rain gardens open up new opportunities for gardeners to select plants they may have admired but didn't have the proper growing conditions for. Some people choose ferns, irises, and pitcher plants; many good selections are available for both color and beauty.

The last step is to top off the area with three to four inches of shredded hardwood mulch. Don't overlook the importance of selecting mulch for your rain garden. Use coarsely shredded hardwood mulch, if available. Double-shredded is okay, but some may float away during rains. Pine bark mulch and pine straw are not recommended because of floating issues.

Rain Gardens Are Growing More Popular

With the implementation of increasingly stringent rules from the federal and state governments regarding stormwater, more rain gardens are being installed in municipalities across the state. North Carolina State University is a leader in helping both homeowners and municipalities address environmental issues through such methods as rain gardens. The university's Department of Biological and Agricultural Engineering conducts research on rain gardens and other environmental practices to handle stormwater runoff. The department also works with North Carolina

Cooperative Extension to sponsor workshops to educate engineers and landscape architects in rain garden design.

More and more gardeners across North Carolina are installing rain gardens, since they offer a chance to creatively use different plants in the landscape and help protect the Old North State's rivers and streams. Rain garden installers and property owners can feel good about doing something positive for the environment.

Twirling, Twining Vines Add Landscape Interest

By Stephen Greer, Forsyth and Gaston Counties

Vines have long been a part of our landscapes, serving many purposes, from aesthetic to functional. North Carolina provides many different growing environments conducive to a variety of attractive vines.

There are three general types of vines. All support themselves as climbers by twining, by attaching rootlike structures to walls, or by attaching to objects by tendrils. Understanding their growth habits and how they attach themselves to nearby objects will help determine what type of support system to put in place. Fences, arbors, and walls are normal means of support. Keep in mind the structure at some time will require maintenance. Likewise, the vine will need your attention from time to time.

Evergreen and deciduous vines are available. Some vines produce flowers. Before selecting a vine for your landscape, do a little research. It's important to know growing requirements. Some vines grow best in the eastern part of the state, while others give their best performance in higher elevations in the west. Will your vine of choice perform at its peak in sun, shade, or a mix of the two? Some vines are grown for fall leaf color or for their unique stem structure after the leaves have fallen off for the winter, thus adding an extra visual effect. In some settings, vines help reduce the energy demands of homes. Proper placement of vines and other plants can help modify the

Clematis
Robert E. Lyons

climate around homes, reducing the workload of the heating and cooling system.

Be aware of the invasiveness of certain vines when selecting and placing them in your landscape. A vine that has created problems in the past by its aggressive growth and reseeding ability is the Chinese wisteria, *Wisteria sinensis*. An alternate is the native wisteria, *W. frutescens* 'Amethyst Falls'. Do your part and research the plant before placing it in your landscape. An invasive vine has the potential to impact your neighbors and community.

Several candidates for consideration are native vines such as Carolina jessamine 'Pride of Augusta' (*Gelsemium sempervirens*); cross vine 'Tangerine Beauty' (*Bignonia capreolata*); and *W. frutescens* 'Amethyst Falls'. A couple of nonnatives are *Clematis* spp. and moonvine (*Ipomea alba*), which is a night bloomer. Another nonnative is *Lonicera sempervirens* 'Leo', which is long blooming and has red to orange-red flowers.

To learn more, visit www.ces.ncsu.edu/depts/hort/hil/hil-633.html.

Wetland Plants

By Toby Bost, Forsyth County

Iris
Robert E. Lyons

Given the current popularity of do-it-yourself water gardens, the growing interest in wetland plants is no surprise. Terms such as *aquascaping* and *rain garden* are finding their way into mainstream horticultural publications.

Whether you need aquatic plants for a backyard water garden or an ornamental planting for wet Carolina soils, the choices are not limitless. Gardeners frequently encounter the same dozen or so plants in the garden center, especially for use in water gardens.

Woody plants suitable for landscaping in wet sites are commonly referred to as "riparian plants." North Carolina Cooperative Extension publication #646, *Qualifiers for Quagmires*, offers a list of plants for riparian landscapes; ask for it at a county Cooperative Extension Center. More than 60 species of woody plants qualify for home-landscaping purposes. Some choice selections include sweetshrub, buttonbush, ninebark, summersweet clethra, inkberry holly, Virginia sweetspire, small anise-tree, waxmyrtle, bayberry, Florida leucothoe, and redosier dogwood.

As with any design project, plants can enhance or detract from the effect you hope to achieve, so it is imperative to follow solid design principles when using wetland plants for the aquascape. Consulting a garden designer or landscape architect is money well spent.

The popularity of water gardening has increased exponentially during the last decade, and rightly so, since water can satisfy our senses by delighting our eyes and ears. Successfully creating an attractive water garden requires organization and planning. Consequently, it is important to address the engineering aspects of a water garden before selecting the plants and powering up the pump.

Aquatic plants for use in water gardens are often classified as floating leafed plants or submerged plants. Submerged plants are the oxygenators of the pond, a must for pond health and for supporting fish. This category of plants includes anacharis, *Elodea*; cabomba, *Cabomba*; and dwarf sagittaria, *Sagittaria*. Water lilies, both day- and night-blooming varieties, are the most popular floating plants.

Most of the aquatic and wetland plants sold by the industry never become problems. However, a few have proven to be highly invasive and have caused significant environmental trouble. Among the plants to avoid when landscaping at home are flowering rush and yellow flag. Also, beware of the few aquatic plants that appear on the noxious weed list. These include creeping primrose, *Ludwigia*; purple loosestrife, *Lythrum*; hydrilla, *Hydrilla*; and water fern, *Salvinia*. Though not currently regulated, a couple others to avoid are water hyacinth, *Eichhornia*, and parrot feather, *Myriophyllum*. Check with your local Cooperative Extension Center before ordering riparian plants offered in mail-order catalogs to avoid future maintenance headaches. A helpful website to visit is www.weedscience.ncsu.edu/aquaticweeds.

Below are aquatic plants to consider:

Water lily—*Nymphaea*

Lotus—*Nelumbo*

Umbrella palm—*Cyperus*

Arrowhead—*Sagittaria* spp.

Water iris—*Iris pseudacorus*

Horsetail—*Equisetum hyemale*

Arrow arum—*Peltandra virginica*

Pickerel weed—*Pontederia cordata*

Variegated rush—*Baumea rubiginosa*

Water garden
Robert E. Lyons

Trees

The Proper Care of Shade Trees

By Michelle Wallace, Durham County

Shade trees are a worthwhile investment. They provide beauty, reduce our energy costs in the summer, define our street corridors, frame our houses, and provide wood for buildings, heat for homes, and homes for wildlife. Since it can take many years for shade trees to reach their full height and potential, it is important to choose trees with superior qualities while taking into consideration site characteristics and location.

Most shade trees have the potential to live more than a century. For that reason, sites should be chosen carefully. Take into consideration properties such as soil type, drainage, environmental conditions (sun, shade, hardiness), and site limitations (power lines, confined root zones, proximity to buildings, underground utilities).

Before selecting the tree species, identify the location for planting and establishing the tree. Select a tree that will thrive under the site's conditions and that will provide the desired characteristics. Some of those desired characteristics include height, habit (pyramidal, oval, vase, rounded), rate of growth (slow, medium, fast), color of fall foliage, fruit (or lack thereof), bark, leaf persistence, and disease and insect resistance. While dozens of species of shade trees are available, not all thrive in every kind of growing condition. For example, many trees do not do well under urban environmental conditions that include drought stress, pollution, and confined root zones. It is therefore necessary to select trees with the desired traits for these conditions.

In order to maximize your investment, follow some basic guidelines to ensure the tree's health and longevity. Choose the best tree variety from a reputable nursery that guarantees its plants. Plant at the preferred time of year—which is fall to early spring—using proper techniques. Water slowly and thoroughly the first year the tree is established. Water one inch every seven to 10 days. Provide a two- to three-inch layer of mulch beginning at the base of the tree to form a ring that is at least three feet in diameter. Make sure the mulch does not touch the trunk. Use proper pruning techniques throughout the tree's lifespan. This will help ensure health, reduce insect and disease problems, and prolong the tree's life.

Proper Planting

Dig the planting hole no deeper than the root ball of the tree. In the case of heavy clay soil, plant the tree "high" so the root ball sits two to three inches above the finished grade. Dig the planting hole two and a half times the width of the root ball. Loosen the soil within the planting hole, and do not add soil amendments until the tree starts to put on new growth. Backfill half of the native soil around the planted tree, then slowly water. Backfill with the rest of the soil and cover with mulch.

If the tree is container grown, make sure it is not root bound before purchasing the plant. Take care to gently loosen up the roots to encourage them to grow out of the planting hole and into the surrounding soil. If the purchased tree is in a wire cage, cut up the wire as much as possible after it is in the planting hole. Remove the ties and ropes when the plant is in the hole. All these extra measures will help to prevent

Caring for new trees
Toby Bost

girdling of the tree, which stops nutrients and water from moving to the different parts of the plant.

Proper Pruning

Shade trees grow to heights of 40 feet and beyond. Occasionally, you may need to remove dead, diseased, or damaged limbs for both the health of the tree and public safety. In addition, there may be times when corrective pruning will improve the shape of the tree or prevent it from growing in an undesired location. Whatever the reason, the size of shade trees means that you may at some point require professional assistance. Many liabilities are connected with the improper removal of limbs. For this reason, hiring a certified and insured arborist is recommended.

For more information on proper planting and pruning techniques, visit www.ces.ncsu.edu/depts/hort/hil/pdf/hil-602.pdf.

Five Common Tree Myths

By Donald Breedlove, Iredell County

Trees enhance our lives in many ways. They are great gifts of nature that add beauty and value to our homes and communities.

Unfortunately, there are lots of myths about tree care. A drive through some communities will readily prove that many people believe these myths. For your trees' sake, learn about proper tree care.

Here are five common tree myths.

Myth: Prune one-third of shade tree branches when planting to balance the top with the roots.
Fact: Most nurseries produce quality plants that are suitable without major early pruning. If it's necessary to prune a newly planted shade tree, it should be done to develop an early framework. Even in this instance, never remove one-third of the

branches. Selectively remove branches that are too close, crossing, or rubbing or are excessive parallels. Don't follow the one-third removal practice.

Myth: Tree seals, wound dressings, and paints prevent disease, decay, and insects and help heal pruning cuts.
Fact: Tree seals, dressings, and paints do not help. Evidence actually exists that sealing a fresh cut traps moisture and can accelerate decay. If a wound is left open, the tree's natural healing defense will work as intended.

Myth: You can add soil around a tree to build up the ground for planting flowers and small shrubs.
Fact: Leave the soil grade surrounding and underneath the tree as is. When excessive soil is placed over the root system, the oxygen level is depleted and the roots suffocate. This can result in the severe decline or even the death of the tree. For conserving moisture, reducing traffic compaction, and suppressing weed competition, use a two- to four-inch layer of organic mulch. Excess mulch can cause problems with rodents, root suffocation, and trunk deterioration. Always leave a gap between the trunk and mulch and avoid the temptation of preparing a flower bed under a tree's canopy.

Myth: A tree company's ads in the newspaper and the yellow pages must mean that it has experts on tree care.
Fact: Anyone can run ads, but that doesn't mean he or she is an expert. Decisions are often driven by what you as a customer want. Tree topping is a prime example. Severe topping is the beginning of decline and death for many a shade tree. The customer normally pays twice—once for topping and later for removal. If your knowledge is lacking as to the best interest of a tree, begin by considering only the certified arborists of the International Society of Arboriculture (ISA). This group of worldwide professionals is dedicated to fostering a greater appreciation of trees and proper tree care. Log on to www.isa-arbor.com. Obtaining a list with contact information is as simple as typing in your zip code. You should get several references and then follow up on them. Always require insurance certificates, a detailed account of procedures, and a written contract. And remember that anyone who recommends or agrees to top your trees is not a professional.

Over-mulching
Toby Bost

Myth: Anybody can plant a tree correctly.
Fact: The idea that you can dig a hole and place manure or compost around the side of the roots and your tree will be happy is wrong. Start the process with a soil and site assessment. Consider the tree's mature height and spread. People often make the mistake of planting in holes that are not the right size for their trees.

Consider Native Trees for the Landscape

By Kevin Starr, Lincoln County

An exciting array of landscape trees is available these days. Many of these trees originated in other countries. Let's not forget, though, about the great native trees we can plant and enjoy.

When it comes to shade trees, the native oaks certainly come to mind. One of the most majestic native trees is the white oak. While the white oak is a slow grower, planting one is a contribution you can make for posterity. Because trees such as the white oak take a long time to reach significant size, it is particularly important to protect them during construction projects. Perhaps the best-known native oak in the landscape is the willow oak. It grows faster than the white oak and can also become quite large. Other popular species include the pin oak, the Nuttall oak, the Shumard oak, and the red oak. The live oak is an evergreen that grows well in the coastal region; it is native to the warmer regions of the South.

The maples are the other big group of native shade trees. The red maple and its varieties, such as 'October Glory', are widely planted and grow faster than the sugar maple. Keep in mind that with faster growth comes weaker wood, though this should not deter you from enjoying the red maple. The maples are good choices for shade and

Redbud
Connie Little

beautiful fall foliage. Other trees of varying sizes that provide outstanding fall color are black gum, sourwood, and sassafras.

One of the most popular native trees in the landscape is the flowering dogwood. The key to success with the dogwood is site selection. Try to provide good soil and partial shade if possible. Remember that the dogwood is an understory tree in the forest, so try to simulate those conditions.

When you think about native trees with showy flowers, the Southern magnolia—a native of the Deep South—has to be on the list. Its shiny evergreen leaves and large, fragrant white flowers make it a classic in North Carolina landscapes. Many varieties are available these days, including some smaller-leaved forms such as 'Little Gem' and 'Teddy Bear'. These are best suited to compact yards.

Mention conifers and the pines usually come to mind first. Different species of pines perform well in each region. The white pine predominates in the mountains but becomes problematic east of the foothills. The longleaf pine does well in the eastern part of the state and is used to a lesser extent in the Piedmont. Check with your Cooperative Extension agent or county forest ranger on which species performs best in your area. A unique conifer is the bald cypress. Don't be surprised when it loses its leaves in the fall. In spite of the fact that bald cypress is native to moist areas in eastern North Carolina, it is an adaptable tree in terms of soil conditions. It has fine-textured foliage and is rather distinctive in the landscape.

If you want a native tree with interesting bark, look no farther than the river birch. Its peeling bark is its primary ornamental feature. This tree is normally grown as a multitrunk specimen. Look for varieties like Dura-Heat™ and 'Heritage'. Birch is best used as a specimen tree and in mulched areas away from foundations and septic fields, due to shallow rooting.

A great source of native tree species is the North Carolina Division of Forest Resources, which sells bare-root seedlings that are dug and shipped during the cold part of the year, when the trees are dormant. The prices are extremely reasonable. A number of species are available. An even greater variety is offered if you order one of the special packages. These include the environmental, wildlife, and wetland-riparian packages. For information on ordering seedlings from the North Carolina Division of Forest Resources, visit www.dfr.state.nc.us/. Click on "Tree Seedling Catalog" under the "Starting a Forest" section.

Don't Top the Trees

By Fred Miller, Catawba County, and Kevin Starr, Lincoln County

Topping is the practice of cutting back trees so that major branches and trunks are left as stubs of varying lengths. This practice is not recommended by tree experts. In fact, when considering the extent of tree disfigurement, decay, and even death caused by topping, the damage caused by this practice is rivaled only by natural disasters such as ice storms and hurricanes.

Tree experts view topping as a very destructive practice. According to the International Society of Arboriculture (ISA), topping is perhaps the most harmful tree-pruning practice known. Yet despite more than 25 years of literature and

Don't top trees.
Toby Bost

seminars explaining its harmful effects, topping remains a common practice.

Why do homeowners have their trees topped? There seems to be a variety of reasons. Some people are afraid of storm damage to their homes caused by the effects of wind or ice on nearby trees. Other folks want to try to limit the size of their trees. Unfortunately, one of the common reasons seems to be that their neighbors had it done. Tree toppers sometimes start working in a neighborhood and then go from house to house for more business, which results in a long line of damaged trees.

Topping is bad for trees for a variety of reasons, not the least of which is that it damages their natural beauty. What took nature years to accomplish can be undone by a chain saw in just a short time. Even if the trees grow back out, they will have an unattractive appearance. The wounds made as trunks and limbs are stubbed off can't heal properly and are ideal places for diseases and insects to get established. A severe topping in the winter will remove most of a tree's leaf buds that were formed the previous season. Those buds would have produced the leaves to make food for the plant through the process of photosynthesis. Thus, the tree has to use up a lot of its stored food and also has to develop new buds to replace the thousands that were lost. Sometimes, such trees are not able to overcome topping and die the first season afterward. Why pay someone to damage your trees?

The appropriate course of action for a homeowner is to consult with a certified arborist. Certification is overseen by the ISA and requires those who become certified to pass a test. This ensures that the arborist has a basic level of knowledge. Ask a qualified arborist about your concerns. Keep in mind that a good arborist knows how to correctly prune a tree without topping it. Consult with as many arborists as you need to feel comfortable. Ask not only about cost but also about things such as insurance and references. The ISA website has helpful links titled "Why Hire an Arborist?" and "Why Topping Hurts Trees." For more information, visit www.treesaregood.com.

These Trees Add Interest to Winter Landscapes

By Paul McKenzie, Vance and Durham Counties

If your landscape seems to have fallen into the winter doldrums, then it's the per-

'Townhouse' crape myrtle
Todd Lasseigne

fect time to think about adding some seasonal interest. Many Carolina gardeners rely heavily on spring bloomers such as dogwoods, azaleas, and daffodils and ignore the possibilities for spicing up the winter garden.

Landscaping for winter interest requires a shift in focus for those who are accustomed to the spring garden. Rather than bright yellows, violets, and pinks, the color palette shifts to golds, browns, shades of dark green, and the occasional splash of red or white. Rather than bombarding the senses, the winter landscape offers subtle contrasts. Differences in texture and form provide a stark beauty.

Trees can add spice to the winter landscape in several ways. Although there are a few winter bloomers such as the Japanese flowering apricot, *Prunus mume*, most winter-interest trees are chosen for interesting bark, attractive form, evergreen foliage, or brightly colored berries.

Choose Trees with Striking Bark

The casual gardener, for example, may fail to notice the striking bark of the crape myrtle. When properly pruned, the smooth, rust-colored stems can become a real centerpiece among the golds and tans of winter. Other trees with exfoliating or peeling bark such as paperbark maple, *Acer griseum*, add striking textures. The lacebark elm, *Ulmus parviflora*, offers mottled patches of tan, rust, and gray. Korean and Japanese stewartias, *Stewartia koreana* and *S. pseudocamellia*, sport patches of green, brown, and gray.

Consider Weeping or Contorted Forms

Many deciduous trees shed their leaves to reveal gracefully arranged trunks and branches. The weeping form of the Japanese flowering cherry, *Prunus subhirtella* 'Pendula', is the classic example. Many of the Japanese maple, *Acer palmatum*, cultivars serve the purpose equally well. Also keep an eye out for trees that come in "contorted" forms with strikingly twisted branches. These are certain to become conversation pieces. Harry Lauder's Walking Stick, *Corylus avellana* 'Contorta', a contorted variety of hazelnut, is sure to please. Contorted mulberry, *Morus australis* 'Unryu', and corkscrew willow, *Salix matsudana* 'Tortuosa', are also worthy contenders that live up to their names. As a bonus, the stems make fabulous additions to winter flower arrangements.

Brighten with Berries

Berry producers add a splash of bright color to the winter landscape, though in some cases the birds may polish off the harvest before you finish enjoying it. Hollies tend to have long-lasting berries. Birds often save them for late winter, after they have exhausted more preferred fare. Cultivars with a tall pyramidal shape and glossy green leaves are the classic form. Also consider weeping yaupon holly, *Ilex vomitoria* 'Pendula', which boasts both abundant berries and a graceful branch structure. Keep in mind that hollies bear male and female flowers on separate trees. If you are purchasing a holly for winter interest, buy it during berry season to be certain you have the right gender. Although some are self-fertile, many varieties require a male plant nearby for pollination or no berries will set.

Don't forget the red berries of the dogwood, and don't limit yourself to *Cornus florida*, the old standard. Kousa, *C. kousa*, and Tatarian, *C. alba*, dogwoods are among those worth considering.

Enjoy the Evergreens

Evergreens offer more than their name implies. By carefully selecting and mixing your choices, you can bring shades of yellow, gold, and blue into the winter landscape. Southern magnolia, *Magnolia grandiflora*, provides large, thick, dark green leaves. If the size of your lot gives you pause at the thought of planting a tree that will eventually reach awesome proportions, consider the sweet bay magnolia, *M. virginiana*, a much smaller cousin.

For large lots, the stately deodar cedar, *Cedrus deodara*, makes a bold statement. This 70-foot evergreen grows in a wide pyramidal form with gracefully extended branches. Hinoki false cypress, *Chamaecyparis obtusa*, grows to 20 feet and is available in a golden-hued form. Try emerald green arborvitae for subtle green shades.

When choosing trees for the winter landscape, consider what they may provide in other seasons. In small urban lots, multipurpose plants that offer something in more than one season are the way to go. The stewartias, for example, provide flowers in the summer and attractive foliage color in the fall. Small trees with multiseason interest will maximize your landscape investment.

Remember, before planting any tree, consult your local Cooperative Extension Center, a reputable nursery, or a good gardening reference book to find out the full-grown height and spread and the preferred environment.

Underused Small Trees

By Michelle Wallace, Durham County

A small tree is one that grows 15 to 20 feet tall with a six-foot central axis. Multistemmed trees such as crape myrtles are also considered small trees. They can be used as specimens, accent trees, and street trees under power lines. While crape

Lacebark maple
Connie Little

myrtles and dogwoods are popular, many less common small trees can add interest to the garden.

Specimen trees grab attention. Used sparingly and placed carefully, they enhance views in the garden year-round. *Betula nigra* 'Summer Cascade' (20 feet tall and 15 feet wide) is a weeping river birch with exfoliating bark. It tolerates both wet and dry conditions. *Acer palmatum* 'Sango Kaku' (20 feet tall and 15 feet wide) is a Japanese maple with coral red bark in winter and palmate golden leaves in fall. It grows in full sun to partial shade and will tolerate drought once established. *Taxodium distichum* 'Cascade Falls' (eight feet tall and five feet wide) is a weeping bald cypress that grows well in full sun and withstands wet and dry conditions.

Accent trees draw attention for a season or two and provide a backdrop for other plants. *Chionanthus retusus* (20 feet tall and 15 feet wide) is an upright fringe tree with white straplike flowers in spring and glossy foliage in summer. It grows in full sun to partial shade and will tolerate drought once established. *Cornus* 'Rutban' Aurora® is a cross between our native flowering dogwood and the kousa dogwood. It has white flowers like its parents but blooms a little later, in mid-spring. Aurora resists dogwood anthracnose and powdery mildew and has spectacular red fall foliage but does not produce fruit. *Cotinus coggyria* (15 feet tall and 10 feet wide) is a smoke tree that produces cloudlike pink flowers in spring and purple foliage in fall. It grows in a wide range of soils and tolerates drought once established.

Small trees can make great **street trees** where overhead power lines loom, provided they are large enough to define the street but small enough not to interfere with the lines, which can be as low as 30 feet. *Robinia pseudoacacia* 'Glode' (20 feet tall and wide) is a black locust with a round habit and yellow fall foliage. It is fast growing and drought tolerant once established. *Koelreuteria paniculata* (30 feet tall and wide) is a rounded goldenrain tree with yellow flower clusters in summer and papery capsules that persist through winter. It has a medium-to-fast growth rate and tolerates drought once established. *Cornus mas* 'Golden Glory' (20 feet tall and wide) is an upright corneliancherry dogwood with small yellow flowers in late winter and reddish purple foliage in fall. It tolerates full sun to partial shade and exfoliates its bark at maturity.

For a more comprehensive list of small trees suitable for North Carolina, visit http://www.ces.ncsu.edu/depts/hort/consumer/quickref/trees/smalltrees.html. Plant something different in the garden.

Food Gardens

Landscape with Style and Good Taste

By Ben Dungan, Gaston County

Edible landscaping merges two schools of thought. Think of it as the family farm meeting the urban gardener. The idea is quite simple: Incorporate some edible plants into the existing home landscape.

Edible plants take many forms. Many of them such as nuts, fruits, and vegetables are familiar. Other types of edible plants include herbs, edible flowers, and bulbs. Incorporating them into the home landscape is quite easy. Many of these plants have desirable features besides the fact that they can be eaten. Blueberries, for example, have showy flowers as well as a nice fall color. They make a beautiful hedge while also providing tasty fruit in mid- to late summer. Many of the tree fruits have beautiful flower displays in early spring.

This edible-landscaping trend is growing for many reasons. For one, nothing beats eating fresh fruits and vegetables harvested directly from the plants. Concern is increasing over the pesticides used on many of the foods we eat. Growing your own food lets you limit the chemicals that are applied to particular plants. The overriding reason many gardeners are moving toward the edible landscape is the desire to be self-reliant. To be able to live off the land and provide for yourself may be the most rewarding aspect of edible landscaping.

Edible landscaping doesn't stray from the basic gardener's rules of thumb. You'll need well-drained soil with lots of compost and organic matter. Addressing the soil before planting will be integral to the success of your garden. You may need a soil test to get you started on the right foot. Lastly, allowing your landscape to receive at least six hours of light per day is ideal.

Edible plants vary in shape and size. Some may be trees and others groundcovers. The beauty of these plants is that they can perform many of the same functions as ornamentals. Simply substituting edible plants for ornamental plants will put you on your way to creating an edible landscape.

Instead of planting begonias and marigolds in your containers, take an edible slant and plant some herbs in pots. Many herbs are drought tolerant and make excellent potted plants. Vines such as Carolina jessamine, climbing roses, and clematis are popular in the landscape. However, grapes and kiwis are great edible vine alternatives. Fruit trees planted in lieu of shade trees are another option. Many edible flowers such as nasturtiums, violas, scented geraniums, and pansies can be incorporated into the mix as well.

Edible landscaping will allow you to incorporate local food plants and hard-to-find varieties that can't be purchased in stores anymore. Many heirloom seeds that

Fig tree
Toby Bost

have been passed down from generation to generation survive well only in our climate. Since these seeds are difficult to find, your edible landscape can have a definite local flavor.

Time and care are required for an edible landscape. The difference between an ornamental landscape and an edible landscape is that a final product is produced in the edible landscape. The challenge is getting that final product before the wildlife in your area does. Edible plants may require a little more pruning, watering, and fertilizing than plants in an ornamental landscape.

Overall, though, edible landscaping is a good option for hobbyist gardeners. If you don't mind standard garden chores, edible landscaping may be for you. Just remember to start small. You don't want to work so hard that you're too tired to harvest your rewards.

Growing Tomatoes in the Home Garden

By Terry Garwood, Surry County

If I had to choose the vegetable that I enjoy the most, it would be the tomato. A thick slice of tomato between two slices of bread with a little salt and mayonnaise and you've got a meal. I have been growing tomatoes for only 25 years, but I'll share some of my techniques for success.

When to Plant

Tomatoes are warm-season plants, so plant them after the last chance of frost has passed. Tomatoes do not like temperatures below 55° F at night. Blossom drop can occur in early spring when daytime temperatures are warm but night temperatures fall below 55°. In summer, blossoms will drop when temperatures exceed 90° in the day and stay above 76° at night.

Garden Site

Plant in a garden site that has full sun and a soil pH between 6.0 and 6.5. It is very important to rotate your sites so that you do not plant tomatoes in the same place the following year. Plant in the same spot every fourth year. Blossom-end rot occurs frequently in North Carolina. The condition is caused by calcium deficiency in the developing fruit. To help provide calcium to the plant throughout the growing season, broadcast about a cup of lime in and around the planting hole while transplanting.

Stake, Fertilize, Water, Weed

Stake your tomato plants for greater success. The plants will take less space and will be easier to pick. And if you have any insects or diseases, they will be easy to identify, remove, or spray as needed. While you can allow tomatoes to grow on the ground, they may be lost due to soil rot, insects, and animals. Staked and pruned tomatoes produce fewer but larger fruit than caged or unsupported plants.

Tomatoes respond well to fertilizer applications, especially phosphorus. Excess nitrogen fertilizer can result in plants with extremely vigorous vine growth but little fruit production. Apply 2½ to 3 pounds of a complete fertilizer such as 5-10-10, 5-20-20, or 8-16-16 per 100 square feet of garden area. Work the fertilizer into the soil about two weeks before planting. Apply additional nitrogen fertilizer after the first fruit has formed and is about the size of a dime. If the fertilizer is applied too soon, the blossoms and small fruit may drop.

Tomatoes are usually determinate or indeterminate in growth habit. Determinate tomato plants grow to a certain height and then stop. They also flower and set all their fruit within a relatively short period of time. This is an advantage if the tomatoes are being grown primarily for canning purposes. Indeterminate tomato plants grow, flower, and set fruit over the entire growing season. Once the plants are established, apply mulch to conserve moisture and suppress weed growth. Pull weeds by hand or remove by shallow cultivation. An even moisture supply is important, especially

Tomato plants
Connie Little

'Spice' globe basil
Robert E. Lyons

when the fruit begins to develop. If the soil becomes too dry, blossom-end rot can be a problem. Too much water at one time may split ripening fruit.

Disease Resistance

Another characteristic to look for when choosing tomato cultivars is disease resistance. Many cultivar names are followed by one or more letters indicating resistance to verticillium wilt (V), fusarium wilt (F), or nematodes (N). Disease resistance can be an important consideration, especially if you have experienced problems with tomatoes in the past.

Cultivars for North Carolina

Hundreds of tomato cultivars are available for the home gardener. I have tried dozens of varieties and usually continue to grow the ones that have been a consistent success. I prefer determinate varieties and will plant a spring crop and another crop in July for fall harvest. I experiment with new varieties each year and observe flavor, yield, and disease resistance. I also prefer tomato varieties that have "keeping" ability. Canned tomatoes provide robust flavor throughout the off-season. I have tried several of the heritage-type tomatoes. While they may be tasty, they are not resistant to any diseases and are the first to die. In addition, the fruit does not keep well and must be eaten quickly.

For recommended varieties for different areas of North Carolina, contact your local Cooperative Extension Center. Here is a short list of tomato varieties that I have had success with in the upper Piedmont of North Carolina:

Fresh market: Carolina Gold, Mountain Fresh Plus, Better Boy, Mountain Spring, Park's Whopper Improved

Cherry: Sweet 100, Sun Gold

Home Orchard Basics

By Terry Garwood, Surry County

A home orchard can be a great family project and can provide fresh fruit for consumption. A well-established and well-maintained home orchard will also enhance the appearance of the landscape. However, there is more to growing fruit than planting the trees and harvesting the crop. Growing high-quality tree fruit requires considerable knowledge about cultivars, planting sites, soil types, planting techniques, training, pruning, fertilizing, and managing pests. Without sufficient and proper care for fruit, quality will be quite poor. Apples, pears, peaches, plums, and cherries can be successfully grown in the home orchard if you follow some basic rules. Here is a brief summary of what it takes to have a home orchard.

Select your site to avoid spring frost, which is the number-one reason for loss of tree fruit in North Carolina. Selecting an elevated site may help avoid frost. Frost moves downhill and fills in low areas, much like water in a pond. A beautiful spring bloom along with frost or freeze equals no fruit.

Asian pear
Michael Parker

Select fruit based on family preference and available space. Available time and pollination requirements also determine the size of the planting. Don't plant more than you can care for properly.

Consider planting several varieties of the same kind of fruit so they mature at different times to prolong the harvest season. Some varieties are best for special uses such as freezing, canning, or other preservation methods. Purchasing some varieties in season from commercial growers may be more economical than growing them yourself.

Cross-pollination is necessary for satisfactory fruit set in many tree fruits. Select varieties that have overlapping bloom dates. To be certain of adequate cross-pollination, plant at least three varieties of apples. Many varieties will not cross-pollinate. Golden Delicious is used by many commercial growers as a pollinizer for other varieties of apples in their orchards.

Plant at least two varieties of pears, plums, and sweet cherries. Japanese- and European-type plums are not generally effective as pollinizers for each other, so plant two varieties of the same type. Home production of sweet cherries is usually difficult in North Carolina. Sour cherries cannot be used to pollinate sweet cherries because they are different species. All of the sour cherry, peach, and nectarine varieties are sufficiently self-fruitful to set satisfactory crops with their own pollen. Apricots are not adapted to North Carolina.

Buying Trees

Obtain the best nursery stock available. Buy only from reputable nurseries that guarantee their plants to be true to name, of high quality, and packed and shipped correctly.

It's best to obtain one-year-old trees. Trees from ⅜-inch to ⅝-inch caliper are preferred. Oversized trees are not recommended for the home orchard. Young trees will bear almost as soon, are easier to keep alive, and develop into healthier, more vigorous trees than do oversized trees.

Orchard Management

Test your soil prior to planting and adjust the pH to 6.2. Add phosphorus, if needed, prior to planting. After planting, apply a complete fertilizer such as 10-10-10 at about three ounces for each year of growth. Apply one-third of the total year's requirement, or one ounce, in early March, one ounce in late April, and one ounce in early June. It is best to spread the fertilizer outside the planting hole.

Mulch young fruit trees until they begin to bear. Eliminate weeds so they will not compete for available moisture and fertilizer. Cultivation must be shallow to avoid injury to roots near the surface. The cultivated or mulched area should extend a little beyond the spread of the branches.

Pest control is essential for the production of tree fruit. Our climate provides the heat and moisture to grow numerous diseases and insect pests that will damage or destroy your fruit. Proper timing and application of pest control sprays early in the season will help bring the fruit to harvest.

Proper Pruning

Proper training and pruning are essential to help regulate growth, to improve fruit size and quality, to control tree size, and to reduce production costs. Pruning is necessary to shape the trees for convenience and to repair damage. Most pruning is done during the dormant season—preferably, just before active growth begins in the spring.

This touches only on the basics. Learn more before you invest time, energy, and money in a home orchard. Contact your local Cooperative Extension Center or visit www.ces.ncsu.edu/depts/hort/hil/ag28.html for a "Home Orchard Production Manual."

Raised-Bed Gardening Yields More Than Lush Plants

By Diane Turner, Henderson County

North Carolinians are blessed with pretty nice weather for gardening, but our soil leaves something to be desired. One common method of correcting soil problems is using raised beds for vegetables, small fruits, and perennials. Raised beds allow gardeners to concentrate on amending soil in small spaces instead of tackling huge areas.

Raised beds are popular for many reasons. Research indicates that a well-maintained raised garden can produce approximately double the conventional yield from planting in rows. This greater production can be attributed to improved soil con-

Raised-bed gardens
J. C. Raulston Arboretum

ditions, including reduced soil compaction. Water, air, and roots all have difficulty moving through soil compressed by tillers and human feet. Gardeners can avoid the problem completely by creating beds narrow enough to work from the sides.

When creating raised beds, make them wide enough to reach across but no wider than four feet. Bed length can be whatever suits your needs. Depth is normally eight to 12 inches if you choose to enclose or frame the bed. If the bed is not framed, it should be about six inches deep with rounded edges to help prevent erosion.

Raised beds are perfect for individuals who find it difficult to bend over. They also make gardening accessible to people in wheelchairs. Benches may be built around raised beds to allow gardeners to sit and work the soil. Supports for poles, trellises, and cages can be mounted to raised bed frames to ensure easy installation and removal.

Pest control is less difficult in raised beds. If burrowing rodents are abundant, line the bottom of the bed with poultry wire or hardware cloth. To discourage rabbits, place a low wire fence around their favorite foods. Weed control can be achieved economically with plastic mulch, as a roll can span the width of the bed.

Raised beds reduce the space for weeds to grow, since the plants are close together. They also allow for water conservation with the use of soaker hoses and drip irrigation systems.

Soil preparation is the key to successful raised-bed gardening. There is no substitute for deep, fertile soil high in organic matter. Humus-rich soil holds extra nutrients and moisture. If the garden soil you have is not deep, double-digging the beds will improve it. Remove the top nine to 12 inches of soil from the bed. Insert a spade or spading fork into the next nine to 12 inches of soil to break up compacted layers. Mix the topsoil that you removed with a generous amount of compost or manure and return the mixture to the bed. It should be fluffy and slightly raised. Continue this action every six to eight inches along the bed.

Treated wood is often used as the construction material for enclosed raised beds. Use the new lumber that is treated with chromated copper arsenate (CCA). This preservative is the safest for gardens because of its very low tendency to leach into soil. Avoid using creosote-treated railroad ties. Freshly treated creosote lumber can leach into the soil for several years and continues to give off vapors over a seven- to nine-year period. Other construction material options include cement blocks, recycled plastic lumber, and bricks. Be sure to keep in mind that cement blocks can raise the soil pH over time.

Start planning or building your raised beds now. There is no better sign of being a successful gardener than eating fresh vegetables from your own garden.

General Gardening Advice and Information

Tidings of Compost and Joy: Gift Ideas for the Gardener

By Stephen Greer, Forsyth and Gaston Counties

Do you have a gardener on your holiday gift list? Giving gardening gifts does not have to be a challenge. Whether you're looking for a gift for a beginner or an experienced gardener, you can turn giving into a simple pleasure.

An interesting fact about people who work with tools is that it seems they can never have enough. Select high-quality equipment that is sturdy and easy to handle. When picking hand tools, think about the handles and how they will fit the person receiving your gift. Look for tools with cushioned grips. Some pruners come with long swivel handles designed to be ergonomically pleasing to use. A kneeling pad or kneeling seat might be useful. Other gifts that help make gardening easier include garden gloves, wide-brimmed hats, garden aprons, and belts for holding tools and cell phones.

Most gardeners have a thirst for knowledge, which places garden-related books and other reference materials at the top of many gift lists. Look for sources that are specific to the growing conditions in North Carolina or the particular region. Some books popular with gardeners are the following:

- *The Carolinas Gardener's Guide* by Toby Bost and Jim Wilson
- *Month-by-Month Gardening in the Carolinas* by Bob Polomski
- *Best Garden Plants for North Carolina* by Pam Beck and Laura Peters
- *The Southern Gardener's Book of Lists* by Lois Trigg Chaplin

Birdhouses make great gifts!
Connie Little

- *Tough Plants for Southern Gardens* by Felder Rushing
- *Growing & Propagating Showy Native Woody Plants* by Richard E. Bir
- *Ornamental Grasses for the Southeast* by Peter Loewer
- *Native Perennials for the Southeast* by Peter Loewer
- *The Plant Hunter's Garden* by Bobby J. Ward
- *The North Carolina Fruit and Vegetable Book* by Walter Reeves and Felder Rushing

New gardeners may need more general plant books that include many visuals along with the descriptive details. Seasoned gardeners may prefer detailed reference materials on topics of interest such as perennials, herbs, or coastal plants.

Several gardening cookbooks connect the garden to the table. You can even add your personal touch in the form of a recipe book filled with gardening pictures to go along with selected recipes. This is a chance to include local flavor such as homemade sauces, jams, jellies, dips, and other culinary goodies.

Look for garden-related gifts that are functional and beautiful. Gardeners and even nongardeners who spend time in the outdoors might enjoy a garden bench, comfortable outdoor furniture, wind chimes, or a small water fountain.

Potted bulbs such as paper whites or amaryllis need little attention as long as they are placed in a room with bright natural light and are watered as needed to achieve bloom. Another idea is jewelry in a floral design. A simple bouquet of flowers can be an elegant, thoughtful gift.

Wildlife in the garden can be the inspiration for other ideas. Consider giving a bird feeder, birdbath, binoculars, a bird identification book, a gift membership to a bird group, or a year's supply of birdseed.

Weather-related equipment for gardeners with an interest in meteorology is a great idea. Weather gifts can run from inexpensive rain gauges made of plastic to ones made of decorative metal to wireless remote digital gauges that can be read through a receiver from the comfort of a recliner. Some gauges can read the wind speed and phases of the moon.

For gardeners who seem to have everything, consider giving a gift certificate or a coupon for your time in the future. This is a fun way to help in the spring with big seasonal garden activities like mowing, mulching, transplanting, weeding, and raking. If you have a truck, a coupon for a delivery of mulch may be a wonderful gift. For gardeners who have a tendency to overdo it and end up tired and sore, a certificate for a massage will work wonders. Many full-service garden centers, on-line companies, and mail-order catalogs are more than willing to provide selected dollar-value gift certificates.

If you are still not sure about a gift, talk to a veteran gardener for ideas. Many public gardens offer memberships and opportunities for donations in honor of some special person. The ideas are just about limitless, so put those creative thoughts to work.

Fall Planting Guide

By Emily L. Revels, Cumberland and Mecklenburg Counties

To many, fall is the most beautiful time of the year, thanks to its painted landscapes. It is a time of harvest and the maturing of the garden. To the gardener, it also is a season full of activity, including planting and preparation for the winter rest. Planting in the fall requires patience and the ability to appreciate delayed gratification.

Most nursery plants are great candidates for fall planting. They usually have well-developed root systems and like cool air temperatures. Trees and shrubs planted in the fall usually perform better the following year than those planted in the spring. Fall planting allows them to put their energy into establishing root systems, since the soil is still warm and they don't have to produce flowers and new leaves. During the fall, most trees and shrubs are entering their dormant periods, so they do not experience as much transplant shock. When spring arrives, these newly planted trees and shrubs are ready to get a jump on growing lush foliage and blooms.

When selecting, keep in mind that small plants establish themselves faster than large plants. It's tempting to select large plants, but often the small ones are better choices.

Complete a soil test to determine the pH of your soil and the nutrient requirements. Prepare your soil by tilling a planting bed and adding compost or organic matter. Do not add sand or peat moss to clay soil.

Right Plant, Right Place

Select the right trees and shrubs for your landscape. The stems, foliage, and bark should look healthy. Avoid plants that are damaged or have insect or disease problems. When possible, look at the roots. Plants should have well-developed roots that are white and do not encircle the root ball.

Answer These Questions

When considering a plant, answer these questions to help determine whether or not it is right for your site.

- What is the plant's mature height and spread?
- Does the plant need sun or shade?
- Does it flower?
- When does it flower?
- What type of maintenance will be required?
- What are the soil requirements?

Transporting Your Plants Home

Do not handle plants by their stems or trunks. Always handle by the containers. Do not stand your plants up in the back of a truck, since wind exposure during transport home can damage foliage. Instead, protect them by laying them down and covering them or wrapping them loosely in burlap or some other cloth. Water the plants as soon as you arrive home. If you are not planting right away, place them in a location away from sun and wind.

Proper Planting Tips

Water the plants prior to planting. Make sure your soil is well drained. Dig a planting hole three to five times wider but no deeper than the root ball. Loosening the soil several feet away from the plant will encourage root growth away from the root ball. Do not plant too deeply; the soil line should be the same as the original soil line

Plant Japanese maples and other trees in the fall.
Connie Little

or a little higher. Gently fill the hole with soil removed from the hole until it is half filled, then water slowly to remove any air pockets. Finish filling the hole with soil. Apply a two- to four-inch layer of mulch, then water slowly and thoroughly.

Do not fertilize a newly planted shrub or tree. Water it slowly and frequently (about every four days in the absence of rain) until the root system is established.

Contact your local Cooperative Extension Center for more information on fall planting. Ask for the Extension's Successful Gardener® *Tree Planting Guide.*

Christmas tree
N.C. Christmas Tree Growers' Association

Holiday Trees: Be Safe and Give Wildlife a Present

By Amy-Lynn Albertson, Davidson County

Christmas trees are grown in two regions of the state. Each produces different species based on climate.

Fraser fir trees are grown in the North Carolina mountains at elevations greater than 3,000 feet. Named for John Fraser, a Scottish botanist who explored the southern Appalachians in the late 1700s, Fraser firs are pyramid shaped and reach a maximum height of 80 feet with a trunk diameter of 1 to 1½ feet. More than 99 percent of North Carolina's Christmas tree production and all wholesale production occur in the mountains.

Holiday trees grown in the North Carolina Piedmont and coastal plain include the Virginia pine (*Pinus virginiana*), eastern white pine (*Pinus strobus*), eastern red cedar (*Juniperus virginiana*), and Leyland cypress (× *Cuppressocyparis leylandii*). Producers of these trees sell on a choose-and-cut basis.

The Fraser fir, balsam fir, Scotch pine, and Douglas fir last longer than other species. Make your choice by looking at, touching, feeling, smelling, and shaking the tree. Remove a ¼- to ½-inch disk from the trunk before placing the tree in a stand that holds water. A tree can use as much as a gallon of water in the first 24 hours and a quart each day afterward for every inch of stem diameter.

Follow some simple rules to keep your tree fresh and safe.

- Don't use lights with worn or frayed cords.

- Never use lighted candles on a tree.

- Don't overload electrical outlets.

- Place your tree away from fireplaces, radiators, televisions, and other heat sources.

- Make sure your tree has plenty of water to prevent drying.

- Always turn off decorations before going to bed or leaving home.

Consider recycling your tree after the holidays. To do so, remove everything, including tinsel, and place the tree outside for birds and other wildlife. The branches provide shelter from wind and cold. Hang fruit, seed cakes, or suet bags on them to feed wildlife. Mix peanut butter and seeds, place it on pinecones, and hang the cones in the tree. Prune off the branches and place them over perennials as winter mulch.

You can recycle your tree as fish habitat by sinking it into a pond or reservoir. The branches will provide fish with shady places to hide from predators. They will also provide habitat for aquatic snails and insects eaten by fish. In a pond, wire the tree to a cement block and drop it in six to 10 feet of water. In a reservoir, place it in 12 to 21 feet of water. Always position it away from swimming areas and mark the location so swimmers and boaters can avoid it.

To find local growers, visit www.ncchristmastrees.com, www.nc-chooseandcut.com, or your county Cooperative Extension Center.

Seed Catalogs Inspire Spring Dreaming

By Amy-Lynn Albertson, Davidson County

In most of North Carolina, we are blessed with mild winter weather that allows us to garden almost all year. However, when we do have those chilly days and nights, we can stay warm indoors while thumbing through the new seed catalogs that come in the mail. Seed catalogs contain more than just photos and plant descriptions. Some of the best are filled with growing tips not found in gardening books, including information about germination, starting times, bloom and harvest times, and ease or difficulty of growing. Many include great recipes as well. The tools and books offered in seed catalogs are usually top-notch. Most seed companies put their entire catalog inventories on their websites, so gardeners can shop online if they prefer.

In catalogs, the language often combines marketing with information. As a result, you can expect some jargon in the mix. Below is a sampling of catalog phrases and their likely meanings.

"Start seeds indoors" is used when discussing seeds that require more care than

Seed catalogs
Mark Dearmon

the average. They may germinate slowly or need warm temperatures, or the seedlings may demand extra time or attention prior to planting outdoors. Many perennials fall into this category.

When a vegetable is "novel" or "unusual" or has "unique" color or shape, you know flavor and texture are secondary. Similarly, "giant" is a clue to vegetables that are grand in size but perhaps better mounted above the fireplace than tossed into a winter stew.

Watch out for anything "vigorous." The word implies that the vine, shrub, or vegetable in question is ready and able to outcompete most plants in its path. If space is limited, look for compact, bush, or dwarf varieties.

Plants that "self-sow readily" are usually annuals or biennials that you plant once and have evermore. Each year, a new crop of seeds germinates and grows without any help from you. Depending on the plant and your attitude, it might become a weed or a favorite companion.

When looking for new varieties, seek recommendations from other experienced gardeners in your area or contact your county Cooperative Extension Center for information. Choose varieties that are resistant to or tolerant of common diseases. For example, tomato names may be followed by "VFN." These letters mean the plants are resistant to verticillium wilt, fusarium wilt, and nematodes, common diseases and parasitic organisms that plague tomatoes. Always order your seed from reputable seed companies. Bargain seed at a local hardware store may be less of a bargain than you counted on because it was probably packaged for the previous year or earlier. Don't save seed from last year's hybrid plants. Most hybrid varieties will not remain true to the variety once they've been planted and produce their own seed. Plants like summer squash also can cross-pollinate with some pumpkin varieties. So if you save the seeds and replant them, you may grow some weird summer squash.

Here is a short list of seed companies. Many more are out there.

Seeds of Change
888-762-7333
www.seedsofchange.com

A great resource for organic gardeners, Seeds of Change offers 100 percent organic vegetable, herb, and flower seeds. It has a huge selection, including several new introductions and many heirloom varieties. Its easy-to-read catalog also features gardening tips and recipes for using produce grown from its seeds.

W. Atlee Burpee & Co.
800-888-1447
www.burpee.com

The grandfather of seed catalogs, Burpee has been selling seeds via mail for over 130 years. This comprehensive resource is packed with new introductions, many of them Burpee exclusives. The company offers thousands of vegetable, herb, and flower seed varieties, as well as seedling plants and summer bulbs.

Park Seed Company
800-213-0076
www.ParkSeed.com

Selling much more than just seeds, Park Seed Company tests more than 2,000 new varieties of flowers and vegetables each year. The ones with the best results make it into its catalog.

Thompson and Morgan
800-274-7333
www.thompsonandmorgan.com

This world-famous 200-page seed catalog contains hundreds and hundreds of full-color photos. This one is a must if you are into flowers. Thompson and Morgan specializes in flower seeds, particularly those featured in English cottage gardens.

Select Seeds—Antique Flowers
800-648-0395
www.selectseeds.com

This catalog contains an interesting selection of seeds and plants. It specializes in heirloom flowers.

Johnny's Selected Seeds
877-564-6697
www.johnnyseeds.com

Johnny's specializes in cold-tolerant vegetable, herb, and flower seeds that are flavorful, disease resistant, and good producers.

A word of caution: Don't forget that winter daydreaming can result in a summertime burden. Resist the temptation to choose more than you can actually manage in your home garden.

What's in a Plant Name?

By Mark Blevins, Gaston County, and Toby Bost, Forsyth County

Garden centers and their plant selections have changed through the years. One of the most notable changes is that more plants are trademarked and patented. Plant images are often copyrighted. Call it shrewd merchandising or an attempt to simplify horticulture for the masses, but branding plants is a hot-button issue in the green industry. Here is a primer for industry jargon.

Patents for Plants

Plants can be patented just like can openers, clocks, and car parts. If a person discovers a plant that is different from all others, he or she can clone that plant and apply for a patent. The rules require invention or discovery in a cultivated state. Hybridizing is acceptable, but finding a plant in the wild isn't. A person has to reproduce the plant asexually by grafting, rooting a cutting, dividing, layering, or otherwise making genetically identical copies.

Plant patents last for 20 years and cost money, but the inventor (the person who discovered or propagated the plant) can control production and propagation or charge a fee when others make money off his plant invention. Nurseries that grow patented plants are required to pay a royalty when they sell them.

Interestingly, most seeds and all tubers are exempt from patents. People who think their seeds and tubers are extra special can apply for protection from the United States Department of Agriculture. Some manufacturers require farmers to follow regulations and legal agreements before planting the genetically modified seed of certain vegetables, like herbicide-resistant corn or soybeans.

Trademarks for Plants

Trademarks are different. They apply more to names than to plants. For example, Endless Summer® is the trademark name of *Hydrangea macrophylla* 'Bailmer'. You will probably never see a sign in a garden center that points people to the 'Bailmer' bigleaf hydrangeas. Instead, retailers put the plants in colorful pots with big tags displaying the trademark name and a premium price. This plant is also patented, so after the botanical name and cultivar, the tag will have the capital letters *PP* and a string of numbers in parentheses.

Similarly, there are many cultivars of Encore Azalea®, each with a cultivar name you may not recognize. The individual trademark names use the word *autumn* and a color description to emphasize that these plants bloom at an unusual time for azaleas. Examples are Autumn Amethyst™ and Autumn Coral™. Trademarks promote a brand or origin and are not technically part of the botanical names of the plants. Cultivar names cannot be trademarked, since they are for public use in identifying plants.

True cultivar names are getting lost in the shuffle as plants are referred to by trademarks—names owned by companies to distinguish their products from others. Cultivar names appear in single quotes and often in a smaller font on the labels.

Groups of plants also can be trademarked. David Austin®, Plants that Work®, and Proven Winners® are examples of plant collections with registered trademarks. Consumers often associate quality or special characteristics with plants under brand names, since lots of research, work, and money went into selecting the particular plants in these named collections. Expensive, colorful signs direct customers to collections of plant groups that offer unique landscaping opportunities. Stepables® may be a great choice where a groundcover is needed. If a customer needs ideas for accessorizing with color in autumn, then Fall Magic® selections just might fit the bill.

Copyrights for Plant Tags and Images

Copyrights are separate. They protect forms of expression. A plant tag or image can be copyrighted so that others cannot legally reproduce and distribute it. Lots of things can be copyrighted—songs, books, dramas, and other artistic forms—but not plants.

Plants without Hype

Keep in mind that plants with common names and unusual characteristics may be hidden beside or behind the flashy brands of trademarked and patented plants. Plenty of groundcovers tolerate some foot traffic. And there is no shortage of plants with fantastic fall color. Just because a collection is trademarked doesn't mean those are the only plants with those features.

Try both patented plants and others without the fancy names. Many plants are dependable, perform well, and look great without the hype. And if you and your gardening friends are thinking of writing a play about a trademarked and patented plant, consult a lawyer.

Plant Information from North Carolina State University

More than 4,000 fact sheets on specific plants can be found by visiting http://www.ces.ncsu.edu/depts/hort/consumer/factsheets/. You can find out about annual flowers, perennial flowers, summer- and fall-flowering bulbs, and plants that attract birds and butterflies. The site contains information on trees, grasses, and almost any kind of plant you can imagine.

Chapter 2

70 Top Plant Choices

Most gardeners are on the lookout for new plants to add to their gardens. These 70 top plant choices include both annuals and perennials and woody plants.

Gardentalk:

"In all things of nature there is something of the marvelous."
Aristotle

Agave parryi
Robert E. Lyons

Annuals and Perennials

Agaves Provide Structural Impact and Boldness

By Mark Blevins, Gaston County

Unique foliage, interesting structure, and occasionally a flower stalk that stretches 40 feet into the air are a few features of agaves. Described as fierce and outspoken, agaves give great bones to the body of your garden. These rugged plants endure brutal summer heat and keep their composure through winter rain and snow.

Often called century plants, this genus is comprised of succulent perennials that patiently grow and accumulate their reserves to put out one grand flower show. Contrary to agaves' nickname, flowering doesn't take 100 years. Agaves typically hold out for five to 10 seasons before producing a monstrously tall stalk of yellow flowers that is well worth the wait—a great gardening event! The second-generation progeny, called "pups," are produced as the originals expire.

Agaves are native to the most challenging desert habitats of Mexico and the southwestern United States. They can survive the hottest, driest summer that North

Carolina can bring. Agaves will benefit from as much sunshine as you can afford and respond well to fertilizer and water in the summer. Keep their feet from staying wet; agaves require very good drainage, especially during our cool, wet winters.

Sunny spots and rock gardens are great places for agaves. Large species such as *Agave americana* grow five feet wide and produce tall flower spikes, while smaller versions and other species such as *A. parryi* can display a more compact stature with equally beautiful, although slightly shorter, flower stalks. Silver, blue, or variegated leaves and colorful spines draw even more attention to this succulent, no matter the size.

Black-Eyed Susans Provide Native Sunshine

By Robert E. Lyons, director and professor at the Longwood Graduate Program at the University of Delaware and former director of the J. C. Raulston Arboretum at North Carolina State University

Black-eyed Susans
Robert E. Lyons

The prairies of Minnesota were the first places I seriously studied wildflowers. Using my camera to create a permanent record and *Newcomb's Wildflower Guide* to identify my slides correctly, I soon discovered my favorites. I was drawn to them time and time again, evidenced by the number of pictures. Without a doubt, one favorite was *Rudbeckia hirta*, the black-eyed Susan. It remains one of my most favored wildflowers to this day.

The range of this North American native stretches from the Rocky Mountains east to the Atlantic Coast states, and from Minnesota in the north to Texas in the south. This rather grandiose residency has yielded some interesting variations to the normally golden, daisylike flower. Wild forms may possess a ring of maroon or rusty brown encircling the flower's central "cone," and entire flowers may be found that lack gold completely, cloaked instead in that same deep maroon or brown color. Garden cultivars seem to have exploited all color possibilities, ranging from the absolutely magnificent 'Indian Summer', whose large, golden flowers and tall, erect stature are virtually without peer, to 'Sonora', which possesses sturdy, multicolored petals and an outstretched posture parallel to the ground.

Black-eyed Susans are short-lived perennials in the garden. They bloom easily their first year from seed and may be treated as annuals. Full sun is a must, and wet soils are their nemesis. Powdery mildew often besieges them late in the season—but late enough, in my opinion, to disregard it as any blemish to black-eyed Susans' reputation for cultivation.

Coralbells Provide Bold, Colorful Foliage

By Mark Danieley, Alamance County

Heuchera 'Pewter Veil'
Robert E. Lyons

Heuchera is an interesting family of perennials comprised of more than 50 species native to North America. *Heuchera*, commonly known as coralbells or alumroot, is hardy from zones 4 to 9, depending on species and cultivar.

Coralbells and alumroot are primarily grown for their foliage, but many species also have attractive flowers that are favored by butterflies. Flowering usually begins in June and continues throughout the growing season. Depending on the variety selected, coralbells can grow in sun or shade. Many varieties develop their best leaf color in full sun. They prefer moist, well-drained soils that have been amended with organic matter like leaf compost or pine bark fines. They are subject to few insect or disease problems, but leaf scorch can be an issue for plants grown in full sun during hot, dry conditions.

The increased interest in coralbells was sparked when *Heuchera micrantha* 'Palace Purple' was selected by the Perennial Plant Association as Perennial of the Year several years ago. Coralbells make a wonderful addition to the garden and can be used as edgings in perennial borders and group plantings. The lighter-colored varieties stand out nicely in lightly shaded gardens.

'Palace Purple' is perhaps the best-known variety, but a number of new varieties on the market are also worth considering for your garden. *Heuchera* 'Amber Waves' has true amber-colored foliage that is brightest in the spring and darkens through the season. *Heuchera* 'Canyon Belle' has clusters of bright red flowers above green foliage and works well in shade gardens. *Heuchera* 'Green Spice' has green leaves with dark purple veins that turn amber in the fall. *Heuchera* 'Plum Pudding' has excellent shiny, deep purple foliage with pinkish white blooms.

Hardy Ferns Add Versatility and Texture

By Donna Teasley, Burke County

Ferns are one of the most popular and versatile groups of plants. Though many of us may think of the fussy little varieties in the plant sections at grocery stores or the ones used in hanging baskets, the hardy ferns are quite different. They are as dependable as any perennial.

Hardy ferns
Connie Little

North Carolina is home to many varieties of hardy ferns. Although they may look delicate and hard to grow, they thrive with very little care or maintenance once they become established in the right spot. Most ferns prefer filtered sunlight, though many can tolerate dense shade or direct sun. Keep the soil similar to a natural forest habitat—evenly moist but not soggy, and rich in organic material.

Hardy ferns come in a large range of colors and textures. They are a good solution when you want to soften the lines of hedges and fences. They provide wonderful backdrops for other plants and can add texture and color underneath existing foundation plantings. Whether in mass plantings or combined with hostas, astilbes, and other shade-loving perennials, they make an interesting addition to any North Carolina garden. Most hardy ferns prefer slightly acidic soil with a pH of 5.5 to 6.5.

One of the finest of the hardy ferns is the Christmas fern, *Polystichum acrostichoides*, an evergreen fern that grows in zones 3 to 9. The hay-scented fern, *Dennstaedtia punctilobula*, does well in zones 3 to 7 and is drought tolerant. It will even withstand salt spray. When its fronds are crushed, they emit a smell similar to freshly mown hay.

You can find these plants in local garden centers and numerous catalog sources. Before making a purchase, be sure to check your site conditions to ensure that you have identified the best plant for that location.

Hellebores Color Winter with Charm

By Linda Blue, Buncombe County

Hellebores are small, lovely evergreen plants that add charm and color to winter gardens. Small enough to be tucked into little pockets of space in a garden, they have blooms and foliage that add a big boost of winter interest.

The most popular member of the *Helleborus* genus is the Lenten rose, *H. orientalis.* The foliage adds a bold texture to the woodland garden. Rising from a central crown, the leaves are large, dark green, glossy, and divided into five to nine segments. The plants stand 12 to 18 inches tall and up to two feet across.

The unique flowers of Lenten rose appear in February, even through a layer of

Lenten rose
Robert E. Lyons

snow. The nodding, five-petaled cups may range in color from cream to light green to pinkish brown, usually with maroon speckling. The flowers, which last several weeks, are followed by interesting seedpods.

Christmas rose, *H. niger*, is quite similar in appearance. Its flowers may not make it in time for Christmas but will probably bloom by January or early February. They are usually creamy white, changing to pink with age. The foliage is not as dark and glossy as that of Lenten rose but is otherwise similar. *H. niger* has a reputation for being more temperamental to grow.

Plant hellebores in at least partial shade. In the mountains of North Carolina, they can tolerate a half-day of sun, but they need shade in the afternoon in the Piedmont and coastal areas. They perform best in a woodland setting with moist, well-drained soil amended with plenty of compost. Lime will probably also be appropriate, as they prefer neutral to slightly alkaline soil.

Joe-Pye Reaches for the Sky

By Royce Hardin, Orange County

Joe-Pye weed, *Eupatorium* spp., is a conspicuous late-summer bloomer that grows naturally in wet or damp meadows, in thickets, and along roadsides. Luckily, it's a natural for gardeners. Few perennials can compare with the showy Joe-Pye weed's ability to create an imposing presence in the landscape. A member of the aster family, the plant is sometimes called feverweed, queen of the meadow, and numerous other common names.

Joe-Pye weed
Robert E. Lyons

A tall wildflower, Joe-Pye weed usually grows five to six feet but under good conditions can reach heights of 10 to 12 feet. Large-sized, whorled leaves adorn the stems like the spokes of a wheel. Joe-Pye weed's huge, rounded clusters of pink-purple fuzzy flower heads are borne on sturdy, unbranched stems, making the plant easy to recognize at blooming time. A dependable nectar source, the showy flower clusters are invariably covered by a variety of insects including butterflies, bees, and various wasps feeding on the sweet blossoms.

In the garden, Joe-Pye performs best in full sun and moist soil, though the plant is tolerant of a wide range of soil types and moisture levels and is even considered drought tolerant once established. The plant should be propagated by division.

Several Joe-Pye weed cultivars are available, including *E. purpureum* ssp. *maculatum* 'Atropurpureum'. Growing up to nine feet high, this Joe-Pye stands up for attention. Its purple-spotted, mottled stems don't require stakes. It makes a great show at the back of a border, thanks to its violet-purple flowers. *Eupatorium purpureum* ssp. *maculatum* 'Gateway', at four to five feet tall, is more compact and bushy. 'Gateway' has graceful, dusty, rose pink flower heads in summer and fall. The stems are wine colored and put out large green leaves. 'Alba' produces white flowers.

'Calicoform' alternanthera
Robert E. Lyons

Joseph's Coat Enhances Other Colors

By Amy-Lynn Albertson, Davidson County

Alternanthera ficoidea is an heirloom plant that was popular during the Victorian era in formal gardens. It has now made its way into our annual gardens, thanks to several new cultivars from Mexico and South America. Joseph's coat is the common name for this plant, which is sometimes confused with a yellow-green form of summer poinsettia that is also called Joseph's coat. Landscapers call the plant chartreuse alternanthera to avoid the common-name confusion. It is also called golden parrot leaf, golden alternanthera, and chartreuse calico plant.

Chartreuse alternanthera has eye-catching yellow-green foliage, compact growth habit, durability, and nonstop color from early spring until fall frost. It grows four to eight inches tall and six to 12 inches wide. It is often used in formal knot gardens or as edging to define plant beds. The plant enhances or echoes other colors, making them appear more vibrant. Alternanthera is grown for its foliage. Its small, greenish white flowers are borne in the leaf axils and hidden by the foliage. Chartreuse alternanthera does best in full sun with moist, well-drained soils. Light pinching will keep the plant compact.

A. dentata 'Purple Knight' is a frost-tender perennial grown for its dark purple foliage. It can be used as a beautiful contrast against other plants in less formal beds and flower borders. The rich color is produced only in full sun and makes a dramatic accent in sunny gardens. To maintain a compact habit, regularly pinch out the growing tips. To keep a formal appearance, use pruning shears to trim the plants in summer. Plant in well-drained soil; water regularly during summer. The growth habit is 18 to 36 inches in height, with an equal spread. The purple leaves excel in high heat and humidity. This plant looks great with rudbeckia and lantana.

Ornamental Sweet Potatoes Add Flavor to the Garden

By Karen Neill, Guilford County

The sweet potato, *Ipomoea batatas*, a tropical root and member of the morning glory family, has taken the landscape industry by storm. Adding another dimension to a plant traditionally welcomed on North Carolina tables, the ornamental sweet potato is popular for its decorative foliage and vigorous growth habit, making it an appealing choice for mixed containers or as a groundcover.

Like so many plants from tropical regions, sweet potatoes like it hot. They need full sun and constant moisture. Plant after the danger of frost has passed. You can then watch them take off when the soil temperature begins to warm.

Look for three main cultivars: 'Blackie', which has purple, almost black foliage and deeply cut leaves; 'Marguerite' ('Sulfur'), which has chartreuse and lime green foliage; and 'Tricolor' ('Pink Frost'), which has shades of pink, green, and white marbled in the same leaf. While these do not flower often, they enhance mixed plantings of shrubs, herbaceous perennials, and flowering annuals.

Perhaps most exciting is the release of four patented cultivars developed by North Carolina State University researchers in cooperation with the J. C. Raulston Arboretum. The Sweet Caroline series names each new cultivar by its color. Plants in the series are characterized by a compact growth habit and reduced root size, which make them better suited than existing cultivars to containers and landscape gardens. They offer all the colors currently available, plus the uniquely hued 'Sweet Caroline Bronze'. The latter is coppery bronze in appearance, especially as the leaves age, and has contrasting deeper-colored veins in its leaves.

'Sweet Caroline Light Green' sweet potato
Robert E. Lyons

Perennial Hibiscus Provides Show-Stopping Appeal

By Emily Revels, Cumberland and Mecklenburg Counties

Hibiscus moscheutos
Robert E. Lyons

Children play hide-and-seek behind it. People leave their cars in the middle of the road to get a closer look. The first time you see the extremely large flowers of the perennial hibiscus, your mouth will drop open and you'll want to attend the party for which Mother Nature created this lovely beauty!

Hibiscus moscheutos, commonly called perennial hibiscus, rose mallow, or swamp rose, is hardy in zones 5 to 9. Though the plant thrives in full sun to partial shade and moist soil that is high in organic matter, it will tolerate wetlands and creek edges and is useful in poorly drained areas. Depending upon the variety, it can reach heights ranging from 18 inches to eight feet. It grows in shrub form.

The most amazing aspect of the perennial hibiscus is its saucer-shaped flowers. A single flower can be six to 12 inches wide in shades of red, white, pink, or bicolor from summer to frost. A little effort with this plant usually reaps big rewards. It grows quickly and is easy to start from seed or to propagate by division. Japanese beetles are its major pest problem.

Use hibiscus as a single plant or massed around a water garden or lake. But be warned that if you plant it in your front yard, this show-stopper compels people to get a closer look at its remarkable flowers! Some common cultivars are 'Disco Belle Mix' (white, pink, red flowers), 'Southern Belle' (red, pink, white flowers), 'Sweet Caroline' (pink flowers with darker centers), 'Anne Arundel' (pink flowers), 'Blue River II' (white flowers), 'Lady Baltimore' (pink flowers with red centers), and 'Lord Baltimore' (red flowers). This North American native hibiscus also works wonders in perennial borders. Consider 'Plum Crazy', which has dusty rose flowers, and 'Kopper King', which has most unusual and complementary purple foliage.

Hibiscus 'Disco Belle Red'
Robert E. Lyons

Muhlygrass
Connie Little

Pink Muhlygrass: Prized for Ornamental Display

By Royce Hardin, Orange County

Considered by many to be one of the most beautiful ornamental grasses, *Muhlenbergia capillaris*, or pink muhlygrass, as it is commonly known in North Carolina, is prized for the fall show it creates. Boasting flowers that look like a purple cloud from afar, this knee-high grass is a native that occurs in eastern North America from Kansas to Massachusetts and south to Florida and Texas.

Given this wide range of adaptation, pink muhlygrass thrives in many environments, from wet prairies and dry savannas at the outer edges of marshes to well-drained upland pine forests. It performs best in full sun. Once established in a dense stand, the plant is remarkable in the late summer and fall when the silky, wispy, purplish pink panicles appear almost overnight. Each panicle is 12 to 18 inches long and up to 10 inches wide, standing tall above the wiry leaves. The color persists for six to eight weeks or until frost, when the ripe seeds that follow give an attractive tan color to the wispy plumes.

The most striking way to plant muhlygrass is in clumps. Each plant consists of wirelike stems that originate from a basal clump. It will get up to three feet tall and just as wide. Plant muhlygrass in borders and perennial gardens where fine-textured foliage is desired to accent bolder specimens. It makes an excellent groundcover for areas with poor soils, or it may be used as a refined specimen grass in natural gardens. It is easy to start from seed and is easily divided to start new plants. Unlike some of the nonnative ornamental grasses, muhlygrass will not displace other native plants and grasses. Leave the plant in the garden over the winter for interest and cut it back to around six to eight inches before new growth in the spring.

From a distance, this grass complements surrounding plants. Up close, its fine texture and bold mass are best appreciated when in full flower.

Rain Lilies Will Make You Wish for Water

By Karen Neill, Guilford County

Zephyranthes 'Stars'
Dennis J. Werner

Zephyranthes and *Habranthus*, or rain lilies, are unobtrusive, summer-flowering small bulbs that can fit into virtually any landscape. They take their name from their habit of blooming several times a season, usually following rains. Despite its common name, the flower is classed as an amaryllis and springs from an onion-like bulb to a height of about 15 inches.

Delightful in rock gardens and naturalized in grassy areas, rain lilies bloom from early spring into fall. Solitary flowers on hollow stalks range in color from the purest of white to yellow, pink, and even apricot. Unlike the more common spring-flowering bulbs, rain lilies have a limited amount of foliage, a feature I particularly like.

While *Z. atamasco*, a southeastern United States native, is the most common, many other varieties are now available. *Z. candida*, a native to South America, has a one-inch, pure white, starlike flower with dramatic golden anthers. It is striking in mass plantings. *Z. citrina*, originating in Central America, can tolerate the worst of weather and soil and seems to go right on blooming its marvelous yellow, goblet-shaped flowers. *Z.* 'Sunset Strain' is an old hybrid with lovely pinkish purple flowers. *Z.* 'Grandjax' is a fast-multiplying stunner with dozens of large, creamy pink flowers with white stars in the center. *Z. grandiflora* is my favorite, featuring three-inch-long rose pink flowers. What an eye-catcher!

Rosemary Provides Landscape Variety, Culinary Delight

By Karen Neill, Guilford County

Rosemary, *Rosmarinus officinalis*, is an attractive, drought-tolerant perennial that should be part of everyone's landscape or herb garden. Steeped in thousands of years of myth and tradition and known as the herb of love and remembrance, rosemary delights both beginners and seasoned gardeners.

Among the many varieties that exist, some are hardy to -10° F, as long as they have time to slowly harden off in the fall. Classified as either upright or creeping, the varieties may grow tall and upright or low and bushy. The upright varieties make a good informal hedge. Prostrate varieties look best in pots or cascading over masonry or rock walls or in rock gardens where the individual branches create interesting edge

Rosemary 'Tuscan Blue'
Robert E. Lyons

patterns. These also can be shaped by selective pruning. All varieties are evergreen. Most bear tiny white or blue flowers intermittently, making rosemary a decorative shrub. Put this together with its value as an herb and this plant is a winner.

Rosemary is native to coastal regions of the Mediterranean and North Africa. The Latin name *Rosmarinus* means "dew of the sea," a reference to the shimmering blue flowers that cover the plant. Like most Mediterranean plants, it needs good drainage and a hot, sunny site.

Popular rosemary cultivars that grow upright include 'Gorizia', 'Tuscan Blue', 'Salem', and 'Arp'. 'Gorizia' has leaves that are double the size of more ordinary varieties. Mature plants may grow to five feet tall and wide. 'Tuscan Blue' has strong, upright, thick stems and can reach heights of seven feet or more. 'Salem' grows to four or five feet and has dark blue flowers reminiscent of common rosemary. 'Arp', considered the winter-hardy variety, grows to about five feet. For the best-looking prostrate rosemary, consider 'Blue Boy'.

Salvias for the Sage Gardener

By Paul McKenzie,
Vance and Durham Counties

Consisting of dozens of species and cultivars and encompassing annuals and perennials as well as herbs, salvias are a staple in many gardens, with good reason. You are certain to find one that is perfect for your garden.

Salvia
Robert E. Lyons

Most gardeners are familiar with scarlet sage, *Salvia splendens*. This annual bedding plant prefers full sun but will perform in partial shade. It should be provided with well-drained soil and consistent moisture. While it is most commonly available in a deep red color, newer cultivars give gardeners a choice of lavender, blue, or white blooms. The big selling point of scarlet sage is its long blooming season, from late spring through the first frost.

Mealycup sage, *S. farinacea*, is another of the annual salvias unless you're in the eastern part of the state, where it may be winter hardy. It reaches a height of two to three feet and has blue, purple, or white flower spikes. 'Victoria Blue', 'Strata', and 'Empire Purple' are some of the newer varieties.

Garden sage, *S. officinalis*, is the choice for herb gardens, thanks to its fragrant leaves that can be used fresh or dried for seasoning meats. Many varieties are available. The foliage ranges from gray-green to purple to variegated forms. Garden sage prefers full sun and well-drained soil but is rather drought tolerant once established. It is winter hardy through most of the state. Pineapple sage, *S. elegans*, is a nice companion, with a scent that lives up to its name.

Mexican bush sage, *S. leucantha*, is a tender perennial that reaches three to four feet and is also drought tolerant. Its flower spikes are long, with purple and white blooms in late summer. Plant it in full sun as a specimen or accent plant.

The hybrid perennial salvias, *S.* × *superba*, are the best choices if you want perennials and live in the Piedmont or the mountain region. Many excellent varieties are available, including 'May Night', 'East Friesland', 'Blue Queen', and 'Rose Queen'.

Remarkable and Versatile Sedums

By David Goforth, Cabarrus County

The rocky cliffs in the mountains of North Carolina have some tough growing conditions. Shallow rock depressions contain thin layers of soil that have formed or washed in over the years. The soil dries to a crisp between rains. Sedums, also known as stonecrops, will tolerate these conditions. And that toughness makes them almost bulletproof in the garden.

North Carolina is home to 10 native or naturalized species of sedums. At least eight species, originally hailing from Japan, China, Korea, and the Caucasus Mountains, are available in local nurseries. Sixty more species and numerous cultivars are available by mail order.

Sedums are customarily divided into low-growing and upright species. Low-growing species such as *Sedum acre* (goldmoss) are traditionally used as groundcovers and in rock gardens. They are a good choice for green roof gardens, a popular trend on flat roof surfaces to improve water runoff while cooling buildings.

Sedum 'Angelina'
Robert E. Lyons

Foliage may be the main reason for planting low-growing sedums, but their flowers can be equally rewarding when selected carefully. The colors vary from burgundy-bronze on some species to pinks, whites, grays, or greens on others. The flowers commonly are yellow or gold, though *S. brevifolium* has pinkish white flowers and *S. sieboldii* 'Dragon's Blood' has red flowers.

Upright species include *S. spectabile* and *S. telephium*, also known as "live forever" or "orpine." These are used as specimens or in mixed perennial borders. The red, pink, or white flowers on upright sedums attract butterflies. The dried seed stalks are persistent and decorative through the winter. *S.* 'Autumn Joy' is a well-known upright cultivar with pink flowers that seem to be a favorite for bees. *S.* 'Vera Jameson' has particularly lovely flowers that stand vibrantly against any surrounding green foliage. All sedums are suitable for containers.

Water Lilies Add Sparkle to Water Gardens

By Darrell Blackwelder, Rowan County

Water lily
Robert E. Lyons

Water lilies are the crown jewels of water gardens and ponds. The image of these floating gems often inspires water garden design. Water lilies not only add beauty, they are necessary for a healthy pond. When properly spaced, they perform a valuable function by limiting the amount of light that reaches the depth of the pool, keeping excessive algal growth in check.

Water lilies (*Nymphaea*) are categorized as tropical or hardy. Tropical water lilies are divided into day- and night-blooming species. Tropical day bloomers include 'Blue Beauty', 'St. Louis', 'Director George T. Moore', and 'Marian Strawn'. For beautiful blooms at night, consider 'Red Cup', 'Red Flare', and 'Texas Shell Pink'. Plant tropical water lily crowns in deep pots. Place the crowns near the top and cover with very little media and one inch of gravel. The growing point should be above the soil and gravel.

Hardy water lilies such as 'Rose Arey', 'Comanche', 'Red Spider', and 'Charlene Strawn' are all day bloomers. Some of the hardy day bloomers add a bit of interest to the garden, in that the flowers change color shades over the life of the blooms. These are often referred to as the "changeables." Hardy lilies grow from rhizomes and should be placed in wide, shallow tubs. Plant them at a 45-degree angle and cover with an inch of gravel, making sure the growing tips are above the soil. Cover both tropical and hardy water lilies with six to 18 inches of water.

Dwarf varieties are available for small or miniature ponds. Look for 'Red Laydeker', 'Aurora', 'Helvola', or 'James Brydon'.

Water lilies should cover 50 to 75 percent of the surface area of the pond, meaning one plant is needed for approximately every 10 square feet of surface area.

To learn more, go to your favorite garden center and look at the stock. Garden magazines list mail-order growers that may be good sources. The International Waterlily and Water Gardening Society offers a wealth of information at http://iwgs.org.

Wild ginger
Robert E. Lyons

Wild Ginger Is the Shade Garden Secret

By Stephen Greer, Forsyth and Gaston Counties

Wild gingers are handsome, low-growing plants that many shade gardeners revere for their deep green or mottled leaves and the "little brown jugs" found hiding under the clusters of leaves. The gingers tucked away down woodland trails largely come from either North America or Asia.

Most wild gingers require moist, rich soil and partial shade. They can tolerate the periods of drought common in the Southeast. The Canadian ginger, *Asarum canadense*, and the 'Callaway' ginger, *A. shuttleworthii* (sometimes known as *Hexastylis shuttleworthii* var. *harperi* 'Callaway'), are becoming more available to gardeners.

Our native ginger, *A. arifolium*, better known as arrowleaf ginger, displays great variability in leaf shape, color, and leaf sustainability. The leaves are often found in the shape of arrows with a mottled or solid green color. This plant is not as showy as its Canadian and European cousins during the winter months, as the leaves tend to become dull and ragged. As spring approaches, it makes up for its winter dullness with a display of fresh new leaves and tan to purplish flower buds.

Two recently introduced gingers come from Japan. *A. splendens* and *A. yakushimanum* display unusually large flower jugs. They are slow to establish but will form a colony. If you want silver-speckled foliage, look for *A. splendens*. For dark, shiny green leaves, consider *A. yakushimanum*.

As the buds give way to flowers or "little brown jugs," many gardeners become kids at heart again. They find themselves on hands and knees, searching under those newly formed leaves for the unusual flowers to pick and show to friends and family. Resist this urge and invite friends into your garden to enjoy them as they should be seen.

Winter Iris Brings Color to the Cold

By Mike Wilder, Nash County

Iris reticulata
Robert E. Lyons

Just when the dark, dreary days of winter seem to drag us down, a small wonder of a plant springs forth to lift our spirits and punctuate the winter gray with a burst of cheerful color. The winter iris is underutilized in gardens, yet absolutely beautiful. And it's the perfect remedy for winter malaise.

The splendid *Iris unguicularis*, also known as Algerian iris, blooms during mild spells from December to February. Native to the eastern Mediterranean, Algerian iris provides a gorgeous splash of blue seldom seen in winter. It prefers sunny locations, is best left undisturbed, and flowers better as the clump grows older.

Just as your Algerian blue-purple passion is winding down, prepare for another bright winter surprise! The Danford iris, *I. danfordiae*, shows off its bright yellow flowers on two- to four-inch stems from February through March. Somewhat fragrant and low growing, it multiplies rapidly and is excellent for borders or rock gardens. This species was introduced from Turkey in 1876.

Keep your spirits up with our next flowering favorite, *I. reticulata*. Also known as dwarf iris or reticulate iris, it typically blooms anytime from late February through mid-March and has short flowers in blue, purple, or dark lavender. They look almost like miniature orchids with lean petals. This bulb is a good companion plant to crocus and Lenten rose. It grows about six inches tall and likes sunny sites with well-drained soil. These small plants have grasslike leaves. The cultivar 'Harmony' has intense blue flowers and is a good companion to flowering quince, forsythia, winter jasmine, vinca, and witchhazel.

You'll find something particularly lovely about any one of these irises lingering amidst a light covering of snow.

Spreading Zinnia Stands Up to Summer Heat

By Toby Bost, Forsyth County

Zinnia angustifolia is ideal for the gardener who dislikes all the care that many annuals demand in our sultry summer weather. This bright little flower, a native of Mexico, will tolerate both heat and long dry spells in full sun. A member of the aster family, it was once known as *Z. linearis*. Spreading or narrow-leafed zinnia bears small, single, one-inch daisy-form blooms continuously from late spring until frost on

Zinnia angustifolia 'Starbright Mix'
Robert E. Lyons

plants 10 to 15 inches tall with an eventual spread of equal size or more.

For years, only gold, orange, and yellow flowering varieties like 'Star Orange' were available. 'Crystal White', a more recent All-America Selections winner, elevated the spreading zinnia's status and got the attention of color bed designers far and wide. This versatile annual can be used as a summer groundcover, at the front of a border, and in hanging baskets or containers on a patio, deck, or sunny porch. Because they resist powdery mildew, the narrow leaves do not become disfigured by white blotches in our summer humidity the way the larger-flowered zinnia species typically do. New hybrid varieties such as the Profusion series offer larger flowers in additional colors, slightly taller plants, a wider lateral spread, and impressive disease resistance.

Spreading zinnia is easy to grow from seed, and easier still from plants from the garden center. Once established with adequate water in fertile soil in a sunny spot, it can thrive through longer periods of hot, dry weather than many other annuals, saving water and work for the gardener. Its flowers can be left in place without deadheading after they fade, as spreading zinnia continues producing new blossoms after the old ones have gone to seed. In annual flowering plant trials at the J. C. Raulston Arboretum at North Carolina State University, the Profusion orange and white varieties have outperformed comparison types by blooming profusely throughout the season without fading in summer heat or showing any sign of powdery mildew disease.

Woody Plants

Anise Belongs in Southern Gardens

By Diane Turner, Henderson County

A rapidly growing, low-maintenance shrub with spectacular foliage offers a combination that's hard to beat. Gardeners will find these winning characteristics in *Illicium floridanum*, a plant to be considered for any Southern garden.

The plant has a multistemmed, upright, compact habit. The foliage of Florida anise or anise-tree is quite attractive and aromatic, smelling similar to anise spice when crushed. The shiny, leathery leaves are olive green in color, while the 1½-inch flowers are dark red. Many petals appear in the early spring.

Illicium species usually reach a height of 10 to 15 feet and should be spaced in the landscape at least five feet apart. Florida anise's natural habitats are the wet, swampy areas and wooded streams with rich, acidic soil from Florida to Louisiana, but it also thrives here in the Carolinas. *Illicium* grows in partial to full shade but reportedly can be acclimated to full sun if well watered. It prefers moist soil and definitely should be mulched and watered during prolonged dry spells, as it has a tendency to wilt. The recommended USDA zones range from 7 to 10. The foliage and fruit of the anise-tree are poisonous to cattle.

Anise-tree
Connie Little

Several cultivars are available, including 'Alba', which has white flowers, and 'Shady Lady', which is variegated. *I.* 'Woodland Ruby', an interspecific hybrid between *I. floridanum* 'Alba' and *I. mexicanum*, produces showy blooms in spring and fall. Also consider *I. simonsii*, a rare yellow-flowered species. Another member of the genus that is native to the Southeast is yellow anise, or *I. parvifolium*, a popular landscaping shrub used especially in hedges. It is more tolerant of sun and dry soil than other species.

Blueberries in the Landscape

By Terry Garwood, Surry County

Blueberries, *Vaccinium* sp., are one of the few plants that offer both beauty and taste throughout most of the year. The actual blueberry fruit is touted by the National Institutes of Health as a way to delay the aging process. Blueberries are nutritional stars, providing a powerhouse boost of antioxidants and nutrients without adding many calories. So why not plant them in your home landscape?

Blueberry
Toby Bost

Blueberries are typically used in the landscape as hedges for screening purposes, but they can also serve in cluster plantings or as single specimen plants. Blueberries are spectacular in the fall, when their brilliant yellow-and-red foliage lights up the landscape. They have attractive, bell-shaped white and occasionally pink flowers in the spring. The summer fruit is a dark purplish blue. An added bonus is their lack of disease and insect problems.

Blueberries require a lower pH than many other small fruit crops and other plants. Therefore, consider grouping them with other acid-loving plants such as hollies, azaleas, rhododendrons, and camellias. Before planting, take a soil test. The ideal pH for blueberries is between 4.0 and 5.0 or 5.5, depending on the cultivar.

Both the highbush and rabbiteye types grow well in North Carolina. The highbush type typically has larger fruit and better fruit quality than rabbiteye but is not as widely adapted to various soil types. The cultivar 'Premier' is an excellent choice for a rabbiteye, boasting the advantage of being self-fruitful, unlike most blueberries, which require cross-pollination for fruit set.

Dr. Jim Ballington, a horticulture professor at North Carolina State University, has developed a series of Southern highbush blueberries that retain the high fruit quality of standard highbush but demonstrate greater adaptation to a wider range of soil types. The 'O'Neal', 'Sampson', and 'Legacy' cultivars are good choices. Little annual attention is required except for occasional pruning.

Camellias for Winter Color

By Donna Teasley, Burke County

As glorious as *Camellia japonica* is in the spring, it is just one of many spring-flowering trees and shrubs. The true camellia stars are those that flower during the winter, when gardeners are starved for bright colors in the landscape. One of the brightest of those stars is *C. sasanqua* 'Yuletide'. This December-flowering camellia features large, bright red single blooms with contrasting yellow stamens that give an eye-catching focus to the winter landscape. Its glossy green foliage offers the perfect backdrop for its spectacular display. 'Yuletide' has an erect, compact growth habit with dense foliage that lends itself well for use as a loose hedge plant or as a focal shrub.

Camellia sasanqua 'Yuletide'
Mark Weathington

As with other sasanquas, 'Yuletide' tolerates drought after it becomes established. Consider its ultimate height of 10 feet and slow growth rate before deciding on an appropriate planting location. It prefers well-drained soil with a pH of 6.0 to 6.5 for best growth. It can withstand the sun but does need protection from drying winter winds. One of the most popular winter-flowering shrubs, 'Yuletide' makes a great addition to any Southern garden.

Another good choice for winter color is *Camellia* × 'Crimson Candles'. This rapidly growing hybrid stands out because of its numerous, small, rose red single flowers in February and March. The new foliage is bronze-red. This plant is vigorous and disease resistant. One of its best features is its sepals, which are red throughout the winter while the buds are maturing. This gives the buds the look of red candles long before the flowers open—hence the name 'Crimson Candles'. Suited for hedge, espalier, topiary, or bonsai, this cultivar can withstand night temperatures in the 20s and is hardy in USDA zones 7 through 9.

Clethra: A Sweet Native Shrub

By David Goforth, Cabarrus County

Summersweet clethra, *Clethra alnifolia*, also known as coastal sweet pepperbush, grows naturally along streams in the eastern United States from Maine to Florida. This upright deciduous shrub has fragrant white flowers arranged in showy three- to five-inch racemes. It blooms in July and August, providing beauty to the late-summer garden as well as food for bees and butterflies. The fruit, though not showy, is eaten by birds.

Summersweet clethra
Toby Bost

Clethra is a good plant for shady, wet sites, where it can grow to eight feet tall and six feet wide. It forms a multistemmed shrub or even a colony. In partial shade or full sun, it has dense, glossy, green foliage that can turn yellow in mid-October. It likes acidic soil and tolerates salt spray but is not a plant for dry sites, where spider mites and dieback can be problems. When planted in the proper site, it is insect and disease resistant.

'Sixteen Candles' is the top seller, though 'Hummingbird' is the best-known cultivar. Both are compact shrubs with white flowers. 'Rosea', 'Pink Spires', and 'Ruby Spice' are three pink-flowered cultivars. 'Ruby Spice' is the darkest pink. This pink color holds even in the coastal plain. 'Sherry Sue', a relatively new introduction, sports white flowers and bright red stems. Another interesting species is *C. tomentosa*, which shows pubescent foliage and very long racemes. Japanese pepperbush, *C. barbinervis*, exhibits beautiful cinnamon-colored exfoliating bark as it matures.

Use clethra for summer flowers in wet, shady areas, particularly where the fragrance can be appreciated.

Crape myrtle
Robert E. Lyons

Crape Myrtles Enhance Our Southern Summers

By Willie Earl Wilson, Union County

Our Carolina summers wouldn't be the same without the blooms of the crape myrtle. Long known by many as the flower of the South, the crape myrtle performs beautifully throughout most of the state.

Crape myrtle, or *Lagerstroemia*, is a favorite small tree or large shrub for many Southern gardeners. It is a versatile flowering plant with many attractive characteristics, such as excellent bark color, texture, form, shape, and fall foliage color, as well as seedpods that persist in the winter.

Specimen tree varieties range from less than three feet to more than 12 feet and are well suited to urban gardens and street planters. The ultimate height for small tree varieties is usually below 30 feet; the roots can exist in restricted areas, making crape myrtles ideal for use under utility lines. To accent the trees' beauty, many homeowners often plant them in garden settings with an underplanting of a favorite groundcover. Gardeners in the cooler regions of the state—zones 6 and 7—are better off planting hybrids with the more cold-hardy *L. fauriei* in their backgrounds. The seeds of *L. fauriei* were collected by John L. Creech on the island of Yakushima, Japan. Plant breeder Donald Egolf introduced 'Hopi', 'Acoma', and 'Natchez', just three in an extensive series. The more commonly planted *L. indica* varieties found in lower elevations of the state will not reliably survive in the mountains.

The trees should be planted at least 10 feet from walls in well-drained soil and full sun. They do not flower well in partial shade and not at all in heavy shade. Powdery mildew can be a problem on the old cultivars, but many new cultivars are disease resistant.

Visit the J. C. Raulston Arboretum at North Carolina State University to see two unique cultivars of the species *L. fauriei*: 'Townhouse' and 'Fantasy'. 'Townhouse' has dark, mahogany red bark and profuse flowers during the summer. It is also noted for its striking winter appearance. 'Fantasy' is named for its elegant stature, beautiful, rusty red exfoliating bark, and profuse display of white flowers in the summer.

Crape Myrtles Are Now in Smaller Sizes

By David Goforth, Cabarrus County

Crape myrtles (*Lagerstroemia* species) are popular mainstays of the Southern garden. Their long bloom period during late summer provides beauty and landscape value when many other plants have succumbed to hot weather. Some people spell the common name with an *e* because the blooms look like crepe paper or the fabric crepe de Chine.

Lagerstroemia indica, *L. fauriei*, and hybrids between these species produce plants that are used as large shrubs or small trees, growing from 15 to 30 feet tall. Upon the introduction of *L. subcostata*, breeding programs began developing dwarf cultivars.

Dwarf crape myrtle
Toby Bost

The National Arboretum introduced a series of crape myrtle cultivars named for Indian tribes. While most of them grow to tree size, two smaller selections, 'Chickasaw' and 'Pocomoke', grow two to three feet in height. Several other active breeding programs across the country are currently developing compact crape myrtles. New introductions include cultivars that are considered groundcovers. The prostrate growth of 'Rosey Carpet' is four to eight inches in height.

A variety of colors including white, red, pink, and purple are available in compact forms. 'Tightwad Red' is generally considered the best red dwarf, although several others such as Cherry Dazzle™ are also available. Others in the Dazzle series include Ruby Dazzle™ and Snow Dazzle™.

Most dwarf crape myrtles flower for many weeks during summer. They can be grown as individual specimen plants in the front of a perennial or shrub border or massed to achieve a groundcover effect. Since these plants are deciduous and have limited winter interest, some gardeners place them in front of evergreens. Like standard crape myrtles, the dwarf forms are reliably cold hardy to zone 7a, and to zone 6b with some protection. 'Rosey Carpet' is rated as winter hardy to 10° F. It can be grown in hanging baskets in the western Piedmont and the mountains but has to be brought inside over the winter.

Most dwarf crape myrtles are resistant to powdery mildew.

Deciduous Azaleas Dazzle with Color

By Kevin Starr, Lincoln County

Deciduous azaleas may not compete with their evergreen relatives in popularity, but they definitely have their place, especially in naturalized landscapes. Such landscapes take advantage of existing native plants like large trees, often incorporating them into mulched areas, which reduces the need for mowing. Deciduous azaleas can add to these settings by providing impact with their flowers without detracting from the natural look. Deciduous azaleas, which botanically are in the genus *Rhododendron*, generally do well in the typical azalea conditions

Deciduous azalea
Toby Bost

of filtered shade and acidic, well-drained soil with high organic matter content.

Unlike evergreen azaleas, some of their deciduous cousins can be found growing wild in the southeastern United States. One of the showiest species is the flame azalea, *R. calendulaceum.* This species and other native azaleas in the mountains are sometimes called honeysuckle. The flowers are frequently bright orange, although they may range into yellow or red. One of the most widely distributed species is *R. periclymenoides* (formerly *R. nudiflorum*), sometimes called the pinxterbloom azalea. It features pink flowers and, like the flame azalea, blooms in the spring. The plumleaf azalea, *R. prunifolium*, is different in that its orange to orange-red blooms arrive in the summer.

Although many hybrid cultivars of deciduous azaleas have been developed, some are not heat tolerant. Among the good choices are species native to your part of North Carolina or named cultivars that have been developed using those species.

Deciduous Hollies Provide Winter Interest

By Jeff Rieves, Union County

Deciduous hollies carry heavy crops of bright red, orange, and occasionally yellow berries well into the winter. The absence of leaves during the dormant season makes the fruit display all the more striking. The berries blaze with color, adding needed punch to the winter landscape.

The most common deciduous holly species are *Ilex verticillata*, winterberry, and *I. decidua*, possumhaw. These two common names are often used interchangeably, though they really should not be. Winterberry has a slightly larger, more rounded leaf than possumhaw, while possumhaw is a glossier shade of green. The most obvious difference between the two is their mature size. Possumhaw is larger, topping out at 30 feet. Winterberry usually reaches no more than 15 feet. Most cultivars will not attain that size in the landscape. *I. verticillata* is slightly hardier, ranging from zones 3 to 9. *I. decidua* is typically hardy only to zone 5.

Native to swampy areas, deciduous hollies are somewhat adaptable to various soils as long as they are not allowed to get too dry. Both species prefer soils with an adequate amount of organic matter. Mulch your plants about two to three inches deep with organic mulch. Deciduous hollies prefer full sun but can set some fruit in shade. The best fruit set is attained by having a male plant in close proximity to the female to ensure adequate pollination. You may see leaf spot or powdery mildew on some plants, but deciduous hollies have no serious pest problems.

Ilex 'Sparkleberry'
Robert E. Lyons

In the garden, deciduous hollies often fade into the background until fall. After the leaves have fallen, the berries shine forth in all their glory, at least until the birds find them. Give these plants a bit of elbow room. They can fill up a small space quickly. In the landscape, they can be used as large shrubs or small trees. The plants often produce suckers from the base, but this is rarely a significant problem.

Popular cultivars include 'Sparkleberry', 'Winter Red', and 'Byers Golden'. Suggested male pollinators are 'Apollo' and 'Southern Gentleman'. American holly, *I. opaca*, will provide pollen for the species and some cultivars.

Deciduous Magnolias Provide Artistic Shapes

By Emily Revels, Cumberland and Mecklenburg Counties

Deciduous magnolia
Robert E. Lyons

Deciduous magnolias offer some of the most beautiful flowers for gardeners. The trees also provide artistic shapes and winter interest. Because some deciduous magnolias grow in shrub form, they offer gardeners the chance to use them in small areas. The biggest problem is that so many bloom early in the season and are damaged by late frosts.

Deciduous magnolias perform best in full sun to partial shade. They like well-drained, porous, organically rich soil with a pH of 5.5 to 6.5. A northern exposure for cultivars that flower in early spring may be most suitable to help delay flowering and possibly avoid frost damage.

Saucer magnolia, *Magnolia* × *soulangiana*, also sometimes called tulip magnolia, generally grows 20 to 30 feet in height and blooms in white, pink, and purple. It can begin blooming as early as February. Star magnolia, *M. stellata*, generally reaches a height of 15 to 20 feet and can bloom as early as late February to early March. Star magnolia flowers are generally white, although some open as pink and then fade to white.

The National Arboretum has developed a group of deciduous magnolias known as "The Little Girls". These cultivars are the result of hybridizing different cultivars of *M. liliiflora* and *M. stellata*. Some of the cultivars are 'Ann', 'Betty', 'Judy', 'Susan', and 'Jane'. These cultivars bloom two to four weeks later than *M. stellata* and *M.* × *soulangiana*, giving them a better chance of not being damaged by late frost. They range in color from white to reddish purple to pink.

The J. C. Raulston Arboretum (JCRA) has one of the most extensive collections of magnolias in the world, including "The Little Girls" cultivars. For a taller tree form, consider 'Spectrum' and 'Galaxy', both of which have pink flowers. Yellow, a newer flower color for deciduous magnolias, is represented well by 'Yellow Lantern', 'Elizabeth', 'Yellow Bird', and 'Butterflies', all easily viewed at JCRA.

Deodar Cedar Adds Grace to the Landscape

By Willie Earl Wilson, Union County

Deodar cedar
Connie Little

The Deodar cedar, *Cedrus deodara*, is one of the most graceful cedars, especially in youth. It has become a favorite among homeowners and landscapers. The tree is broadly pyramidal with graceful, pendulous branches that become wide spreading and flat topped in old age.

The tree's foliage ranges from light blue to grayish green to silvery in color. The cones are three to four inches long by approximately three inches broad on short branchlets. The Deodar grows about two feet in a year when young. If root-pruned, the Deodar transplants easily. The tree prefers well-drained, somewhat dry, sunny locations and protection from sweeping winds.

Many evergreen nurseries have expanded their catalog lists to include *C. deodara* cultivars. Three interesting cultivars are 'Kashmir', a hardy form with silvery blue-green foliage that can withstand temperature drops to below zero; 'Kingsville', which is similar to 'Kashmir' but possibly hardier; and 'Shalimar', which boasts good blue-green color and excellent hardiness and grows nine to 15 feet in 10 years from a cutting.

The Deodar cedar's fine-textured foliage allows light and water to penetrate the grass or groundcovers that grow below. The few needles that drop are easy to clean up. You won't have to worry about a solid mat of fallen leaves that may threaten to smother other plants. Deodar cedar is a good substitute for white pine but is subject to cold injury in zone 6.

The Deodar cedar is well represented at the J. C. Raulston Arboretum. The more than 30 different cultivars in its collections range from those with prostrate habits to those with a bluish cast to their foliage to those exhibiting pendulous, drooping branches. This is truly one species with tremendous possibilities for the landscape!

Dwarf Yaupon Is a Plant for All Conditions

By David Goforth, Cabarrus County

Every landscape needs its working-class plants that perform year after year with first-class results. Dwarf yaupon is such a plant. Though writers often get snobbish around working-class plants like dwarf yaupon, these are the very plants gardeners need to meet. Let me introduce dwarf yaupon, *Ilex vomitoria* 'Nana'.

Dwarf yaupon is a carefree, three- to four-foot-high evergreen shrub with fine-textured foliage that allows the gray stems to show off. It looks great anywhere from full-sun areas to partial shade. This shrub can grow to a round mound five feet high and slightly wider. Dwarf yaupon doesn't require heavy pruning but will tolerate it if you are compulsive with a pair of pruners in your hand. It is a good choice for clipped hedges or as a sheared plant to use in formal designs.

The plant tolerates poor soil and wet or dry conditions. *I. vomitoria* 'Nana' was the first plant in my first landscape plan. Twenty-five years later, it still contributes landscape value every day. It grows well in sticky, yellow clay where other species crash and burn. It is resistant to diseases and insects and grows throughout the state, though it's especially popular in coastal areas. In the northwestern Piedmont and points west, unusually long, cold winters can injure this shrub. However, most recover by summer.

Dwarf yaupon holly
Toby Bost

Eastern Redbud Is a Striking Tree with North Carolina Roots

By John Vining, Polk County

When naturalists and gardeners think of spring, the native redbud tree has to come to mind. One of North Carolina's most underrated small flowering trees, the eastern redbud, *Cercis canadensis*, is native from northern Florida to New Jersey.

Effective as a single specimen plant or in groupings in shrub borders, the redbud has a place in nearly every landscape. It is especially nice in naturalized and woodland locations.

'Hearts of Gold' redbud
Robert E. Lyons

Eastern redbuds grow in a wide range of soil types except those that are continuously wet. Their adaptability makes them well suited for home gardens. They grow 25 to 30 feet in height and have a spread of similar proportions.

The highlight of this small tree's gardening year comes in early spring before its leaves unfold. Eastern redbuds have reddish purple buds that open to purplish pink flowers. Some years, their bloom coincides with that of another showy native tree, the white flowering dogwood. Together, they create a spring display second to none.

Today, many new redbuds are available in the North Carolina nursery trade. Among them are 'Forest Pansy', which has purple foliage; 'Alba', which has white flowers; 'Appalachian Red', which has bright, rosy pink flowers; 'Silver Cloud', which has green-and-white variegated foliage; and 'Covey', an extraordinarily attractive weeping form. 'Hearts of Gold' is a new cultivar discovered by former J. C. Raulston Arboretum employee Jon Roethling in a North Carolina landscape. This outstanding and unique form is distinguished by its striking, intense, golden yellow spring foliage that gradually changes to chartreuse as the summer advances. These, along with additional cultivars from another redbud subspecies, the Texas redbud, *Cercis canadensis* var. *texensis*, make this an exciting landscape tree for Carolina gardeners.

The J. C. Raulston Arboretum at North Carolina State University has one of the most comprehensive collections of redbuds in the country, if not the world. Cultivars continue to evolve; see Chapter 6, "Tried-and-True and Hot New Plants for Carolina Gardens."

Edgeworthia Lends Blooms and Fragrance to Winter

By Donald Breedlove, Iredell County

Edgeworthia
Piedmont Carolina Nursery

Edgeworthia chrysantha, also known as the paperbush plant, provides superb winter interest and fragrance. This well-branched shrub begins blooming in December, when it's nothing but a bare silhouette in the garden, and continues through the winter. Although the individual florets are tiny, a few dozen make up a 1½- to 2-inch cluster that will simply knock you sideways. One characteristic of edgeworthia, which is related to daphne, is that you can smell it from a great distance before you ever see it. The fragrance is a bit like gardenia with a slightly spicier element thrown in.

Edgeworthia thrives in partial shade and appreciates well-enriched, moist soil. In spring, after the blooms pass, it sports lovely bluish foliage with silvery undertones that are both eye-catching and soothing. In summer, it has a beautiful shape and form similar to rhododendron, though the foliage is not as lush green as that of a rhododendron grown in a shaded area. In autumn, the foliage turns rich shades of yellow.

This shrub grows in zones 7 to 9 and in protected areas of zone 6. It eventually grows seven feet high and wide and makes a nice stand-alone specimen or back-of-the-border choice. Space these plants about seven feet apart in partial shade and rich, moist soil. You may want to plant edgeworthia within reach of passersby because the foliage invites handling. Be sure to snip a few blooms to keep the house fragrant through the winter.

Edgeworthia is now making its way into retail garden centers but may still be a bit hard to find. Look for 'Gold Rush', 'John Bryant', and 'Red Dragon'.

Barnes & Noble Booksellers #2126
5959 Triangle Town Blvd
Unit 2107
Raleigh, NC 27616
919-792-2140

R:2126 REG:001 TRN:5817 CSHR:Douglas H

irkle
0736970320168 T1
(1 @ 29.95) 29.95
nth-By-Month Gardening in Carolinas
9781591862345 T1
(1 @ 24.99) 24.99
ccessful Gardener Guide
9780895875150 T1
(1 @ 19.95) 19.95
uble Fudge
9780142408780 T1
(1 @ 6.99) 6.99
G
9780142410387 T1
(1 @ 6.99) 6.99
ink and the Ultimate Thumb-Wrestling S
9780763664237 T1
(1 @ 4.99) 4.99

btotal 93.86
les Tax T1 (6.750%) 6.34
TAL 100.20
SA 100.20
Card#: XXXXXXXXXXXX3646
Expdate: XX/XX
Auth: 07867A
Entry Method: Swiped

MEMBER WOULD HAVE SAVED 9.40

Thanks for shopping at
Barnes & Noble

1.35B 02/14/2015 10:28AM

CUSTOMER COPY

the date of return, (ii) when a gift receipt is presented within 60 days of purchase, (iii) for textbooks, or (iv) for products purchased at Barnes & Noble College bookstores that are listed for sale in the Barnes & Noble Booksellers inventory management system.

Opened music CDs/DVDs/audio books may not be returned, and can be exchanged only for the same title and only if defective. NOOKs purchased from other retailers or sellers are returnable only to the retailer or seller from which they are purchased pursuant to such retailer's or seller's return policy. Magazines, newspapers, eBooks, digital downloads and used books are not returnable or exchangeable. Defective NOOKs may be exchanged at the store in accordance with the applicable warranty.

Returns or exchanges will not be permitted (i) after 14 days or without receipt or (ii) for product not carried by Barnes & Noble or Barnes & Noble.com.

Policy on receipt may appear in two sections.

Return Policy

With a sales receipt or Barnes & Noble.com packing slip, a full refund in the original form of payment will be issued from any Barnes & Noble Booksellers store for returns of undamaged NOOKs, new and unread books, and unopened and undamaged music CDs, DVDs, and audio books made within 14 days of purchase from a Barnes & Noble Booksellers store or Barnes & Noble.com with the below exceptions:

A store credit for the purchase price will be issued (i) for purchases made by check less than 7 days prior to the date of return, (ii) when a gift receipt is presented within 60 days of purchase, (iii) for textbooks, or (iv) for products purchased at Barnes & Noble College bookstores that are listed for sale in the Barnes & Noble Booksellers inventory management system.

Opened music CDs/DVDs/audio books may not be returned, and can be exchanged only for the same title and only if defective. NOOKs purchased from other retailers or sellers are returnable only to the retailer or seller from which they are purchased pursuant to such retailer's or seller's return policy. Magazines, newspapers, eBooks, digital downloads and used books are not returnable or exchangeable. Defective NOOKs may be exchanged at the store in accordance with the applicable warranty.

Returns or exchanges will not be permitted (i) after 14 days or without receipt or (ii) for product not carried by Barnes & Noble or Barnes & Noble.com.

Policy on receipt may appear in two sections.

Return Policy

With a sales receipt or Barnes & Noble.com packing slip,

Fringe Tree: A Natural for Carolina Landscapes

By Carl Matyac, Orange and Wake Counties

Fringe tree
Connie Little

Native trees are excellent choices for North Carolina landscapes, since we know they have survived the stresses of our environment for hundreds of years. Most of us, however, want trees to do more than just survive. We often look for trees that can fit into small spaces, that have few disease and insect problems, and that offer features that give them special interest. All of these criteria describe the fringe tree, *Chionanthus virginicus*. This tree is native to North Carolina and has a range from New Jersey to Florida and as far west as Arkansas and Texas. In the wild, it grows along stream banks and wetlands.

Considered a large shrub or small tree, the fringe tree can grow to about 20 feet in height and width at maturity. It produces dark green, glossy leaves in the spring, along with beautiful, slightly fragrant flowers that feature airy, drooping, four- to six-inch-long clusters of fringelike, creamy white petals. These flowers give the tree its common name, as well as other names such as old man's beard. When in bloom, the entire tree looks like it is glowing, due to the soft, airy nature of the flowers. The flowers give way to clusters of olivelike fruits that ripen to a dark bluish black in late summer and are a food source for birds and other wildlife.

The fringe tree grows easily in moist, fertile, well-drained soil in full sun to partial shade. It may be difficult to transplant a specimen once it is established. It's best to plant a balled-and-burlapped or container-grown plant early in the spring in a well-prepared site. The tree seldom needs pruning and is a beautiful specimen shrub. It also does well in groups and borders and near large buildings. Because it is tolerant of air pollution, it can thrive along streets and highways. The slow-growing nature of this tree results in strong, dense wood that is able to withstand the bending stresses associated with wind and ice storms.

C. virginicus is an excellent choice for the urban landscape, the native garden, or container planting, or as a utilitarian tree under power lines.

'Green Giant' Western Cedar Stands Tall among Evergreens

By Carl Matyac, Orange and Wake Counties

Thuja plicata 'Green Giant' is a vigorously growing, pyramidal evergreen with rich green color. The genus is more commonly referred to as arborvitae, which is known for its lustrous, dark green leaves in summer with a bit of bronzing in the winter months. 'Green Giant' has the added feature of a faint white streak on the bottoms of its leaves, giving the entire tree a slight but noticeable accent of color.

This cultivar has been available in the United States for 30 years, having been imported from Denmark. While 'Green Giant' is not a big seller for North Carolina nurseries, it is gaining in popularity as an excellent substitute for Leyland cypress. Many lower-growing cultivars also are available and make good landscape additions.

Western cedar
Toby Bost

Mature specimens can grow up to 40 feet tall with an eight-foot spread, so be sure to give them plenty of room. 'Green Giant' is best used in multiple plantings to create a living frame for your landscape, lending a feeling of formality to the garden. When the trees are planted in rows, the frame also may function as a screen to create privacy. 'Green Giant' is also effective as a single specimen that functions as an evergreen sentinel.

Like most of its relatives, 'Green Giant' is not troubled by any significant insect pest or disease problems. It tolerates a wide range of soil types and hardiness zones. Because of its popularity in the Pacific Northwest, few gardeners realize that it has great potential for landscape use in North Carolina. Growth rates of two to four feet per year have been reported at the J. C. Raulston Arboretum in Raleigh. All of this makes 'Green Giant' a plant with many favorable characteristics.

Hardy Palms Create a Tropical Feel

By Will Strader, Franklin County

Windmill palm
Toby Bost

When people think of palm trees, they envision tropical beaches and sultry climates laden with towering plants. Some palms grow quite well in North Carolina's coastal plain and Piedmont. With a little effort, you may be able to grow a few of your own.

The windmill palm, *Trachycarpus fortunei*, which is native to the Himalayan region, has a reputation as one of the world's hardiest palms. It has an amazing ability to survive even when completely defoliated. It grows to about 40 feet tall and develops a solitary trunk covered with matted fiber. The palmate leaves of the windmill palm can grow to four feet wide; they are deeply divided and have drooping tips. This palm should be planted on a well-drained site that is protected from winds. It performs best when planted in partial shade as an understory plant or where it receives afternoon shade. It is not hardy in North Carolina's mountains.

Another hardy palm native to the Himalayas is new to the landscape trade and quite difficult to find. The windamere palm, *T. latisectus*, grows fast once it develops a trunk. It can attain a height of 40 feet with a trunk diameter of six inches to one foot. The light gray trunk shows faint rings. This palm has large, leathery leaves with very wide leaflets.

Our own native dwarf palmetto palm, *Sabel minor*, is easier to find at local nurseries. This evergreen palm has a slow growth rate and reaches 10 feet in height at maturity. It prefers light shade and moist to wet soil but can tolerate considerable drought. *S. minor* produces small white flowers in large branched clusters in summer. *S.* 'Birmingham', commonly accepted to be a hybrid of *S. minor*, makes a nice show in the landscape as well.

No matter what your travel schedule looks like, including a couple of hardy palms in the landscape will let you experience that tropical feel year-round.

Hollies Are a Landscape Mainstay

By Diane Turner,
Henderson County

'Helleri' holly
Robert E. Lyons

Mention hollies in December and most people think of the spiny evergreens that are used to deck the halls for the holidays. But when it comes to the landscape, the diversity within the holly (*Ilex*) genus is never ending. These sturdy beauties can be evergreen or deciduous; they can be small and spineless or large and spiny. They are available in numerous shapes such as columnar, pyramidal, and rounded. Homeowners use these plants for screens, hedges, mass plantings, and specimen plantings.

Hollies are dioecious, meaning that males produce pollen and females produce berries. Good fruit production can normally be expected if the male and female grow within 30 feet of one another. The resulting berries can be red, orange, yellow, or black, depending on the species. Hollies fall within the easy-to-care-for category. They prefer full sun and well-drained, slightly acidic soil with the pH between 5 and 6. To maintain healthy plants, gardeners should fertilize and mulch. The common insect pests of hollies include leaf miners, scales, and red mites. Some of the Japanese cultivars can be very susceptible to root rot diseases.

Two favorite dwarf evergreen hollies are *I. crenata* 'Helleri' and 'Soft Touch'. These Japanese hollies survive well in most environments, especially in foundation plantings, although they may be susceptible to root rot in poorly drained sites. Another attractive choice is *I. cornuta* 'Carissa'. This Chinese holly has one single leaf spine, which makes for an interesting form. It is more compact than its Burford holly cousin and seldom fruits.

The blue holly (blue boy and blue girl combination), *I.* × *meserveae*, is popular for its lustrous black-green foliage. A good deciduous holly is *I. decidua*, possumhaw holly, which has beautiful winter color and grows to a small tree. Many cultivars are available. Another great deciduous holly is the common winterberry, *I. verticillata*.

Hydrangeas: Hallmarks of the Southern Garden

By Darrell Blackwelder, Rowan County

Hydrangeas, an old favorite, are ever more popular, thanks to the new hybrids. The more than 100 different varieties include climbing hydrangea, dwarf container plants, large oak-leaved varieties, red-stemmed choices, and hydrangeas with pure white blooms. There are too many cultivars to list, but hydrangeas are usually placed in three basic categories: *Hydrangea macrophylla*, also called bigleaf, mop head, or French hydrangea; *H. quercifolia*, or oakleaf hydrangea; and *H. paniculata*, often referred to as PeeGee hydrangea.

'Annabelle' hydrangea
Robert E. Lyons

The most popular is bigleaf hydrangea, *H. macrophylla*. This older cultivar is usually pink or blue, depending on soil pH, which affects the available aluminum uptake responsible for color change. However, a few white cultivars are available. Acidic soils produce blue flowers, while alkaline soils produce pink petals. Newer cultivars such as 'Endless Summer' and 'Blushing Bride' are touted as everblooming plants. When planting, locate big-leaved hydrangeas in semishaded spots where the soil is moist and drains well.

Oakleaf hydrangea, *H. quercifolia*, is a dramatic, white-blooming shrub with four seasons of interest. It is noteworthy for its fall foliage color, leaf texture, and bark interest. It thrives in much drier locations than its cousins.

H. paniculata types boast blooms that are usually panicle shaped (somewhat cone shaped), rather than ball shaped. Often in late summer, the blooms develop a pink shade as they age, extending their beauty into the fall. PeeGees are desirable because they tolerate pruning well. Prune at any time except when they begin forming bloom heads in the summer. PeeGees often get very large; some are the size of small trees in the mountains. However, compact forms for smaller spaces are now appearing in nurseries.

Japanese Flowering Apricot Brightens Winter

By Linda Blue, Buncombe County

Japanese flowering apricot
Todd Lasseigne

A flowering tree any time of year is a glorious gift. A flowering tree in winter is pure delight. When winter days seem especially dreary, Japanese flowering apricot, *Prunus mume*, produces beautiful, delicate flowers with a rich fragrance that's certain to boost spirits.

Most varieties of Japanese flowering apricot bloom sporadically in late winter and early spring. Their season ranges from mid-February through mid-March in most of the state. Although the flowers may be frozen by a sudden cold snap, another flush of blooms will usually open with the next warm spell. The flowers may be white, pink, or red. In addition to providing flowers when little else is in bloom, most varieties will easily perfume a small garden. The branches can be cut to bring early-spring blooms and fragrance indoors.

Japanese flowering apricot reaches about 25 feet. Plant habit, size, flower color, and fragrance vary depending on the variety. It flowers best in full sun. The soil should be fairly well drained and have a pH between 5.5 and 6.5.

This relatively new plant has not been thoroughly tested for cold hardiness. However, plants at the J. C. Raulston Arboretum (JCRA) in Raleigh have come through temperatures as low as -7° F with minimal damage, so Japanese flowering apricot should be hardy even in most of the North Carolina mountains. Considering its winter flowers and fragrance, it is certainly worth a try, especially near a patio or entryway.

JCRA holds one of the most extensive collections of *Prunus mume* cultivars in the eastern United States. These beautiful trees provide vibrant and welcome color throughout the winter months. Look for new or distinctive cultivars such as 'Matsurabara Red', which has double pinkish red flowers; 'Tojibai', which has white flowers; 'W. B. Clarke', which has a weeping form and double pink flowers; and 'Bridal Veil', a weeping tree with white flowers.

Threadleaf Japanese maple
Connie Little

Japanese Maples Provide Form and Foliage Treasures

By John MacNair, Mecklenburg County

Elegant form, ornate leaf pattern, and striking leaf color establish Japanese maple as the most peaceful and eye-pleasing small tree in the landscape. It is perfect for today's residential homes, providing graceful beauty and enough shade for small patios, porches, and gardens. The tranquil appeal of many cultivars comes from their downcast, closely layered branches, which provide cascading sheets of leaves that yield the image of a foliage waterfall. Most grow 15 to 20 feet high and wide and are considered slow growers.

When planted in the right place, Japanese maples have few problems. Dappled shade is ideal. Too much shade and they are less vigorous and may even perish. They can be planted in full sun if they are watered during drought, though some cultivars may exhibit scorched leaves in such bright light. Whether you plant in clay, sandy, or rocky soil, prepare the soil well and make sure it's on the acidic side, with a pH level of 6.

Japanese maples are grouped into several varieties, according to size and leaf shape. The most popular cultivar is 'Bloodgood'. It tolerates heat, retains its conspicuous purple foliage in the summer, and turns a dazzling red in the fall. Its eye-catching, papery red fruit is an added bonus. Those labeled "dissectum" somewhere in their scientific names have finely threaded leaves and provide the familiar manicured look found in formal Japanese gardens.

An incredible array of Japanese maple cultivars is on the market. 'Oregon Sunset', 'Crimson Queen', and 'Osakazuki' are three examples among the plethora available.

The Japanese maple is the signature plant of the J. C. Raulston Arboretum at North Carolina State University. There is a good chance you will see one from any vantage point in the arboretum. For a listing of the arboretum's cultivars, visit www.ncsu.edu/jcraulstonarboretum. Click on "Horticulture" and then "Current Plantings"; type in *Acer palmatum*. Just watch how many come up. Then go and see them firsthand!

Kousa dogwood
Robert E. Lyons

Kousa Dogwood Prolongs Spring's Beauty

By David Barkley, Brunswick County

Few plants herald spring like the common flowering dogwood, *Cornus florida*. But the plant that prolongs spring's beauty is another dogwood, *C. kousa*. Bursting into bloom two to three weeks after the common dogwood, kousa is a stunning tree with creamy white flowers and green foliage. The pointed or tapered white petals are actually modified leaves called bracts. They surround clusters of tiny yellow flowers and cover the tree for a striking spring display.

Kousa dogwood is in demand for its grower friendliness and is an excellent substitute for the common flowering dogwood, particularly since it is resistant to the dogwood borer and dogwood anthracnose problems that have plagued common dogwoods in recent years.

This handsome small tree adds year-round beauty and is particularly attractive in small spaces and urban gardens. The bark is initially smooth and light brown. It later exfoliates into small patches that form a tan-and-brown camouflage or mottled pattern. This mottled, exfoliating bark creates interest in wintertime. After kousa blooms in mid-May, its red raspberry–like fruit appears during late summer, hanging down among the green leaves. The fruit persists into autumn, complementing the purplish red fall foliage. The fruit is sweet and edible but somewhat mealy.

Kousa does best in partial shade but will tolerate full sun. It grows to 15 to 25 feet with a 25-foot spread. It grows in climatic zones 5 to 8 and prefers being planted in well-drained, acidic soil.

The beloved kousa dogwood will stretch your imagination when you visit the diverse collection of cultivars at the J. C. Raulston Arboretum. From the weeping forms of 'Pendula' and 'Lustgarten Weeping' to the slightly rosy floral display of 'Satomi' and the subtle fall color interest of 'Autumn Rose', you will find that kousa dogwood takes a backseat to nothing!

Lilacs for the South

By Kevin Starr, Lincoln County

Many of us remember those fragrant lilacs that grew in the gardens of our parents or grandparents. But we may not remember all the problems that afflicted those plants. The plant that most of us identify as a lilac is the common lilac, *Syringa vulgaris*. Some varieties of common lilac do pretty well in the North Carolina mountains.

Unfortunately, they do not like the heat they encounter in the warmer parts of our state and often become afflicted with powdery mildew and borers.

Lilac
Piedmont Carolina Nursery

That fact has led horticulturists to look at other species. 'Miss Kim', a cultivar of *S. patula*, has been publicized as a lilac that can take hot Southern conditions. Another lilac mentioned as a candidate is *S. oblata* var. *dilatata*, a variety of the Korean early lilac.

Dick Bir, a retired researcher and North Carolina Cooperative Extension specialist, wanted to find lilacs that "look and smell like lilacs." He conducted trials on lilacs for 20 years at the Mountain Horticultural Crops Research and Extension Center in Mills River. His long-term observations led Bir to conclude that some of the best lilacs for the Piedmont and coastal plain of our state are the cultivars in the *S.* × *hyacinthiflora* group. This hybrid species is the result of crossing *S. oblata* and *S. vulgaris*. Many garden centers in the state have some of these cultivars available in the spring. As for *S. oblata*, Bir said it flowers too early to consistently avoid frost and freeze damage in the upper Piedmont and mountains. For warmer areas, *S. oblata* selections and hybrids deserve a try.

'Little Gem': A Magnificent Southern Magnolia in a Smaller Form

By John MacNair, Mecklenburg County

The Southern magnolia may be a favorite plant for many but is totally unrealistic for today's small lawns. If you want to enjoy the beautiful evergreen leaves and large, creamy white blossoms that are features of the Southern magnolia but don't want the tree to totally dwarf your landscape, then the 'Little Gem' magnolia, a cultivar of Southern magnolia, is the plant to consider.

'Little Gem' grows 20 feet high by 10 feet wide in 10 years, making it a long-lasting screen plant. It also makes a regal stand-alone specimen without taking up the entire property.

Magnolia 'Little Gem'
J. C. Raulston Arboretum

The glossy green leaves have bronze undersides. The fragrant, creamy white flowers are six inches wide and begin when the tree is only two or three years old. Abundant flower production arrives in May and June and tapers off sporadically into November. Although 'Little Gem' is tolerant of shade, plant it in full sun for a profusion of flowers and to show off the leaves. The honeycombed fruit husks have attractive red seeds that ripen in fall and are ravenously eaten by birds. The tree suffers no serious insect or disease problems. Occasionally, woodpeckers create shallow holes in rows, but this should not damage the plant unless the holes are numerous. Broad-leaved evergreens including 'Little Gem' drop older yellow leaves in late spring, so don't worry that you have a problem when the leaves fall.

Other cultivars of Southern magnolia to consider are 'Gold Strike', which has yellow variegated leaves; 'Bracken's Brown Beauty', which has cinnamon brown leaf undersides; the dwarf 'Teddy Bear'; and 'Baby Doll', which is round shaped instead of pyramidal.

Loropetalum Creates a Dramatic Display

By Mark Blevins, Gaston County

Few plants are as useful in so many landscape situations as this beautiful spring-flowering shrub. You can't go wrong with Chinese fringe flower, though its white or pink flowers and green, variegated, or burgundy leaves make it hard to decide on just one.

It can serve in foundation plantings, tall hedges, borders, and low screens. Left alone, this evergreen shrub will grow 10 feet tall and wide and present a thick, layered appearance. Compact forms exist, and more are being developed. Chinese fringe flower will endure pruning but is beautiful left to grow naturally in a sunny or partially shaded spot. On a large, mature plant, one option is to remove the lower limbs, which will reveal a beautiful structure and create a pleasant spot to relax. This technique will produce a delightful small tree that creates as much drama as a Japanese maple.

Easy to find at garden centers and nurseries, loropetalum prefers acid to neutral soil; its leaves may yellow in alkaline soil. Transplanting from a container is no problem, but give the plant adequate moisture during the first season to ensure survival.

Burgundy leaf loropetalum
Connie Little

The varieties (discovered in nature) and cultivars (found in cultivation) growing at the J. C. Raulston Arboretum give a glimpse into the wide world of *Loropetalum chinense*. Names such as 'Green Elf', 'Blush', and 'Zhuzhou Fuchsia' suggest colors from far and near. Excitement drips off plant tags listing 'Snow Dance', 'Sizzlin' Pink', 'Daybreak's Flame', and 'Fire Dance'.

Loropetalum flowers in late winter or spring. Its long, narrow petals resemble soft ribbons. These strap-shaped flowers are common to the witchhazel family, *Hamamelidaceae*, and can be fragrant. Each flower consists of only four petals. But because three to six flowers cluster together at many points along the branches, they create a spectacular overall display.

Wait until after flowering to prune. Scattered flower production may occur in fall, but don't be alarmed. This shrub is just pleasantly reminding you to wait for more flowers come spring. And come they will.

Oakleaf Hydrangea Boasts Bold Features

By Carl Matyac, Orange and Wake Counties

Hydrangea quercifolia, oakleaf hydrangea, provides bold texture and beautiful, fragrant flowers in the summer and great leaf color in the fall, characteristics most of us want in our gardens. Old-fashioned big-leaved hydrangeas have been in gardens throughout the country for decades, but this one is less known.

Oakleaf hydrangea
Robert E. Lyons

The olive green leaves of this woody ornamental are tropical in appearance and are sure to get attention. The leaves can reach eight inches long and six inches wide with deep lobes. The leaves alone make this plant a unique attraction. But that is just the beginning. The plant's creamy white, fragrant, erect flower clusters appear in May, June, and July. They are huge—sometimes one foot long and six inches wide. The flowers persist just like those of the old-fashioned hydrangeas and can be used in dried arrangements. In the fall, the leaves change to shades of red, orangish brown, and purple, providing beautiful color well into the season.

Oakleaf hydrangea prefers moist, fertile, well-drained soil but will tolerate more poorly drained conditions. Full sun or partial shade is best, especially if the roots are kept cool. It does not do well in very dry areas. Oakleaf hydrangea suffers no serious pest or disease problems, with the exception of a Japanese beetle now and then.

This plant's bold features make a striking statement in the garden. Be sure to find a place where it will not overpower smaller plants. Many gardeners do not realize that it can grow up to eight feet in height and spread at least that wide. Cutting the canes back every three years can help manage the overall size. The plant will produce suckers from its roots and continue to expand if allowed. If you want a single-stemmed plant, keep the suckers in check. For small gardens, look for dwarf varieties such as 'PeeWee' or 'Sykes', which grow to about four feet.

River Birch in Weeping Form

By Kevin Starr, Lincoln County

'Summer Cascade' weeping river birch
Thomas G. Ranney

Horticulturists are always looking for plants that are new and different. Many cultivars are developed, but few gain marketplace popularity. A new type of river birch, 'Summer Cascade', looks to be one of those special plants that is unique enough to make its mark in North Carolina landscapes.

'Summer Cascade' is a weeping form of river birch that was discovered by John and Danny Allen at Shiloh Nursery in Harmony, North Carolina. The river birch is one of our landscape mainstays, characterized by its handsome peeling bark. A weeping form promises something really special. Because of their unique growth habit, weeping plants are often used as specimen plants in the landscape. River birch, like many native plants, is very dependable and has few major pest problems. 'Summer Cascade' is considered to be a fast grower. It will form a mounded shrub or small tree if left untrained, or it can be provided with trunk support and trained into a tree form.

The development of this tree is a good example of how significant achievements can be realized when a private business and a land-grant university work together. Shiloh Nursery worked with Dr. Tom Ranney, a North Carolina State researcher at the Mountain Horticultural Crops Research and Extension Center in Mills River, to determine how easily the plant could be propagated. Plants that are difficult for nurserymen to propagate are likely to be limited in commercial availability, regardless of how many features they possess. Dr. Ranney found that 'Summer Cascade' can be rooted easily from stem cuttings.

A number of North Carolina nurseries are now growing 'Summer Cascade'. Specimens can be seen at the J. C. Raulston Arboretum in Raleigh, the Mountain Horticultural Crops Research and Extension Center, and the North Carolina Arboretum in Asheville.

Rockspray Cotoneaster Accents Walls, Covers Slopes

By Emily Revels, Cumberland and Mecklenburg Counties

Rockspray cotoneaster, *Cotoneaster horizontalis*, is a lovely choice to consider when you are looking for a plant to cover a bank or drape over a wall. The stem grows in an interesting fishbone or herringbone pattern, which creates flat growth

Rockspray cotoneaster
Toby Bost

and a layered effect. The plant is also a good selection for rock gardens or espaliers.

This versatile plant brightens fall and winter with its red berries decorating the stiff, spreading branches. It is generally thought of as semi-evergreen, though it sometimes is considered evergreen or deciduous. The plant grows to a height of two to three feet with a spread of five to eight feet and has small, fine-textured green leaves that turn purplish red in fall. In May, it has small, whitish pink blooms ¼ inch in diameter.

C. horizontalis, widely used in England, is worthy of more frequent consideration in our landscapes, particularly for its hardiness and nice features throughout the year. It is related to apples, pears, and hawthorns. This cotoneaster grows in zones 6, 7, and 8 and tolerates coastal areas. Because of their sparse root systems, container-grown plants should be planted in well-drained, fertile soil in either full sun or partial shade. The plant is a slow grower.

Some possible insect problems are caused by lace bugs, mites, and scales. Fire blight can be a disease problem. If you have a deer problem, though, this plant is a good one to consider, as it is not a deer favorite.

A variety to look for is 'Variegatus', named for its variegated leaves edged in white, which turn rose red in fall. Other varieties include 'Ascendens', 'Dart's Splendid', 'Robustus', and 'Wilsonii'.

The multiseason landscape value of the cotoneaster sets it apart from many other plant choices.

Roses Are Now More Hardy

By Mike Wilder, Nash County

The rose's timeless and classic beauty has ensured its place as the queen of flowers in the hearts of gardeners. New rose varieties are in test trials across the country. Many are crowned as All-America Rose Selections. Experts evaluate hybrids over a two-year period for color, fragrance, disease resistance, and hardiness.

In 2000, the Knock Out® rose received rave reviews and recognition as the Rose of the Year. Rose lovers worldwide soon discovered the staying power of this red-flowering rose. The term *landscape rose* was quickly coined, and the rest is history. Other than deadheading and watering, this rose requires very little of the gardener.

Knock Out® has a high disease resistance among AARS selections. Touted as maintenance free, this landscape shrub rose provides a continuous bloom cycle from spring until late fall. The deep cherry red blooms are 3 to 3½ inches in diameter, with a petal count of five to seven. Newer introductions, among them a yellow rose, vary widely in flower color. Knock Out® has a medium rounded form. It is three feet high

Knock Out® Rose
Robert E. Lyons

by four feet wide or better and has clusters of three to 15 blooms. The foliage is glossy green-purple with a swirl of burgundy.

Shrub types such as Knock Out® and Carefree landscape roses can be used as borders or short hedges, in beds or foundations, on patios, and along walks or fences. Clearly, if you are searching for a fragrant cutting rose, you will be well advised to stay with the standard hybrid tea and floribunda rose varieties.

Serviceberry: A Drought-Tolerant Tree for North Carolina

By David Goforth, Cabarrus County

The serviceberry (*Amelanchier* spp.) is a small tree or shrub with white, airy blooms that make it a desirable landscape plant. In the Piedmont, *A. arborea* beats other spring beauties to the punch, blooming earlier than dogwoods and often earlier than redbuds.

Serviceberry
Piedmont Carolina Nursery

The berries are the size and shape of blueberries and have a distinct taste. They can be eaten fresh or used in pies and jams. If you prefer feeding wildlife, birds seem to consider the berries fine cuisine.

The species and most cultivars have good fall

color, which also contributes to their landscape appeal. Fall foliage varies from yellow to red. The smooth, grayish white bark of young trees and the reddish purple buds add winter interest.

When looking for this tree for your landscape, be aware that its common names include serviceberry, sarvisberry, shadbush, shadblow, and juneberry. *Amelanchier* is sometimes called a currant by people unfamiliar with real currants (*Ribes* sp.). Though the names can be confusing, most named hybrids have *A. arborea* or *A. laevis* in their parentage. These perform well in North Carolina. A natural hybrid called *A.* × *grandiflora* is good for edible landscaping. *A. alnifolia* is a Northern species and doesn't do as well in North Carolina. *A. arborea* is often incorrectly sold as *A. canadensis*, which is a small, suckering shrub.

Amelanchier does well in full sun to partial shade and thrives in most landscape situations. In nature, *A. arborea* often grows on dry ridges with shallow soils, which means it is drought tolerant once established. Insects usually are not a problem. Overfertilization may cause some fire blight. Rust may sometimes occur, which may reduce the yield but will not kill the plant.

Showy Spireas Update the Heirloom Classic

By Toby Bost, Forsyth County

The old, garden-variety Vanhoutte spirea must now take a bow to the compact, colorful Bumald spireas. Garden designers are getting the message out that contemporary landscapes are better served by the showy foliage and myriad textures provided by interesting woody ornamentals. The Bumald spirea hybrids, a cross between *Spiraea albiflora* and *S. japonica*, have demonstrated that they are here to stay in our Carolina landscapes. These dwarf species encompass numerous cultivars that can light up gardens with golden yellow, bronze, or lime green foliage and contrasting pinkish or multicolored flowers. Mainstream selections such as 'Little Princess', 'Goldflame', 'Goldmound', and 'Limemound' can now be found at most Piedmont nurseries.

'Crispa' spirea
Robert E. Lyons

The dwarf spireas are as tough as their heirloom cousins and offer color in the summer, when most shrubs are showing the hot-weather doldrums. Most cultivars grow three to four feet high with a similar spread and need virtually no care. You will find that these deciduous shrubs are right at home in low borders or used en masse. The colorful varieties can be placed to draw attention to an entrance or garden gate.

Container-grown plants are easy to transplant and are adapted to a wide range of soil types. Avoid low, wet sites. Give the plants full sun in an open area and they will be delightful companions. Spireas have few pest problems and are considered drought tolerant when established. Keep the plants low by pruning them after they bloom. Creeping junipers are good companion plants.

The newest cultivars that can be used for botanical accents in the landscape include 'Neon Flash', which has reddish purple new growth and vivid red clusters of flowers, and 'Golden Sunrise', which offers the brightest yellow foliage yet.

Spicebush Provides Fall Color and Fragrant Scent

By Karen Neill, Guilford County

Spicebush
Bryce Lane

The name spicebush brings to mind fragrance. In fact, the plant is named for its spicy scent. The Northern spicebush, *Lindera benzoin*, is a fairly common large shrub (or sometimes a small tree) that is found on northern slopes, river bottom lands, and woodland stream banks in scattered locations from Florida to Canada.

Spicebush is dioecious, meaning that males produce pollen and females produce berries. It spreads slowly by suckers and reaches a height and spread of 10 to 20 feet. When used in the landscape, it is a good shrub for borders or natural areas. Besides being extremely fragrant, the brilliant scarlet fruit of the female plants is eye catching in the autumn landscape. The foliage is a favorite of the spicebush swallowtail caterpillar.

For best landscape performance, situate spicebush in a semishady spot in moist soil. *Lindera* is difficult to transplant because of its coarsely fibrous root system. It is also somewhat slow to reestablish.

The 80 other species of *Lindera*—some evergreen, others deciduous—have been praised by such plantsmen as the late J. C. Raulston. *L. glauca* and *L. angustifolia* have spreading habits with blue-green leaves in summer. The narrow, elliptical leaves change to brilliant shades of yellow, apricot, and crimson in fall. The foliage then changes to tan and persists through winter, giving the shrub the appearance of a small beech tree. *L. glauca* has yellow flowers in early spring that are followed with black, pearl-sized fruit in the fall. Birds find this fruit very appealing after it matures in September.

Sugar Maples Accent Autumn

By Toby Bost, Forsyth County

Sugar maple
Toby Bost

Of the many maples recommended for planting in North Carolina landscapes, none produces more wonderful fall color than the sugar maple, *Acer saccharum*. Its dull green summer leaves turn a gorgeous orange and yellow with the first frosts. Because of its colossal height of greater than 60 feet and its similar spread, it is not a tree for a courtyard or a small residential property. This beauty is a great tree for large yards.

Given plenty of room and years to mature, a sugar maple is almost unsurpassable as a shade tree in the cooler regions of the Tar Heel State. The sugar maple, like the Norway maple, is best adapted to the Piedmont Triad and points west unless a heat-tolerant cultivar is selected. Though it is a slower-growing tree than are red and silver maples, this beauty has a desirable symmetrical form that matures into an upright oval to round tree. Its strong branches hold up well in ice storms, unlike those of the silver maple. The branches are distinguished by smooth gray bark that provides winter interest. Unfortunately, you will not see this tree lining many city streets, as it is adversely affected by air pollution in urban environments.

The newer heat-tolerant cultivars offer more latitude when planted in warm zone 8 landscapes. 'Legacy' has proven superior in the South and appears to be the best of the drought-tolerant cultivars. Of equal reputation is Green Mountain®, which offers dark green, leathery foliage with good scorch resistance. If space is at a premium, columnar forms are available, among them Apollo™, a slow-growing tree that reaches 30 feet in as many years.

Sweetshrub Provides Alluring Fragrance, Subtle Charm

By Mark Danieley, Alamance County

Calycanthus, commonly known as sweetshrub, sweet bubby, or simply calycanthus, is a favorite of many gar-

Sweetshrub
Connie Little

deners. An old-fashioned deciduous shrub, it has been overlooked in recent history but is now making a comeback. It is best known for its maroon or red fragrant flowers that open before the leaves emerge in the spring. People in the know plant sweetshrubs around patios or decks where they can enjoy the strawberry-scented aroma.

Sweetshrubs are easily transplanted and can be grown in sun or shade. They can get tall and leggy, growing six to nine feet in height, but pruning them after they flower will keep them presentable. They prefer deep, well-drained, loamy soil, though they are tolerant of less-than-perfect soil conditions. Sweetshrubs are tough plants that have few insect or disease problems.

One species of *Calycanthus* is native to North Carolina. The Carolina sweetshrub is commonly found growing as an understory shrub in woodlands and along streams. Sweetshrub can be propagated by seed, but some seedlings may not be true to type and may not have fragrant flowers. Softwood cuttings taken in late spring and summer and treated with a rooting hormone will root readily for most cultivars.

Varieties such as 'Hartlage Wine', 'Athens', and 'Michael Lindsey' are good choices for fall color. New hybrids are being developed at North Carolina State University using a combination of different *Calycanthus* species. One of the most promising varieties is a selection called 'Venus', produced by crossing three different species. 'Venus' features large, ivory yellow buds on a medium-sized shrub. The buds open into large, upright white flowers that resemble magnolia blooms. The spring blooms are very fragrant and much showier than those of the native sweetshrubs.

'Tangerine Beauty' Adds Surefire Sensation to Gardens

By Leah Chester-Davis, North Carolina Cooperative Extension Specialist

A surefire sensation in any garden is the 'Tangerine Beauty' crossvine, a showy, long-flowering cultivar of the native American vine *Bignonia capreolata*. 'Tangerine Beauty' has garnered attention as a J. C. Raulston Arboretum Selection™ plant for regional gardens. In order to be named a J. C. Raulston Arboretum Selection™ plant, 'Tangerine Beauty' had to prove itself in trials at the J. C. Raulston Arboretum at North Carolina State University, and it did just that.

'Tangerine Beauty' crossvine
Dennis J. Werner

The vine's trumpet-shaped flowers, borne in profusion from late spring through early summer, are a rich shade of orange-red outside and tan-yellow inside. A vigorous grower capable of reaching 10 feet in a single year, it grows well in both sun and shade, but it flowers much more intensely in full sun. A two-year-old plant at the J. C. Raulston Arboretum stopped visitors in their tracks when it first bloomed, its masses of tangerine-colored blooms totally obscuring its leaves. This flowering vine is native to the moist coastal woodlands of North Carolina. Crossvine is considered evergreen but may be semi-evergreen in the mountain region. It tolerates planting in a wide range of soil types. The lightly scented, trumpet-shaped flowers that appear in mid-spring are especially attractive to hummingbirds.

'Tangerine Beauty' has no serious pests and is drought tolerant once it is established. It can climb wire or wood trellises and fences, as well as tree trunks and wooden or stone walls. To keep it in check, prune annually after it finishes blooming.

'Tangerine Beauty' is a reintroduction of a plant sold only for a short time in the 1950s by Wayside Gardens. Other colorful cultivars include the red-flowering 'Jekyll' and the orange-blooming 'Velcyll'.

Versatile, Vibrant Viburnums

By Mike Wilder, Nash County

Viburnum
Piedmont Carolina Nursery

"A garden without a viburnum is akin to life without music and art," says Dr. Michael A. Dirr, noted horticulturist. Choices abound. More than 150 viburnum species and cultivars range in size from low shrubs to small trees. They offer white or pink flowers and many fruit colors. They are suitable for wet or dry areas and formal or natural settings. They are noted for their inspiring fall color. The leaves of viburnums vary in shape, texture, and size. Flowering may occur from autumn to June, depending on the species. Viburnums are versatile, fitting into woodland plantings, borders, patios, and public areas.

Natives *Viburnum alnifolium*, known as hobblebush, and *V. cassinoides*, Witherod viburnum, prefer moist to wet soils and shaded woodland. Both grow to about six feet in height and have white flowers. Hobblebush has red to black summer fruit and deep red foliage in autumn. Witherod viburnum turns heads with its variable fruit colors ranging from green to pink to red, then blue to black. Other natives prefer drier or well-drained soils. Black haw, *V. prunifolium*, can survive in full sun or heavy shade. Downy arrowwood, *V. rafinesquianum*, will tolerate many soil types and cold winters. Native viburnums provide food for wildlife and are among the toughest of landscape plants.

Another attribute of some viburnums is a sweet fragrance. While a few are real stinkers, many of the exotic species provide a memorable experience while in bloom.

Seasoned gardeners favor Koreanspice, *V. carlesii*, and the cultivar *V.* × *burkwoodii* 'Mohawk' for their delicious spicy fragrance and striking fall foliage. *V.* × *carlcephalum* 'Cayuga' has pink buds that open to five-inch, fragrant, white, waxy flowers in spring. Leatherleaf viburnum, *V. rhytidophyllum*, lives up to its common name in cool climates. Its leaves are distinctly corrugated and deep green.

V. awabuki 'Chindo' was introduced by J. C. Raulston, a North Carolina State University professor and the founder of its arboretum. The leaves are lustrous and dark green. It will survive in all but wet soils. At a height of 10 to 15 feet, it is one of the most desirable evergreen screening plants for sunny or shady areas.

Virginia Sweetspire: A Great North Carolina Native

By Carl Matyac, Orange and Wake Counties

Virginia sweetspire, *Itea virginica*, has the characteristics we all look for when we hear the word *native*. Easy to establish, sweetspire is insect and disease resistant and drought tolerant. It has great leaf and flower color and works well in naturalized sections of the urban landscape. This deciduous shrub is considered homegrown not just in North Carolina but from the Pine Barrens of New Jersey to the Florida wetlands and west to Missouri.

Virginia sweetspire
Piedmont Carolina Nursery

Sweetspire produces white, fragrant flowers in May or June on racemes from three to six inches long. It flowers on the previous season's wood and so should be pruned immediately after the blooms fade. Fall color is superb when the green foliage, which is oblong and slightly serrated, turns to hues of yellow, orange, crimson, and purple. It remains on the plant until December. One drawback is sweetspire's tendency to spread. A mature plant might be only three to five feet in height but will spread up to 10 feet in width. This tendency to take up space makes this a perfect choice for mass plantings in tough locations such as slopes or hillsides where junipers would frequently be used. Sweetspire can handle plenty of sun but develops a thinner canopy in light shade. Though this plant tolerates dry sites, it prefers moist, fertile soil.

Look for some of the nursery selections such as 'Henry's Garnet' and 'Little Henry', which have a more restrained growing pattern. These selections have the characteristics noted above, but their spread is limited to 1½ times the height of the specimen.

Weeping Blue Atlas Cedar Serves As a Landscape Accent

By Carl Matyac, Orange and Wake Counties

Weeping blue atlas cedar
J. C. Raulston Arboretum

Many gardeners are familiar with the wonderful ornamental attributes and landscape use of deodar cedar, *Cedrus deodara*, with its beautiful blue-green leaves and graceful habit. Its unusual-looking cousin, weeping blue atlas cedar, *C. atlantica* 'Glauca Pendula', deserves recognition as well. This is truly a unique plant. Its branches feature a flowing effect; they are sometimes described as cascading like water over a bed of rocks. This wonderful weeping conifer has the same bluish evergreen needles as the common deodar cedar. The weeping, twisting, long branches crowded with bright blue needles fall down around the trunk.

In consideration of its unusual characteristics, weeping blue atlas cedar is a perfect candidate as a specimen plant. It deserves a special place where it will be sure to catch the eye and hold the interest of any visitor to the garden. It can be trained, trellised, espaliered, and even grown as a bonsai to fit the need and size of the garden. Its twisted branch habit gives it year-round interest.

As with most cedars, weeping blue atlas cedar does best in loamy soil and full sun but will tolerate other soils except those with poor drainage. It is a moderate- to slow-growing evergreen that reaches 10 feet in height and 15 feet in width. Since weeping blue atlas cedar is somewhat difficult to transplant, it is best to plant container-grown trees. Staking and training young trees is necessary to establish the desired form.

Blue atlas cedar is resistant to serious pest and disease problems. Be sure to protect trees from strong winter winds, since cold temperatures can injure or kill the tops of established trees.

Winter Daphne Tickles Spring's Fancy

By Darrell Blackwelder, Rowan County

Daphne odora, or winter daphne, is a winter-flowering shrub that can withstand fickle weather that may be balmy one day and downright cold the next. This plant's irresistible fragrance, sweet nosegay-type flower clusters, and glossy foliage brighten the winter landscape.

Winter daphne is an attractive, sparsely branched evergreen shrub that reaches about three feet in height and spread. The most common cultivar, 'Aureomarginata', has leaves with a narrow, irregular yellow margin. From February to early March, the plant produces terminal clusters of small flowers that are crystalline white inside and deep purplish pink outside. The flowers of winter daphne are highly regarded

Winter Daphne
Piedmont Carolina Nursery

for their strong scent—possibly the most delightful of any flowers. The scent is very similar to that of *Osmanthus fragrans*, which blooms in the fall. The flower clusters keep well in water, allowing gardeners to appreciate the scent indoors. In the landscape, winter daphne is best located near a well-traveled path or an outdoor courtyard, where its fragrance can best be appreciated.

Winter daphne can be challenging to grow. It does not tolerate soils with poor drainage. Root rot diseases associated with poorly drained soils are likely the major cause of its failure in the landscape. Ideally, deep, well-drained woodland soil with plenty of humus is best for this shrub. Plant it in a slightly raised bed in amended soil to ensure adequate drainage. Winter daphne can tolerate full sun but does best in protected areas that provide moderate shade. Although the plant needs to be irrigated during periods of drought, it is considerably tolerant of drought episodes. It does not heal well from cuts into mature wood, so it is best to avoid pruning. However, "pinching" or taking cuttings from the tips of long shoots on the current year's growth will make the plant fuller and more floriferous.

Wisteria 'Amethyst Falls' Offers an Elegant Alternative

By Kevin Starr, Lincoln County

Wisteria is a plant that, for some, evokes images of garden pergolas laden with fragrant, cascading blooms. Mention the plant to gardeners, though, and they can't seem to run fast enough to sharpen their pruning shears! Though pruning shears are a necessity to keep Chinese wisteria in check, there is an alternative that offers beauty without the need for constant manicures: 'Amethyst Falls' American wisteria, a J. C. Raulston Arboretum Selection™.

Wisteria 'Amethyst Falls'
Robert E. Lyons

'Amethyst Falls' is a cultivar of *Wisteria frutescens*, a species native in much of the southeastern United States. It was first released by Bob and Bill Head of Head-Lee Nursery in South Carolina. This deciduous, flowering vine has dark green foliage and a more restrained growth habit than the more familiar Chinese wisteria, *W. sinensis*. While Chinese wisteria has beautiful flowers, most gardeners know that it is extremely aggressive and has become naturalized in many spots in the state. 'Amethyst Falls' has hanging clusters of lavender or purple flowers that are produced abundantly in the spring and sporadically through the summer.

This cultivar adapts well to a variety of soils and is disease and insect resistant, though it is bothered occasionally by Japanese beetles. It flowers best when located in full to partial sun. 'Amethyst Falls' is a good choice for small garden settings as a nonvigorous vine grown on an arbor or other small structure. It is hardy in USDA zones 5 through 9.

Witchhazel: The Gardener's Missing (Winter) Link

By John MacNair, Mecklenburg County

'Ruby Glow' witchhazel
Robert E. Lyons

While most plants are hibernating for the winter, witchhazels delight the senses with a tantalizing array of delicate, often fragrant flowers. A wonderful winter accent, these small- to medium-sized shrubs complement other plantings in the landscape. Depending on the species and the named variety, witchhazels bloom from late fall through early spring. To cope with blustery weather, their flower petals curl up and then reopen on warm, sunny days. The flowers, which have threadlike petals somewhat akin to bee balm, vary in color from tinges of yellow to red to orange.

The leaves resemble those of hazelnut. The fruit provides further winter interest. Witchhazels are upright, loosely branched shrubs or small trees that need room to branch out. They grow 10 to 15 feet in height and width. Pruning is not necessary except for infrequent shaping.

If you prefer natives, *Hamamelis virginiana*, which blooms in the fall, and *H. vernalis*, which blooms in late winter, are available. Hybrid cultivars such as 'Arnold Promise', 'Ruby Glow', and 'Primavera' are best for consistent flowering, scent, and fall color.

The edge of a natural area or a mixed shrub border with improved soil, good drainage, and occasional irrigation is ideal for these plants. They look most attractive when used to heighten areas of a garden that already are inviting. They're perfect for established landscapes, especially historic homes and gardens.

Chapter 3

Seasonal Gardening Calendar

North Carolina gardeners are blessed to live in a state where we can garden year-round. Because conditions vary from the mountains to the Piedmont to the coast, we include a calendar to recommend the best timing for gardening tasks in each of the three areas of the state. We thank the Extension Master Gardener Associations in Brunswick, Buncombe, and Forsyth counties for their timely gardening tips and calendars, which helped frame this chapter.

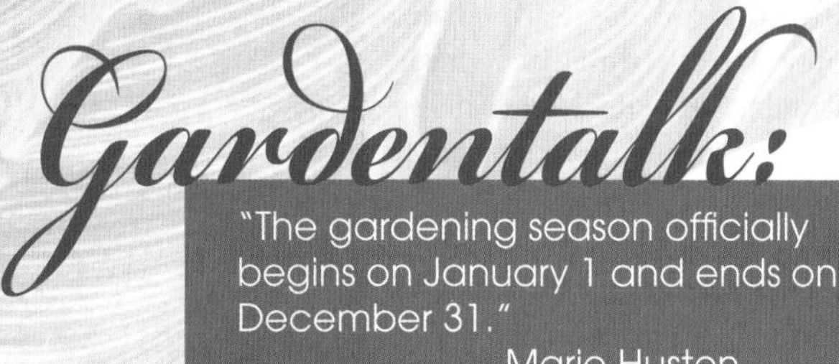

"The gardening season officially begins on January 1 and ends on December 31."
Marie Huston

Mountain Region

Spring—March, April, May

Lawns

Treat sunny lawns that have been infested with crabgrass in the past with a preemergent herbicide to prevent germination of this annual grassy weed. Don't use preemergent herbicides in combination with spring seeding.

While cool-season lawns are best seeded in early fall, March is an acceptable time to sow grass seed and begin laying sod. Keep seeded or sodded lawns well irrigated in spring.

Complete spring fertilization by mid-March. Weed-and-feed products can help manage juvenile broadleaf weeds; spray applications of herbicides are effective.

Mow frequently enough to avoid removing more than one-third of the height of the grass with each mowing. Research shows that proper mowing height helps manage weeds.

Ornamentals

Do not remove foliage from spring-blooming bulbs until after the leaves are partially brown.

Plant container-grown trees, groundcovers, rosebushes, and evergreen shrubs.

Prepare flower beds with organic matter. Plant annuals after the danger of frost has passed. Continue to pinch flower plantings to encourage bushy plants and more summer blooms.

Do heavy pruning in March on hedges and rosebushes.

After the soil has warmed up, apply a fresh three-inch layer of mulch on beds. Mulch helps manage weeds and conserve moisture.

If spring-flowering shrubs need pruning, do so soon after the blooms fade.

Shape or prune summer-flowering shrubs and trees to improve flower display.

Crocus
Dennis J. Werner

Evergreen trees and shrubs do not need fertilization every year. Test the soil or use a slow-release fertilizer or organic product to maintain health and vigor.

Edibles

Plant and prune fruit trees, blueberries, and cane berries. Thin fruit on bearing fruit trees.

Fruit trees benefit from annual applications of fertilizer. While only nitrogen fertilizer may be needed, apply one pound of 10-10-10 fertilizer per year of tree age (up to five pounds for mature trees) in lieu of a soil test.

Remove weeds from strawberry beds, then mulch with straw in late March.

For high-quality tree fruit, apply a fungicide/insecticide spray routinely as recommended on the product label. Always remove diseased fruit (mummies) at the end of the season. Follow good sanitation practices in backyard orchards.

Select vigorous crowns and plant asparagus in well-prepared garden soil. Follow bed preparation information closely to enjoy this perennial crop for many years.

Start seedlings of tomatoes, peppers, and herbs indoors.

Don't till garden soil that is too wet. Wait a week after rain before working the soil. Better still, prepare new ground in early winter. Spade in rotted leaves and lime the soil.

Summer—June, July, August

Lawns

Brown patch disease and other spring fungal blights appear at this time of year. Mow when the grass is dry. Avoid fertilizing cool-season lawns. Use a fungicide as a last resort on lawns that will be irrigated regularly.

Do not water a tall fescue lawn unless you can continue to irrigate throughout the summer. Allow it to go dormant (brown); irrigate every three weeks to keep lawn alive.

Test the soil of problem lawns that will be reseeded in September.

Eliminate Japanese beetle grubs with a recommended soil insecticide.

Fertilize and irrigate zoysia grass lawns in the summer months.

Campsis grandiflora 'Morning Calm'
Robert E. Lyons

Ornamentals

Woolly and green aphids arrive. They may indicate overfertilized plants. Either ignore them, since they are food for birds and beneficial insects, or control them with an insecticidal oil. Or you can hose them off using a forceful stream of water.

Control Japanese beetles by handpicking them and placing beetle traps. Otherwise, apply organic pesticides or liquid Sevin or a similar approved chemical.

When needed, apply insecticides carefully and late in the evening to avoid bee kills.

Continue to pinch back herbs and deadhead flowers. Irrigate blooming flowers regularly.

Eliminate encroaching Bermuda grass with grass killer herbicides such as Vantage or similar products.

Use Roundup® or similar glyphosate product to spot-spray difficult-to-control weeds. Beware of wind drift to sensitive vegetables and nearby plants.

Irrigate spring-planted shrubs and trees. Soak the ground to 10 inches.

Edibles

Thin strawberry plants to 12 inches apart. Remove runners; fertilize and weed beds. Remove beds older than three years and replant next spring.

Irrigate small fruits during the harvest season if dry weather persists.

Watch for yellow jackets nesting in gardens. Locate nests and use an approved insecticide to treat at dusk when the bees return to the ground.

Continue to plant successive crops of vegetables. Side-dress (fertilize) vegetables six weeks after planting and monthly as needed. Use two cups of calcium nitrate or similar nitrogen product per 100 feet of row.

To prevent early blight and leaf diseases, spray tomatoes weekly with a fungicide.

Vegetables need one inch of water per week. Irrigate early in the day; keep foliage dry late in the evening. Consider using mulch and drip irrigation to conserve water.

Squash plants succumb to vine borers if the stems are not treated. Scout for vegetable insects routinely. Use the least toxic products available for edible crops.

Fall—September, October, November

Lawns

Core aerify and renovate cool-season lawns. During the cool months, ensure that seed and sod are established well ahead of winter. Use three pounds of grass seed per 1,000 square feet when overseeding and six pounds for new lawns.

Apply two pounds of nitrogen fertilizer per 1,000 square feet in the fall; split applications between September and November.

Keep fallen leaves from accumulating on newly seeded lawns.

Wait until after the third mowing before applying broadleaf weed killers on new grass seedlings.

Irrigate newly seeded lawns twice weekly until established.

Ornamentals

Purchase spring-flowering bulbs for planting in November. Use a bulb fertilizer at planting time to encourage longer bulb life.

Till deeply to eliminate soil compaction problems. Incorporate topsoil, organic matter, and limestone before planting winter annuals and bulbs. Finish with a two-inch layer of mulch. Plant mums and pansies for seasonal decorations.

Sun coleus and mums
Robert E. Lyons

Continue planting trees, perennial flowers, and shrubs. Remember to loosen roots in containers that are pot-bound.

Groom perennial beds. Divide crowded plantings; share them or create new beds.

Construct a compost bin. Collect leaves and yard debris to make leaf compost.

Delay heavy pruning of hedges and shrubs until late winter. After a killing freeze, begin pruning back damaged perennials and rosebushes.

Edibles

Order fruit trees and grapevines for winter planting.

Do not prune young fruit trees until buds swell as spring approaches.

Clean gardens by removing old vegetable plantings. Plant leafy greens and lettuce. Protect them during frosty nights by using a row cover fabric.

Till a spot for planting early-spring vegetables. Consider planting ryegrass as a winter cover crop. Use leaves to protect the soil over the winter months.

Winter—December, January, February

Lawns

Garden in winter
Robert E. Lyons

Remove winter weeds such as wild onions and dandelions from cool-season lawns (tall fescue, Kentucky bluegrass, fine fescue) by hand-weeding using an appropriate tool. Spot-spray with a postemergent herbicide. Surfactants help chemicals stay on the waxy leaves of many weeds for better control.

Fertilize cool-season lawns in February with one pound or less of actual nitrogen per 1,000 square feet. Slow-release lawn fertilizer products are ecologically friendly and yield good color.

Note that turf-type tall fescue blends improve grass density and tolerate shade better than Kentucky 31 fescue.

Mow lawns at 2½ or 3 inches. Leave grass clippings to recycle nutrients and add organic matter to the soil.

Irrigate lawns during dry periods, especially in early winter.

The presence of moles in the lawn may indicate a white grub problem. Wait until late spring to evaluate and treat grubs. Spear-type traps are the most effective method of eliminating moles.

Ornamentals

Plant deciduous trees and shrubs when the ground is not frozen. Plant balled-and-burlapped trees and bare-root plants in their dormant season. Plant evergreens as the temperature rises in early spring.

Mulch perennial beds and tender shrubs as the ground cools down.

Prune trees and evergreen shrubs as needed. Follow the "4-Ds"—remove dead, dying, diseased, and dangerous branches. Make clean cuts using well-sharpened loppers or shears.

Don't prune spring-flowering shrubs; wait until after they bloom.

Consider using sand, sawdust, or kitty litter on walks and driveways in lieu of deicing salts. Some salt products pollute streams and injure landscape plantings.

Peruse mail-order catalogs for new releases or varieties for the garden. Visit arboreta, nurseries, and local garden centers for design ideas and plant selections.

Consider using a live Christmas tree; plant it in your landscape in early January. Consider a family visit to a choose-and-cut farm. Store cut trees in the shade and provide lots of water.

Trim groundcovers such as liriope in late winter before new growth appears.

Choose landscape plants based on their cold hardiness and mature size. Select small-sized trees—dogwoods, crape myrtles, or Japanese maples—when planting near utility lines.

Consider deciduous hollies and other berry-producing plants that offer birds a cold-weather treat.

Fertilize spring bulbs after new growth is visible above ground.

Edibles

Sow seeds for early vegetables such as lettuce, radishes, onions, and spinach in a cold frame. Monitor seedlings closely and ventilate frame on sunny days.

Test new garden soils. Check with your Cooperative Extension Center for free soil test boxes and instructions. Till or turn soil before spring rains. Lime is inexpensive but pays big dividends when incorporated to reduce acidity.

Utilize compost and aged manures to enhance garden soils.

Take advantage of downtime to design a drip irrigation system; install rain barrels or cisterns to capture summer rains.

Control overwintering insects on fruit trees by applying a horticultural oil on a warm day in early winter.

Plant garden peas and onion sets in late February.

Repair gardening equipment; tune up mowers and rototillers.

Piedmont Region

Spring—March, April, May

Lawns

Manage crabgrass with a preemergent herbicide to prevent germination of this annual grassy weed. Most such products cannot be used in combination with spring seeding.

While cool-season lawns should be established in early fall, early March is the next best time to sow grass seed and lay sod. Keep seeded or sodded lawns well irrigated in the spring.

Complete spring fertilization before mid-March. Weed-and-feed products can help manage juvenile broadleaf weeds. Spray applications of herbicides are very effective. Liquid fertilization by professional turf companies is acceptable for irrigated lawns in the off-season.

Mow frequently enough to avoid removing more than one-third of the height of the grass with each mowing. Proper mowing height will help manage weeds, especially crabgrass.

Mow tall fescue and bluegrass lawns at a 2½ to 3 inches, and higher in summer.

April is a good month to lay sod or sprig warm-season lawns of hybrid Bermuda grass, zoysia, centipede, or St. Augustine.

Fertilize Bermuda grass and zoysia two weeks after green-up. Avoid adding nitrogen fertilizer to centipede lawns.

Ornamentals

Plant container-grown trees, groundcovers, rosebushes, and evergreen shrubs.

Prepare flower beds with organic matter. Plant annuals when the danger of frost has passed.

Continue to pinch flower plantings to encourage bushy plants and more summer blooms.

Do heavy pruning in March on hedges and rosebushes.

When the soil warms up, apply a fresh layer of mulch, using three inches on beds. Mulch helps manage weeds, conserves moisture, prevents erosion, and improves soil health.

If spring-flowering shrubs need pruning, do so soon after the blooms fade.

Shape or prune summer-flowering shrubs and trees to improve flower display.

Fertilize summer-flowering bulbous plants that are beginning to emerge. Apply a bloom booster (high phosphorus) product or follow a soil test report when preparing new beds.

Layer new plants by lowering a branch of your favorite shrub and covering it with soil and a brick or stone to encourage root development.

Bleeding heart
Robert E. Lyons

Plant and stake peonies, Oriental lilies, dahlias, Belle hibiscus, and heady perennials.

Prune rosebushes in March and begin fungicide sprays on hybrid tea roses. Prune Knock Out® roses to remove blighted canes and encourage vigorous growth.

After the last frost, plant tropical bulbs and plants such as cannas, caladiums, and elephant ears.

In containers and planters, refresh old soil with organic matter, or use new potting soil containing moisture-holding materials to reduce watering frequency.

If azaleas and pieris suffer from lace-bug attack, treat the plants with an insecticide, horticultural oil, or soap-spray application to the undersides of the foliage canopy.

Slugs can ruin tender annuals. To kill slugs, use prepared gels or place baits in plastic containers to protect pets.

Refresh mulch in spring as you groom foundation, entrance, and color-bed plantings.

Edibles

Plant cold-tolerant vegetables such as broccoli, cabbages, onions, and peas in March.

When planting a vegetable garden, remember to rotate the locations of plant families to reduce disease and insect pressure. Include flowers to attract beneficial predator bugs.

Plant and prune fruit trees, blueberries, and cane berries. Thin the fruit on bearing fruit trees.

Fruit trees benefit from annual applications of fertilizer. While only nitrogen fertilizer may be needed, apply one pound of 10-10-10 per year of tree age (up to five pounds for mature trees) in lieu of a soil test.

Remove weeds from strawberry beds, then mulch with straw in late March.

For high-quality tree fruit, apply a fungicide/insecticide spray routinely as recommended on the product label.

Select vigorous crowns and plant asparagus in well-prepared garden soil. Follow bed preparation information closely to enjoy this perennial crop for many years.

Start seedlings of tomatoes, peppers, and herbs indoors. Closely monitor moisture, sunlight, and heat buildup in cloches and cold frames.

Be prepared for frost protection. Floating fabric row covers, milk jugs, and old bedsheets can reduce the loss of tender transplants in March and April.

Summer—June, July, August

Lawns

Brown patch disease and other spring fungal blights appear. Mow when the grass is dry. Avoid fertilizing cool-season lawns. Use fungicides as a last resort and only on lawns that will be irrigated regularly.

Do not water a tall fescue lawn unless you can continue to irrigate throughout the summer. Allow it to go dormant (turn brown). Irrigate every three weeks to keep it alive.

Get a soil test on a problem lawn that you plan to reseed in September.

Control broadleaf weeds like lespedeza by spot-treating infested areas using an ap-

Sphinx moth feeds on four o'clock.
Dennis J. Werner

proved broadleaf herbicide. Water lawn the day before applying the product.

Eliminate Japanese beetle grubs by using a recommended soil insecticide.

Fertilize and irrigate Bermuda grass and zoysia lawns in the summer months.

Ornamentals

Watch for spider mites, which can become a problem during hot, dry conditions. Make a thorough spray application using insecticidal soap or a miticide in the morning hours.

Control woody weeds such as kudzu, trumpet creeper, and wisteria by repeated pruning and by spraying basal sprouts with a glyphosate herbicide or similar vegetation killer.

Maintain roses by deadheading, fertilizing, watering, and applying fungicides.

In late summer, sow perennial seeds such as hollyhock, delphinium, and stokesia to produce flowers next spring.

Deadhead annual and perennial flowers to encourage successive blooming.

Control Japanese beetles by handpicking and placing beetle traps. Otherwise, apply organic pesticides or liquid Sevin or a similar approved chemical.

When needed, apply insecticides carefully and late in the evening to avoid bee kills.

Edibles

Follow good sanitation practices in backyard orchards, especially by managing weeds that harbor insects. Always remove diseased fruit (mummies) by the end of the harvest season.

Thin strawberry plants to 12 inches apart. Remove runners; fertilize and weed beds. Remove beds older than three years; replant next spring.

Irrigate small fruits during the harvest season if dry weather persists.

Beware of yellow jackets nesting in gardens and mulched beds. Locate and drench nests with an approved insecticide; treat at dusk when the bees return to the ground.

Continue to plant successive crops of vegetables. Side-dress (fertilize) vegetables six weeks after planting and monthly as needed. Use two cups of calcium nitrate or similar nitrogen fertilizer per 100 feet of row.

Spray tomatoes weekly with a fungicide to prevent early blight and leaf diseases.

Vegetables need one inch of water per week. Irrigate early in the day; keep foliage dry late in the evening. Consider using mulch and drip irrigation to conserve water.

Squash plants succumb to vine borers if the stems are not treated. Scout for vegetable insects routinely. Use the least toxic products available for edible crops.

Fall—September, October, November

Lawns

September is the optimal time to start new lawns and renovate tall fescue lawns. The new turf-type tall fescue blends have a finer texture than Kentucky 31, offer better shade tolerance, and produce dense, green lawns often with less fertilizer.

Color bed
Robert E. Lyons

Core aerify and renovate cool-season lawns. During the cool months, ensure that seed and sod are established well ahead of winter. Use three pounds of grass seed per 1,000 square feet when overseeding and six pounds for new lawns.

Control winter annual bluegrass and chickweed by applying a select preemergent herbicide in September. Do not seed lawns when applying these herbicides, as they prevent seed germination.

Apply two pounds of nitrogen fertilizer per 1,000 square feet. Split between September and November applications.

Keep fallen leaves from accumulating on newly seeded lawns.

Aerify and overseed Bermuda grass lawns with perennial ryegrass in early fall. Fertilize warm-season lawns with a winterizing product.

Ornamentals

Purchase spring-flowering bulbs for planting in November. Use bulb fertilizer at planting time to encourage longer bulb life. Mix Perma-Till™ into the soil to discourage the voles (pine mice) that eat valuable spring bulbs and hostas.

Till deeply to eliminate soil compaction problems. Incorporate topsoil, organic matter, and limestone before planting winter annuals and bulbs. Finish with a two-inch layer of mulch. Plant mums and pansies for seasonal decorations.

Continue planting trees, perennial flowers, and shrubs. Remember to loosen roots in containers that are pot-bound.

Groom perennial beds. Divide crowded plantings; share them or create new beds.

Collect leaves and yard debris to make leaf compost. Construct a compost bin.

Delay heavy pruning on hedges and shrubs until late winter. After a killing freeze, begin pruning back damaged perennials and top-heavy rosebushes.

Stockpile municipal leaf compost for mulching throughout fall and winter. Remember to keep mulch back a few inches from basal stems of shrubs and young trees to prevent rot and vole injury during the winter season.

Clean and properly store garden tools and hummingbird feeders.

Get a head start on next season's pest problems by spraying bug-prone shrubs with a horticultural oil before the holiday season.

Edibles

Till a spot for planting early-spring vegetables. Consider planting ryegrass as a winter cover crop. Use leaves to protect the soil over the winter months.

Problems with vegetables, especially cucumbers and tomatoes, may be related to soil-inhabiting nematodes. Collect a soil sample for analysis; take it to your local Cooperative Extension Center.

Order fruit trees and grapevines for winter planting.

Do not prune young fruit trees until spring; keep them watered and weeded during fall.

In September, clean and groom the garden, removing old vegetable plantings. Plant leafy greens, mesclun, spinach, and lettuce; protect them on frosty nights with a row cover fabric.

Winter—December, January, February

Lawns

The only adequate way to judge soil acidity (and the need for limestone/calcium) is a soil test. Winter is a good time to submit samples from your lawn or garden beds. Most soils can benefit from an application of 20 to 40 pounds of lime per 1,000 square feet every three or more years to offset the negative effects of fertilizers and rainfall.

Zoysia and Bermuda grass lawns can benefit from dethatching; rent a power rake to assist you.

Areas of the landscape that are too steep to mow or are getting too much shade can be converted to groundcovers. Select the best groundcover for the site.

Remove winter weeds such as wild onions and dandelions from cool-season lawns (tall fescue, Kentucky bluegrass, fine fescue) by hand-weeding, using an appropriate tool. Spot-spraying with a postemergent herbicide is preferred in cases of serious infestation. Surfactants help chemicals stay on the waxy leaves of many weeds for better control.

Fertilize cool-season lawns in February with one pound of actual nitrogen or less per 1,000 square feet of lawn. Slow-release fertilizers are ecologically friendly and yield good color.

Note that turf-type tall fescue blends improve grass density and tolerate shade better than Kentucky 31 fescue.

Mow lawns at 2½ to 3 inches. Leave grass clippings to recycle nutrients and add organic matter to the soil.

Irrigate lawns during dry periods, especially in early winter.

The presence of moles in the lawn may indicate a white grub problem. Wait until late spring to evaluate and treat grubs. Spear-type traps are the most effective method of eliminating moles.

Ornamentals

Plant deciduous trees and shrubs when the ground is not frozen. Plant balled-and-burlapped trees and bare-root plants in their dormant season. Plant evergreens as the temperature rises in early spring.

Mulch perennial beds and tender shrubs as the ground cools down.

Prune trees and evergreen shrubs as needed. Follow the "4-Ds"—remove dead, dying, diseased, and dangerous branches. Make clean cuts using well-sharpened loppers or shears.

Don't prune spring-flowering shrubs until after they bloom.

Consider using sand, sawdust, or kitty litter on walks and driveways in lieu of deicing salts. Some salt products pollute streams and injure landscape plantings.

Peruse mail-order catalogs for new releases or varieties. Visit arboreta, nurseries, and local garden centers for design ideas and plant selections.

Hippeastrum 'Safari'
Robert E. Lyons

Trim groundcovers such as liriope in late winter before new growth appears.

Choose landscape plants based on their cold hardiness and mature size. Select small-sized trees such as dogwoods, crape myrtles, or Japanese maples when planting near utility lines.

Consider deciduous hollies and other berry-producing plants that offer birds much-needed food.

Fertilize spring bulbs after new growth is visible above ground.

Edibles

As soon as the soil is prepared, sow early vegetables such as lettuce, radishes, onions, and spinach in a cold frame. Monitor seedlings closely and ventilate frame on sunny days.

Test new garden soils. Check with your local Cooperative Extension Center for free soil test boxes and instructions. Till or turn soil before spring rains. Lime is inexpensive but pays big dividends when incorporated to reduce acidity.

Utilize compost and aged manures to enhance garden soils. Cover fallow ground with leaves for later tilling into the soil.

Take advantage of downtime to design a drip irrigation system; install rain barrels or cisterns to capture summer rains.

Control overwintering insects on fruit trees by applying a horticultural oil on a warm day in early winter.

Plant garden peas and onion sets in late February.

Consider a rotational plan for your garden. If possible, plant cover crops.

Repair gardening equipment; tune up mowers and rototillers.

Coastal Region

Spring—March, April, May

Lawns

Always properly identify weeds before using pesticides. Some products interfere with weed seed germination, while other herbicides kill established weeds.

Weed-and-feed products can help manage juvenile broadleaf weeds; spray applications of herbicides are very effective and are often preferable to granular products. Apply preemergents for crabgrass control when forsythia is blooming in March.

Fertilizing warm-season lawns requires knowledge of the varieties of turfgrass. Call your local Cooperative Extension Center to request a copy of the "Lawn Maintenance Calendar."

Fertilize warm-season lawns beginning two weeks after green-up. Centipede is sensitive to nitrogen fertilization; don't fertilize these lawns without a soil test.

Before green-up, remove dormant grass leaves by mowing to 2½ inches with a rotary mower with a well-sharpened blade; hand-rake or use a power dethatcher. Fertilize later in May.

Plant warm-season grasses such as Bermuda grass, centipede, zoysia, and St. Augustine.

Dethatch lawns to reduce compaction.

Bellflowers
Robert E. Lyons

Ornamentals

Plant summer-flowering bulbs and herbaceous perennials early in the season. Remove cool-season annuals to make room for summer annuals. Groom and fertilize flower beds.

Apply preemergent herbicides to freshly mulched landscape beds. Hand-pull winter annual weeds such as bittercress and chickweed that pop up in clean beds.

Prune spring-flowering woody ornamentals immediately after they bloom. Remove weak or diseased twigs and branches from other trees and shrubs.

Prune up crape myrtles to create single or multitrunk specimen trees. Prune other summer-flowering plants such as hibiscus, lantana, rose-of-Sharon, and oleander.

Groom evergreen shrubs such as camellia, gardenia, nandina, and loropetalum.

Repot houseplants that have overgrown their containers and are root bound. Houseplants moved outdoors need time to acclimate under shade trees, out of direct sunlight.

Mulch to a depth of two to three inches when using double-ground or finer hardwood. Use pine needle mulch to a depth of four to six inches. Mulch is an effective weed barrier.

Always wear chemical-resistant gloves and goggles when handling a pesticide. Follow the label for personal protective equipment advice.

Never burn poison ivy after removing this weedy vine. Protect hands with gloves.

Edibles

Start and maintain a spray schedule for fruit trees. Fire blight is a common bacterial disease of quince, apples, and pears; prune blighted twigs or spray streptomycin.

Plant container-grown fruits and keep them well watered. Choose a full-sun location. Delay fertilization until they are established.

Every garden needs a fig tree and a couple of blueberry plants. An arbor of muscadine grapes is a treasure for down-east gardeners. Proper spacing is important for abundant fruit.

Set out transplants of herbs and vegetables after the danger of frost has passed.

Sow beans, corn, cucumbers, and squash. Avoid planting melons, okra, sweet potatoes, and gourds until the soil has warmed to a temperature above 75°.

Indeterminate tomato plants will continue to grow and fruit until autumn frosts. Construct wire cages for them for higher yields and less blossom-end rot.

Employ soaker hoses and other drip irrigation systems to conserve water and encourage roots.

Summer—June, July, August

Lawns

Soil testing is recommended for lawns that will be reseeded in September.

Control broadleaf weeds such as spurge, lespedeza, and plantain by spot-treating infested areas using an approved broadleaf herbicide. Water lawn the day before applying herbicide in order to get better chemical uptake, and thus improved weed kill.

Eliminate Japanese beetle grubs with a recommended soil insecticide.

Fertilize and irrigate Bermuda grass and zoysia lawns in the summer months.

St. Augustine is sensitive to 2, 4-D and MSMA herbicides. Large patch fungus disease can show up on these lawns. Watch for signs of chinch bug infestation.

Mow warm-season lawns such as Bermuda grass and zoysia with a reel mower set at

Hibiscus 'Kopper King'
Robert E. Lyons

¾- to 1-inch height. Leave clippings on lawns. Mow centipede lawns at 1 inch.

A yellow appearance in centipede lawns can indicate iron deficiency or soil pests. Spray iron sulfate (two ounces per 1,000 square feet) or a chelated iron product. Avoid staining walks and driveways by hosing them off promptly.

Irrigation is important in fast-draining, sandy soils. Apply the equivalent of ½ inch of water every third day if rainfall is lacking.

Ornamentals

Watch for aphids and whiteflies on gardenia, hibiscus, and impatiens. Use soft, organic products like horticultural oil and soap for early-morning spray applications.

Start pulling weeds from landscape beds before they get a foothold. Don't let weeds flower or they produce seeds that perpetuate maintenance problems.

Powdery mildew disease is a chronic concern on native dogwoods, crape myrtles, and garden phlox. Treat varieties that are not disease resistant with an approved fungicide.

Replant container gardens with annuals throughout the summer; water well. To avoid staking flowers, select compact cultivars of dwarf dahlias or spreading zinnias.

Properly space ornamental grasses for effect. One rule of thumb is to space them according to their heights. For example, plant three-foot-tall grasses like 'Morning Light' on three-foot centers. In other words, plant them in a grid pattern using the grass height as the spacing distance, giving them plenty of room to sway in the wind.

Prune perennial plantings of mums and asters for more flowers later. Divide daylilies and irises; transplant them while the colors can be identified.

Propagate semi-hardwood cuttings of your favorite ornamentals; use a rooting hormone. A soil mix of equal parts peat moss or vermiculite and perlite will serve the purpose.

Hand-remove and discard leaf gall (swollen leaves) on azaleas and camellias.

Protect honeybees by applying chemical insecticides late in the day to manage Japanese beetles and chewing bugs.

Plant annual vines to attract hummingbirds and beneficial predator insects.

Edibles

Plant warm-season vegetables like Southern peas, peppers, and melons in June.

Scout for garden pests routinely. Birds and other natural predators will reduce the number of insects.

Thin peach fruits every four to six inches for larger, high-quality fruit.

Tip-prune culinary herbs to keep their flowers from going to seed prematurely. Harvest regularly at the peak of flavor. Water with a soaker hose to reduce the likelihood of leaf diseases.

Remove suckers from the lower portions of tomato plants to encourage large fruit and reduce leafspot diseases. Mulch plantings if using overhead irrigation. Tomato suckers can be rooted in a semishaded location for planting later.

The vegetable harvest peaks in August; visit a farmers' market for local produce.

Fall—September, October, November

Lawns

Prepare to winterize coastal lawns. To repair centipede grass, make an application of potash (no nitrogen) in September. Test the soil every three years.

Bermuda grass is the only warm-season grass that can be overseeded with ryegrass for

Autumn anemone
Connie Little

winter color. Continue to mow at the recommended 1½-inch height.

Do not fertilize lawns after September. Cut back on irrigation as well in autumn.

Apply a preemergent herbicide to prevent broadleaf weeds in lawns that have a history of problem weeds such as chickweed and henbit. Otherwise, spot-spray weeds as necessary.

Rake fallen leaves from lawns or use a rotary mower to mulch them.

Clean spray equipment, lubricate parts, and store for the winter.

Ornamentals

Do not prune trees and shrubs until cold weather. Pruning may disrupt the plants' internal process of preparing for winter dormancy.

Fall is the time for planting trees, shrubs, perennials, and cool-season annuals. The roots have time to establish before the onset of growth in spring. Consider adding plants for fall color.

Planting guides and landscaping classes are available at Cooperative Extension Centers and community colleges. Consider taking a class to increase your knowledge of ornamentals.

Bring houseplants and tropicals inside when the temperature dips below 50°. Inspect and treat for insects that hitchhike via plants on the move.

A killing frost will signal when it is time to groom herbs and herbaceous perennial beds. Cut back wilted growth and refresh mulch if needed. Make notes if you keep a plant journal.

Secure plans for constructing a solar greenhouse if you enjoy plant propagation.

Fill a few containers with colorful winter annuals to decorate your porch or patio. Add a few bulbs such as snowdrop, crocus, or tulip for interest.

When buying mums for fall color, select varieties that can be planted as perennials. Hardy herbs for planting include comfrey, lamb's ear, catmint, sage, and lavender.

Edibles

Set out transplants of cole crops such as broccoli, cabbage, and collards in September. Plant seeds for a winter crop of lettuce, onion sets, radishes, spinach, and leafy greens.

Prepare beds for planting strawberries. Set plants in spring or fall.

Herbs for fall planting include calendula, cilantro, dill, garlic, leek, parsley, and rosemary. Enrich the soil with an organic fertilizer and limestone.

Collect and dry herbs for cooking and crafts. Place gourds in a ventilated location to cure.

Use fabric row covers made of spun-bound polyester for frost protection.

Spray horticultural oil in gardens to eliminate overwintering scales and mites.

Winter—December, January, February

Lawns

Sandy soils can dry out during the winter months. Irrigate Bermuda grass lawns overseeded with ryegrass during dry periods as the temperature allows.

Let other warm-season lawns rest. This is a good time to play a round of golf!

Ornamentals

Don't toss out that old Christmas tree without considering opportunities to recycle it. Possible uses include hanging suet and other bird treats from its branches, removing branches to shred for mulch, sinking the tree in a pond for a fish habitat, or using it as a trellis for planting garden peas.

Winter dreaming
Mark Dearmon

Wash soiled pots using a mixture of one part household bleach to nine parts water. Place them in a sunny location and cover with a clear plastic sheet to keep them clean and solarized for disease prevention.

Use downtime to stockpile mulch and manage compost bins.

Construct deer fencing as a deterrent to browsing deer. Specifications for fencing are available from Cooperative Extension Centers and state wildlife officers.

Continue planting trees and other landscape plants, especially field-grown balled-and-burlapped specimens, during the dormant season. Stake trees for the first three months or until they are established; monitor straps and other guylines to prevent girding injuries to trunks. It is not necessary to put fertilizer in the planting holes unless it is formulated for such use.

Rodents and rabbits can damage ornamental plantings. Use wire hardware cloth to craft cylinder-like plant collars for shrubs. Or cover bulb beds with the small-mesh wire.

Move aquatic plants into deeper parts of the pond or water garden after they die back.

Edibles

Plan a spring garden on paper. Peruse catalogs for new All-America Selections; choose the most pest-resistant cultivars. Place orders ahead of scheduled planting times.

Soil testing is a priority during the winter and summer seasons. Pick up kits from a county Cooperative Extension Center. Remember that limestone takes time to work when applied to the soil.

Incorporate organic matter to prepare a raised bed for asparagus planting.

Plant early-spring vegetables such as edible-podded peas, onions, and lettuce from early January through late February.

Use tree guards to protect young fruit trees from rodents, rabbits, and string trimmers. Purchase plastic tube-shaped guards that are long enough to wrap around entire trunks. Pull mulch away from trunks to discourage pesky voles (pine mice).

Growing your own seedlings indoors can be challenging without sufficient light. Locate plans for building a portable light stand made of PVC pipe and fluorescent light ballast.

Attract more birds to your garden with woody plants that produce edible fruits. Some possible selections include blueberry, viburnum, wax myrtle, deciduous and American hollies, juniper, birch, dogwood, and serviceberry.

Chapter 4
Enviro-Tips

"Enviro-Tips" shares ways we can implement best management practices to minimize our carbon footprint, ensure sustainability, and take care of precious natural resources.

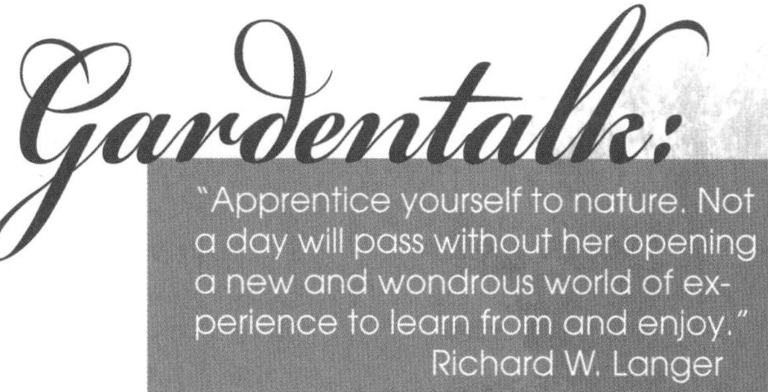

"Apprentice yourself to nature. Not a day will pass without her opening a new and wondrous world of experience to learn from and enjoy."
Richard W. Langer

Buffers for Waterfronts

By David Barkley, Brunswick County

Waterfront buffer
USDA-ARS

Runoff into our waterways can carry pollutants that wreak havoc in sensitive estuaries and marshes. Dislodged particles of soil and water-soluble materials—whether nutrients or other chemicals—can move across even gentle slopes and flow into ditches or canals, ultimately ending up in our waterways. Buffer strips help to filter out most pollutants and can trap sediment and other particles before they enter our streams.

Living plants along the shoreline protect property from erosion and provide cover and habitat for fish, birds, and other wildlife. Undisturbed natural shorelines also protect water quality by trapping excess nutrients and sediment. Home construction often involves stripping away vegetation and cutting the land to a final grade. Water crossing bare ground carries sediment and other materials to our streams. But a 50-foot border of groundcover will halt most of the pollutants from entering the water system, according to scientists.

Removal of shoreline vegetation can cause shallow-water temperatures to rise. This can adversely affect fish. The loss of trees and shrubs, wetlands, beaches, banks, and underwater grass impacts habitat and water quality.

Be sure to plan ahead during any construction activity along waterways. Use temporary silt fences until groundcovers can take over. Plant mixed vegetation that includes trees, shrubs, groundcovers, and vines. Mixed plantings are better for wildlife than grass alone and can be arranged to create an aesthetically pleasing landscape. Be sure to plant adaptive species for your climate. Check with your local Cooperative Extension Center for the best waterfront plants to use in your area.

Green roof
Bill Hunt

Green Roofs Reduce Runoff

By Darrell Blackwelder, Rowan County

When I think about green roofs, I usually think of algae and excessive shade. Some homeowners, however, are adapting a building practice that has been used since the Middle Ages. Green roofs can add color to the surroundings *and* aid the environment.

Germany leads the world in green roofs and rooftop plantings. About 10 percent of Germany's buildings have some type of green roof. Green roofs are now becoming popular in the United States, especially in cramped urban settings.

A green roof can be as simple as a rooftop planter with flowers and vegetables or as elaborate as a deep-soil system that supports a lawn and small trees. Green roofs decrease the total amount of stormwater runoff by retaining more than 50 percent of rainwater and gradually releasing it back into the atmosphere. They also minimize heating and cooling costs, reduce the urban heat-island effect, and increase wildlife habitat. One challenge with green roofs is to minimize the amount of nitrogen and phosphorous in the runoff. This can be done by carefully selecting planting media and minimizing the use of fertilizers.

Green roofs can be expensive. Most homes cannot be retrofitted to accept the extra weight. Maintenance is another factor. Even low-maintenance green roofs must be fertilized and watered if a drought occurs. Not every structure can support a green roof. Most roofs are not flat enough, nor can they handle the weight. If you have the right slope, a sturdy-enough structure, and access to your roof, you may be able to cultivate a roof garden.

For more information on green roofs, visit http://www.bae.ncsu.edu/stormwater/PublicationFiles/BMPs4LID.pdf.

Rain Gardens Capture Runoff

By Carl Matyac, Orange and Wake Counties

After a little rain on most soils in North Carolina, runoff begins to flow to low spots in the landscape. Runoff often carries sediment and pollution from driveways to nearby streams, which affects water quality. Rain gardens offer a solution.

Rain garden
Toby Bost

In rain gardens, plants and soil work together to absorb and filter pollutants and return cleaner water through the ground to nearby streams. Rain gardens also reduce flooding by absorbing runoff. And they can provide habitat for beneficial insects and wildlife.

Size your rain garden to accommodate a one-inch rainfall by measuring the roof and any parking area draining to the site. Divide the square footage by 20 to determine the proper square footage for your garden. Dig the garden four to six inches deep with a slight depression in the center. Use the removed soil to create a berm on one side that will retain water during storms. If the garden is on a slope, locate the berm on the downhill side. To prevent erosion, cover the berm with mulch or grass.

Use plants that tolerate fluctuating soil wetness. To help them survive extended wet periods, plant them on the edge of the rain garden or on mounds within it to elevate the roots above the pooled water level. Planting several species can create a long flowering season and add depth and dimension.

A rain garden has different wetness zones. Place plants that can withstand a few days of flooding at a time in the deepest part. In the shallow parts and on the edges, use more typical landscape plants.

Using little or no fertilizer or pesticide helps protect water quality. Add mulch two inches deep, but avoid burying new plants. Hardwood mulch is best because it will not float away.

For complete instructions, sizing recommendations, and a plant list, visit http://www.bae.ncsu.edu/topic/raingarden/.

The Right Plant Helps Reduce Diseases and Insects

By Michelle Wallace, Durham County

Falling in love with a plant is easy. It probably happens every time you go to the garden center. Whether it is the foliage, the flower, the shape, the size, or the fruit that makes you want a particular plant, do your homework first to see if it is really suited for the location you have in mind.

Juniper in nonirrigated bed
Toby Bost

Each plant has special growing requirements. Taking them into consideration will help to ensure success. These requirements address the plant's ability to withstand environmental conditions such as cold temperatures, humidity (or lack thereof), sun, shade, water (or lack thereof), and wind. They also address soil type. When you take all growing requirements into consideration prior to selecting a plant, your chance for success increases. To further ensure success, you can look for plant varieties that have been bred for disease and insect resistance, which will reduce the need for preventive pest management.

North Carolina is characterized as having three general plant hardiness zones: zone 6 in the mountains, zone 7 in the Piedmont, and zone 8 at the coast. Plant hardiness zone maps help categorize the regions by the average annual minimum temperatures. The lower the number on the hardiness scale, the lower the average minimum temperature of the region. Find out what the plant hardiness zone is for your region and the range of hardiness for the plant before making a selection.

Conduct a thorough inventory and analysis of your property to identify the existing conditions. Choose plants based on how well adapted they are to those conditions. You will find that many wonderful plants are available that will thrive under the environmental conditions on your property, have the characteristics you seek, and have few insect and disease problems.

Pesticide Safety at Home

By Jeff Rieves, Union County

Whether pesticides are commonly or infrequently used products around your house and garden, their safe use is of the utmost importance. Here are a few questions to ask and answer before you apply any pesticide.

Do you know how to identify problems? Not all insects are bad, nor are all undesired plants weeds. Determine if a problem exists, then find a specific solution.

Do you really need to spray a pesticide? Many insects such as aphids can be removed from plants with a stream of water. Weeds can be smothered with mulches, pulled, or mowed. Diseased parts of plants can be pruned away.

Can you tolerate the damage from the pest? Just because you see some damage from a pest doesn't mean you need to use a pesticide. This is especially so if the damage is light.

Pesticide safety
North Carolina Cooperative Extension Service

If you need to apply a pesticide, do you already have something at home to use? Instead of running to the store for a new pesticide, why not use what you have? Make sure both the pest to be managed and the plant to be treated are on the label of the pesticide.

Have you read the label on the pesticide? Take a few minutes to read the label before you apply any pesticide. Follow the label instructions. This is the safest thing you can do to protect you, your family, and the environment.

Do you know that you are required by law to follow all the instructions on the pesticide label? You are, so read the label.

How much pesticide do you need, and how should you apply it? The old saying "More is better" does not apply to pesticides. Often, using too much or applying the product incorrectly can damage the plant you are trying to protect. Remember, you are required to use no more than the amount of pesticide recommended on the label.

What kind of personal protective equipment should you wear? Many gardeners disregard the need to use any type of personal protective equipment, especially if the product doesn't smell bad. But odor has no bearing on toxicity. Read the label to determine what type of protective equipment you must use. The recommendations are there for your safety. Follow them and be healthy and safe.

After you apply a pesticide, can you keep kids, pets, and others away from the treated area? The majority of pesticides are most toxic in their liquid state. Once a product dries, it is more difficult to get residue on clothes or skin. Check the label to determine the reentry time.

Did you clean up? After every application, clean sprayers and protective equipment. Wash clothes worn to apply pesticides separately from other clothes. After laundering, run a cycle of hot water through the washer to clean it out. This will protect you from any possible contamination.

Asking and answering a few questions before you grab a pesticide and begin spraying can make a happier, safer, and more successful gardener.

Plants for Slopes

By David Barkley, Brunswick County

Plants for slopes
Connie Little

When establishing plants on a slope, you should consider many factors. How steep is the slope? Would a retaining wall be a better solution? Does water move quickly across the slope, causing erosion concerns? Does any of the water make it into the rootzone of the plantings? What are some of the other climatic factors—rain, irrigation, sun, shade—you need to deal with in making your plant selections?

When plants are used on slopes, their roots help anchor the soil. Getting them established, however, can be difficult. Seeds and mulch may wash away. Wildflowers, clump-forming ornamental grasses, and other perennial native plants usually adapt quickly to slopes and unimproved soil.

South-facing slopes tend to dry out quickly. Choose a variety of drought-tolerant plants. Try a mixture of spreading shrubs, ornamental grasses, perennials, and herbaceous groundcovers for effective slope stabilization. The tried-and-true selections of groundcovers often center on liriope, mondo grass, and English ivy. However, other options exist. The Brunswick County Botanical Garden, a project of North Carolina Cooperative Extension, tests a number of plants on slopes and has had success with a variety of ornamental grasses including muhlygrass, *Muhlenbergia capillaris*; pampas grass, *Cortaderia selloana*; blue fescue, *Festuca glauca*; fountain grass, *Pennisetum alopecuroides* 'Hameln'; and feather reed grass, *Calamagrostis brachytricha*.

For perennials, try gaillardia, coneflower, daylily, evening primrose, globe thistle, yucca, wild indigo, coreopsis, yarrow, black-eyed Susan, and sedum.

Consider hollies, Indian hawthorns, and junipers. Annuals such as the ornamental sweet potato and the Wave petunia provide a lot of coverage but not long-term erosion control. An interesting combination is a red Knock Out® rose with the ornamental sweet potato vine running underneath. The Scotch Petite Rose cascading down a slope is another attractive choice.

Recycle Newspapers in Your Garden

By David Barkley, Brunswick County

Where do all the newspapers go that are delivered to or brought into households each day? Many are recycled, and many end up in landfills. An inexpensive way to control weeds in your garden is to use leftover newspapers for mulch material. Newspaper mulch can provide adequate weed control, improve plant growth, improve fruit cleanliness, increase yields, and help conserve soil moisture. Gardeners often don't think about the cooling benefits that mulches can provide. However, cooler soil temperatures may help certain crops grow better. One of the best reasons for using newspaper mulch is that it takes a recyclable material out of the waste stream, which could help extend the life of a landfill site and allow land to be put to better use.

Recycled newspapers enhance beds.
Robert E. Lyons

When using newspapers as mulch in the garden, lay down several layers. Four to five sheets should be sufficient. Fill a wheelbarrow with water, moisten the pieces of newspaper to the point that they are soaking wet, then lay them out over the area to be mulched. Place the sheets flat and at least two inches away from the stems of your plants. Avoid keeping the area near the stems too wet, so as to prevent rotting.

Another method is to place dry newspapers where you need them and then soak them with water from your hose. Add a layer of heavy grass clippings or other mulch materials on top of the newspapers to hold them in place. Avoid using garden soil for this purpose, since weed seeds may be in the soil. Newspaper mulch controls weed seeds by excluding the sunlight necessary for them to germinate. Most colored inks used in newsprint are soy based, not petroleum based, so they are safe to use.

For more information about recycling, contact your county Cooperative Extension Center.

Not All Insects Should Bug You

By Jeff Rieves, Union County

Gardeners normally wage what seems a never-ending battle with insects, mites, and other so-called pests. But many bugs are beneficial to nature and man.

All of us are familiar with butterflies, moths, and bees. They are the pollinators of many of our fruits and vegetables. They also provide beauty and interest to our gardens. One of the lesser-known benefits of many insects is pest control. Lady beetles, praying mantises, wasps, and spiders all play a role in controlling the voracious appetites of other bugs like aphids. The larvae of lady beetles consume aphids, mealybugs, and even some soft scales. Praying mantises hunt down and eat anything

Butterfly and bee
Toby Bost

they can find, including each other. Small wasps lay eggs inside many caterpillars, and the young destroy the caterpillars as they hatch. Spiders love to catch any type of bug they can and make a meal of it.

How can we encourage all these great garden helpers? One way is to lessen the amount of pesticides we use, and to use all pesticides carefully. Identify the insect that is causing you trouble, and use as specific a pesticide as possible. Accepting a bit of damage will often give predator insects time to do their work. Washing the bugs off the plants with water will also lessen the chance of killing predator insects.

Many plants host populations of beneficial insects among their foliage. Dill, borage, Shasta daisy, fennel, and parsley are just a few of the plants that provide food and shelter for many such insects. Water also helps attract beneficial insects to the garden. Shallow pools of cool, clear water will provide for many insects.

Observation and patience are your two best tools for developing populations of beneficial insects. Look for the presence of these helpful insects before you spray, and spray only as needed. Give your beneficial neighbors time to do their work before you do anything.

The Value of Leaves in the Landscape

By Mary Helen Ferguson, Randolph County

One way to manage fall leaves is to mow them and thereby return nutrients into the soil. Composting is another way to recycle the nitrogen, phosphorus, potassium, and other elements found in leaves. Leaves can be composted with other yard waste like grass clippings (if they are too plentiful to leave on the lawn), pruning waste, fruit and vegetable scraps, coffee grounds, egg shells, and manure from herbivorous animals like rabbits, chickens, cattle, and horses. If you compost leaves alone or with other low-nitrogen materials like sawdust or woodchips, you may need to add nitrogen fertilizer so that the microbes that break down the materials will have a decent ratio of carbon to nitrogen in their diet and be able to work efficiently.

Leaves for compost pile
Toby Bost

Recycling nutrients is one of the main ways that leaves contribute to the landscape. Another of their important functions is serving as mulch. When gathered and applied to tree and shrub beds, flower beds, and vegetable gardens, leaves can help suppress weed growth and limit the need for hand-weeding and herbicide use. Between two and four inches of mulch are generally recommended. Other materials like pine bark, which is typically purchased, can be used for mulch. But why buy mulch if you can get it from your yard?

A note of caution regarding the use of leaves for mulch: Some trees produce chemicals that are allelopathic, meaning that they affect the growth of plants around them. Black walnut is a prime example. Using uncomposted black walnut leaves as mulch can cause some plants to wilt and die. Regardless of the type of mulch you use, avoid direct contact between mulch and tree trunks.

Protecting Plants from Deicing Injuries

By Diane Turner, Henderson County

While most areas of the state have minimal snowfall throughout the winter months, North Carolina is occasionally hit with both snow and ice. Knowing how to properly get rid of snow and ice will help gardeners prevent permanent damage to plants.

Ice-ladened holly
Robert E. Lyons

Sodium chloride, or rock salt, is used as a common deicer. Its drawback is that it can burn plants and corrode metal and concrete. If you must use salt, use it judiciously. Erect barriers by using plastic fencing, burlap, or snow fencing to protect sensitive plants and minimize contact with salt. Reduce salt damage by mixing salt with sand and by removing snow before salting.

When possible, use deicing agents containing calcium chloride or calcium magnesium acetate (CMA), a salt-free melting agent made from limestone and acetic acid. Cat litter or sawdust can help create traction on sidewalks.

Do not pile snow that contains salt around plants. Avoid piling it where runoff will flow over root zones. Many plants can recover from occasional salt spray. If it is a yearly occurrence, however, the death of the plant may result. Place salt-tolerant plants near roadways and sidewalks. Contact Cooperative Extension about salt-tolerant plants for your area.

If salt buildup occurs, water liberally before spring growth by applying two inches of water over a two- to three-hour period. Repeat a few days later to flush the sodium from the soil.

Pest-Tolerant Roses Require Fewer Pesticides

By Mark Danieley, Alamance and Orange Counties

Knock Out® rose
Nancy Doubrava

Roses have long been a garden favorite. But the amount of work required to keep them looking good discourages many gardeners. Black spot and powdery mildew can quickly ruin beautiful roses. There is hope, however, for homeowners who want roses without the continuous maintenance of hybrid tea roses. If you are looking for a low-maintenance rose, the shrub rose could be the answer. Shrub roses have good disease resistance and require little, if any, chemicals. They also need little pruning. Knock Out® and Carefree are two popular series of shrub roses that have good disease resistance. The flower forms range from single and semidouble to double.

Knock Out® roses have a long cycle of bloom, from early spring until late fall. The growth habit is compact; they reach a height of about three feet. They work well for hedges, borders, and mass plantings. The Knock Out® roses are available in cherry red, pink, blushing pink, and sunny yellow.

Carefree roses also offer nonstop blooming all season. The growth habit is medium and bushy; they may reach four to five feet in height, depending on the variety. Carefree roses work well for borders and mass plantings. They are available in lemon yellow, several pink tones, and double-flower types.

While shrub roses have good disease resistance, proper site selection is still important. Roses need six to eight hours of direct sunlight each day, plus good air movement. If you do not have a full-sun site, morning sun is more important than afternoon sun. Morning sun helps dry the dew from the leaves quickly. Limiting the amount of time the leaves stay wet reduces the incidence of black spot.

A discussion of pest-tolerant roses would not be complete without mentioning the Lady Banks' Rose, a vigorous climber that has white to yellow blooms in April and May. It has a relatively short bloom period but offers the advantage of being an evergreen vine. Lady Banks' Rose is often sold as the cultivar 'Lutea'.

Alternatives to Gas-Powered Mowers

By Mark Danieley, Alamance and Orange Counties

Lawns are a main element of most North Carolina landscapes. Well-maintained lawns add value to homes. They also help clean the air and filter surface-water runoff. Mowing lawns on a regular basis helps keep them healthy, but using gas-powered mowers can contribute to air pollution. Manual reel mowers and electric mowers are alternatives.

Manual reel mowers work well on small lawns. A lawn area of less than 8,000 square feet can be maintained reasonably well with a reel mower. It typically takes 50 percent longer to mow with a reel mower than with a power mower. Reel mowers can be used to mow larger areas, but the time and effort required takes the fun out of the job.

Some advantages of reel mowers are quiet operation, low maintenance costs, and environmental friendliness. Reel mowers do have some disadvantages. The biggest is mowing height. Most reel mowers have a maximum cutting height of 1½ inches. That height may be acceptable for some warm-season grasses but would be a real problem with tall fescue. Tall fescue should be mowed at least 3 inches high, and 3½ inches is better. The other main disadvantage is the difficulty reel mowers have with tall grass and weeds. Tall vegetation tends to lie down and not get mowed. It also becomes more difficult to push the mower when the grass gets tall.

Electric mowers may be a more desirable alternative to gas-powered mowers. They are quieter than gas-powered mowers and will mow taller grass and weeds than reel mowers. Electric mowers are also best suited to small lawns. Corded models are more powerful than battery models, but the cord can be aggravating to handle and limits your range from the outlet. Battery models provide more freedom of movement but have a limited run time before the batteries need recharging.

Alternatives to Traditional Pesticides

By Royce Hardin, Orange County

Many homeowners ask what they can use instead of synthetic pesticides to control various pest problems around the home. Consider these options.

Baits and Traps

Instead of ant and roach sprays, use bait systems. These contain materials that prove fatal when the culprits either ingest them or carry them back to their homes. These products eliminate the problem of spray drifting to nontarget surfaces. "Roach motel"–type traps are also effective.

Meal moth traps contain pheromones that attract moths. Once moths enter the traps, they cannot escape.

Sticky traps are available for various insects such as flies, ants, and whiteflies. Traps also are available for wasps.

Dehydrating Materials

Diatomaceous earth and silica gels actually kill small insects by drying them out. Take precaution to prevent inhaling these materials, as they can be quite bad for the lungs. Always wear a protective mask during application.

Organic Controls

Bacillus thuriengiensis (Bt) and *Bacillus thuriengiensis israelensis* (Bti) are effective in controlling, respectively, caterpillars and mosquito larvae.

Horticultural Oils and Insecticidal Soaps

These products help control scales and many soft-bodied insect pests.

Lastly, learn how to identify beneficial insects such as ladybeetles, green lacewings, encarsia wasps, and praying mantises. Protect these natural predators.

Irrigation Tips for Wise Water Use

By Stephen Greer, Forsyth and Gaston Counties

With water restrictions becoming more common in cities across the state, the proper use of irrigation systems is critical. There are ways to apply irrigation water efficiently and effectively. One proper irrigation method is to water based on plant needs. Do not assume all plants need the same amount of water or frequency of application. The best landscapes are those in which plants that have similar water requirements are grouped together in planting zones.

Rain monitoring system
Toby Bost

Once a tree or shrub planted in the low-water-use zone has made it through the initial 12- to 18-month establishment period, little or no supplemental water may be necessary, so an irrigation system may not be needed in this area. Many such areas are watered via the garden hose in the first year.

Moderate-water-use plants need water only during stressful times of the year—in the heat of summer and when rainfall is scarce. A seasonal system such as a soaker hose or hand-watering with a garden hose may be all that is needed to manage plants in a moderate-use area.

At the extreme end of irrigation is the high-water-use zone, which might include the lawn, annual flower beds, and other plants with high moisture needs. High-use areas may need a permanent automated irrigation system. Several different types of systems are available. The choice includes drip systems that apply irrigation water to individual plants, systems with a choice of spray heads and precipitation-rate nozzles that water groups of plants, and turf-type spray-head systems.

The key to wise water use is to water infrequently and for a long duration, just to the point of runoff, and no more than one inch per week. This is an approximate amount of water for lawns. More or less water may be needed in your setting.

Protect Water Quality with Proper Fertilizer Use

By Carl Matyac, Orange and Wake Counties

Fertilizer can provide essential nutrients to maintain optimum turfgrass growth, resulting in a lawn that is able to recover from insect and disease attacks. A healthy lawn also will compete better with weeds, thereby reducing the need for pesticides. However, it is important that the nutrients applied to the lawn stay in place and do not contaminate streams, lakes, and rivers. Follow these guidelines to have a healthy lawn and to maintain water quality.

Proper fertilizer use protects water for recreational and other uses.
Toby Bost

Soil Test: A soil test will determine the amounts of nutrients needed.

Slow-Release Fertilizers: Apply fertilizers that are comprised of slow-release sources of nitrogen. Avoid applying fertilizers where sandy soils are prevalent, near surface water, and where the water table is shallow.

Apply water-soluble or quick-release fertilizers at half the recommended rate in two applications about 10 days apart to lessen the chances of water contamination. Water lightly immediately following application to wash the material into the soil, where the nutrients can be used by the grass plants. This will also reduce the potential for surface runoff.

Water Slowly: Water lightly and frequently on slopes immediately following fertilizer application to reduce runoff. When working with slopes, natural drainage areas, or soil that is compacted, allow water time to penetrate. You may need to aerate the soil.

Drop Spreaders: Use a drop-type (gravity) spreader rather than a centrifugal-type (rotary) spreader near water to minimize the possibility that fertilizer will enter the water.

Shut off the spreader when passing over unplanted or bare ground surfaces. Fill the spreader over a hard surface for easy cleanup. Make sure to sweep fertilizer that falls on the driveway and the walk onto the lawn.

Rain Barrels Save Water

By Paul McKenzie, Vance and Durham Counties

Recent droughts have many of us thinking about ways to conserve water. Rain barrels can be a big part of the effort. Do you realize that it takes only about 1/10 of an inch of rain to collect 60 gallons of water from an average roof?

Although rain barrels are easy enough to construct from large drums, the manufactured variety look better and are easier to install. Many come with an attachment that connects directly to a downspout. A spigot allows you to attach a standard garden hose. Also be sure the barrel has some type of overflow system to direct water away from your house if it fills before the rain stops.

Rain barrel
Connie Little

You won't be able to irrigate your whole landscape with water from rain barrels. But if you combine them with other water savers such as mulching and drought-tolerant plants, you should be able to make a big dent in your water usage. Ideally, you should place a rain barrel at each downspout, though installing only one can still be of great benefit. Just keep in mind that you'll have to rely on gravity to move the water, so make sure the spigot of the rain barrel is higher than the bed or plants you'll be watering. The biggest problem is mosquitoes, but these are easily controlled with a fine screen over the barrel. Otherwise, treat the water with a pelleted insecticide containing *Bacillus thuringiensis* (Bt).

During dry spells, use the stored water strategically on the plants that are most susceptible to drought. These include flower beds, potted plants, and recently planted trees and shrubs.

Some county Cooperative Extension Centers sell rain barrels to help the public with water conservation. Contact your local center for information on where to purchase barrels.

Protect Water Quality by Following These Practices

By Jim Monroe, Mecklenburg County

Water quality is important to all citizens in North Carolina. Most of us can take steps to help ensure that our lakes, streams, and groundwater won't suffer from careless practices around our homes. Nitrogen and phosphorus, essential nutrients for a healthy landscape, can degrade water if they aren't used properly. Excess amounts of these nutrients can promote the growth of undesirable aquatic weeds such as algae. By implementing the following "Best Management Practices," we can maintain turfgrass while reducing negative impacts on the environment.

Water is one of our most precious resources.
Robert E. Lyons

Test your soil and follow soil test recommendations to promote ideal plant growth. Healthy plants can resist stress and pests. Use a soil test to determine the amounts of phosphorus and nitrogen needed. Generally, the best time to apply phosphorus is in the fall after coring and seeding. Apply nitrogen only when the grass is actively growing; use slow-release nitrogen sources to reduce leaching and runoff.

Always sweep or blow

fertilizer and grass clippings from streets, sidewalks, and other impervious surfaces back onto the lawn. Stormwater carries nutrients and pesticides directly into surface water.

Recycle grass clippings back into the turf. "Grasscycling" reduces nitrogen needs and does not contribute to thatch.

Scout for pest problems and apply pesticides only when needed.

Perform practices such as fertilizing and overseeding at the proper times. Lawn maintenance calendars for the major turfgrasses used in North Carolina can be found at www.turffiles.ncsu.edu.

Reducing Water Use in the Landscape

By Linda Blue, Buncombe County

It's too bad we often don't think about how much water we use in the landscape until dry weather arrives. We can conserve water a lot more effectively with some planning.

One of the best ways to help plants survive droughts is to ensure they have strong, deep root systems. Good soil preparation before planting is key. Adjusting the pH and phosphate levels according to soil test recommendations is an easy way to enable your plants to develop good root systems. Working plenty of organic matter into the planting area also can be a great help. Materials like pine bark soil conditioner, compost, and manure are quite effective in not only loosening and aerating the soil but helping retain moisture as well. When dry conditions set in, plants with extensive root systems will survive best.

After planting, add a layer of organic mulch to help prevent moisture from evaporating from the soil. Apply the mulch while plenty of moisture is in the soil, so as to retain what is already there. Mulch should be about three inches deep, and no more than four inches deep around trees and shrubs.

Healthy lawns can survive several weeks without water. Fescue and bluegrass lawns that are allowed to go dormant need only one inch of water every three weeks to keep the roots alive. If you water your lawn or landscape areas, do so only when needed, not just because you always run the sprinklers on Wednesday.

Prepare for droughts by deciding what your watering priorities are. Annual flowers can be replaced next year. Turfgrass can be replaced less expensively than trees and shrubs. If you have made a large investment in shrubs in the last two years, you may want to protect that investment. Herbaceous perennial beds may come next on the list.

Water is one of our most precious resources. We can be successful gardeners without unduly taxing the water supply.

Safe Winter Storage of Pesticides and Fertilizers

By Amy-Lynn Albertson, Davidson County

As the fall gardening season slows to a halt, it's time to put up pesticides and fertilizers for the winter. Finding a safe storage area for your gardening pesticides and fertilizers is important for many reasons, including protecting the environment and human health, as well as maintaining the chemicals' effectiveness.

Use a winter storage area that is secure from children, animals, and any other unwanted visitors. Good lighting is helpful for sorting and other tasks. Ventilation is important to keep volatile chemicals from contaminating other materials in storage and for the health of the applicator. Separate the chemicals by type—herbicides, fungicides, insecticides, and fertilizers—as additional insurance against contamination.

The storage area needs to be safe from dampness and possible flooding. Water damage and dampness can reduce the shelf life of many chemicals and degrade metal and paper containers. Do not store chemicals on the floor. Temperature also can affect the shelf life of chemicals. Heat increases the volatility of stored chemicals, while a freeze can cause some containers to rupture. Check the labels to see if specific temperature ranges are needed for storage of specific chemicals.

Make sure your storage site allows for the containment of spills and leaks. Store cleanup materials nearby. Store flammable liquids outside living areas and away from any sources of ignition. Make sure chemicals and their containers are in good condition before storing them. The product labels should be legible and attached to the chemical containers. Never store excess fertilizers or pesticides in empty food containers. Do not store pesticides with or near food, medicine, or cleaning products.

Keep an inventory of stored pesticides and fertilizers in order to plan purchases for next spring. Be sure to include the product names, active ingredients, dates of purchase, volumes, and dates stored. One way to minimize storage hassles is to plan ahead and buy only pesticides and fertilizers for one season at a time. Sometimes, small containers that seem more expensive will save you money and time in the long run.

Decay-Resistant Hardscape Material

By David Goforth, Cabarrus County

The wood many homeowners once bought for landscape projects is no longer on the market. Treated with chromated copper arsenate (CCA), the wood raised suspicions about arsenic that the industry could never quell. Even though no research-based evidence ever proved arsenic used in this manner caused problems, the industry voluntarily removed CCA from the market.

Wood is now treated with alkaline copper quat, copper boron azole, or acid copper chromate. Gardeners building arbors, retaining walls, and other projects with these new products won't see much difference. They may notice a different initial

Decay-resistant hardscape material
Toby Bost

color. Buyers may also notice a slightly higher cost.

The higher cost of treated wood has steered some gardeners to stone, concrete, and block. Even metal is being used. Plastics, particularly recycled plastics, are also more competitive. Plastic resin composites are also available. Some of the plastic products, however, are not suitable for structural components. In addition to plastic resin composites, wood resin composites are available in some markets.

Some trees have decay- and insect-resistant wood. For ground contact, the best local woods are red cedar (heartwood only), bald cypress (heartwood), and black locust. More options are available for outdoor uses when the wood doesn't come in contact with the ground. Oak has some decay resistance when used above ground, although it is a rare gardener who can afford it. A few ornamentals such as osage orange, yew, honey locust, and photinia have decay-resistant wood.

Some tropical woods are naturally insect and decay resistant, but avoid them unless you are sure your purchase doesn't encourage environmentally unsound or unsustainable forestry practices.

The Pruning "4-Ds" Can Reduce the Need for Chemical Controls

By David Barkley, Brunswick County

Proper pruning minimizes problems.
Toby Bost

Pruning is one of the ways to handle plant pest problems without resorting to chemical controls, making it an environmentally friendly control method. What is the best way to prune to maintain your plants' health? To answer that question, it's best to know the plants you need to prune. Prune some plants at the wrong time of year and you will end up with specimens that won't bloom. However, most plants will tolerate pruning just about any time of year, provided you don't remove more than one-third of the foliage.

A good rule of thumb for gardeners to follow is the "4-Ds of Pruning." This rule works every time without question. No magical moment or waiting is involved—just prompt, quick, decisive action.

The "4-Ds of Pruning" are as simple as follows. Prune immediately whenever you see (1) dead, (2) diseased, (3) dying, or (4) damaged plant parts.

This simple rule is important in preventing plants from suffering further losses. According to the "4-Ds," it is important to prune all damaged plant parts.

If we were to add another "D," it would be for desired characteristics such as enhanced flowering, higher yields and fruit quality, and preferred shape and form. This type of pruning requires that you know about the growing habits of plants.

To learn more about pruning landscape plants, check with your county Cooperative Extension Center.

"Grasscycling" Helps the Environment

By David Barkley, Brunswick County

When you throw away grass clippings, you're getting rid of lots of valuable nutrients that your lawn could use. Why throw away those clippings when you can grasscycle instead?

Grasscycling simply means leaving grass clippings on the lawn so the water and nutrients they contain go back into the lawn when they decompose. Grass clippings are about 80 to 85 percent water and break down rapidly.

Grasscycling is a natural way to use 50 percent of all yard waste while helping the environment. It reduces the need to apply nitrogen fertilizer to your lawn by 25 percent.

Another reason to grasscycle is that state law prohibits yard waste, including

Grass clippings recycle nutrients.
Toby Bost

grass clippings, from being discarded in landfills.

If you properly mow, water, and fertilize, grasscycling can actually produce a healthier-looking lawn. Cut the lawn frequently to produce small clippings that will fall between the standing blades and decompose quickly. If a lawn is not cut frequently enough and long clippings are left, your landscape may have a "haylike" look that can be unsightly.

Any mower that is in good working condition and has a sharp blade can grasscycle. Mulching mowers may be better than traditional mowers for those who cannot mow on a regular basis. These mowers tend to cut grass into finer pieces, allowing it to filter down among the standing plants. Whatever the mower, a dry lawn produces the best results.

If bad weather causes you to miss a scheduled mowing, the grass might be too long for you to leave the clippings. Raking and composting the clippings is another way to use them. Use grass clippings to mulch around trees, shrubs, and flower beds. Do not use them as mulch if you have applied herbicides to the lawn recently.

Some people believe that grass clippings left on the lawn cause thatch. Not so. Research shows that grass roots are the primary cause of thatch, as they contain materials that decompose slowly. Thatch is also caused by excessive growth from overfertilizing, by allowing grass to get too high before mowing, and by incorrect watering. Some grasses such as Bermuda and zoysia are more thatch prone than others.

A small amount of thatch (approximately ½ inch) is actually beneficial to a lawn. It provides insulation to roots and serves as a mulch to prevent excessive water evaporation and soil compaction. It may also create a cushioning effect for lawn play. Too much thatch, however, may lead to disease problems that can damage the lawn.

Eliminate Standing Pools of Water to Control Mosquitoes

By Emily Revels, Cumberland and Mecklenburg Counties

Mosquitoes often interfere with outdoor activity and can transmit diseases to people and domestic animals. They are most active during the twilight hours and at night. They need water to complete their life cycle and can breed in almost any water source.

The most important factors in mosquito control are locating and eliminating their breeding sites. This involves searching the yard for areas where water collects. These can include birdbaths, saucers under plant pots, tarps, pet water bowls if water is not changed daily, children's toys that sit outside, and any other areas where water can pool. Keep your gutters free of leaves and other debris so water will drain, and eliminate standing water around such areas as air conditioners and faucets.

To keep mosquitoes out of your home, make sure all screens on doors and windows fit securely. Caulk cracks and crevices to prevent mosquitoes from entering the house.

When it comes to natural control, make friends with bats and purple martins. Both consume mosquitoes as part of their diet, so creating nesting areas for these species may help with control.

Periodiocally monitor and clean birdhouses and fountains.
Toby Bost

Citronella candles are one repellent used for mosquito control. Place them on decks and patio areas and be aware that they work best if used during times of little air movement, since air disperses the chemical quickly. Personal repellents include products that contain DEET, which can be applied to exposed skin but not the hands and face. Repeated use of repellents over a short period of time is not recommended, especially for children. Be sure to follow all label directions.

Homeowners treating small garden pools or birdbaths may want to try a bacterial insecticide called Mosquito Dunks, which contains Bti (*Bacillus thuringiensis israelensis*). This product kills mosquitoes but does not harm fish, birds, or other wildlife. Electronic traps such as "bug zappers" are not effective in reducing mosquito populations. Studies show that less than 1 percent of insects killed in electronic traps are biting insects. Bug zappers also tend to kill nontargeted beneficial insects.

Why IPM Is Important for Your Garden

By Donna Teasley, Burke County

No method of pest management provides complete control of pests in the garden. For many years, chemical control was the most-used method, but overuse of pesticides in the garden has resulted in some pests developing resistance to chemicals. The use of chemicals has caused the decline of beneficial insects, too. While the correct use of pesticides is safe for consumers, public perception is becoming increasingly negative.

Integrated pest management (IPM) is the practice of combining cultural and biological controls with pesticides to manage the level of insects that can be present without causing unacceptable damage to a crop. In other words, some insects can be present in the garden without ruining the crop. IPM helps keep pests to an acceptable level by using methods such as timing and rotating crops, planting resistant varieties, and introducing beneficial insects.

Parasitized hornworm
Toby Bost

IPM also recognizes the importance of combining these methods with some chemical use and educating gardeners on the importance of regular monitoring of crops to catch problems early. Good garden maintenance is important in helping plants grow vigorously so they will be better able to withstand some insect presence.

The willingness to accept less-than-perfect crops is an important part of IPM. A small flaw on a fruit or vegetable does not make it worthless. Gardeners who really want to lessen the use of chemicals will come to terms with minor imperfections and take immense satisfaction in the fact that their gardens are using lower amounts of chemicals.

Tap the Sun's Energy to Control Pests

By David Barkley, Brunswick County

Want to know how to control some of your plant pests just by using the sun? Solarization is a practical, nonchemical technique that traps radiant heat energy from the sun and raises the temperature of the surrounding environment, which causes physical, chemical, and biological changes in the soil. These changes help suppress soil-borne plant pathogens such as fungi, bacteria, nematodes, and weeds.

Solarization also provides other benefits. When soil is prepared for the solarization process, soil tilth often improves, which helps plants grow. The benefits of higher yields, improved quality, and reduced use of pesticides help make up for the inconvenience associated with solarization.

How to Solarize Soil

Till and then rake the soil free of debris and large clumps. If the soil is dry and powdery, be sure to water. Do not oversaturate. Add just enough water to make the

Plastic helps solarize the soil.
Robert E. Lyons

soil moist. Next, place a one- to six-mil piece of plastic over the soil and bury the edges about 12 inches deep in a trench. Clear plastic is preferable, though colored plastic may be used.

Timing

Long, hot, sunny days are needed to reach the soil temperatures required to kill soil-borne pests and weed seed. The longer the soil is heated, the better and deeper the control will be of all soil pests. In North Carolina, mid-June through mid-August is the best period for getting the desired results. Leave the plastic on the soil for four to six weeks. This will heat up the soil to the point of killing most of the plant pests and pathogens to a depth of almost eight inches.

Natural ways to control pests are very popular. Add "Best Management Practices" to your pest-control regimen to minimize the amount of pesticides you use. Contact your local Cooperative Extension Center for more details.

Proper Herbicide Use

By Paul McKenzie, Vance and Durham Counties

Herbicides are powerful tools in the home landscape. The results will be disappointing, however, if you don't use herbicides properly.

It's important to get uniform coverage of the site. If you're applying a granular herbicide, evenly distribute the granules. With liquid herbicides, uniform coverage of the leaf surface is the key to success.

When using a product that claims to kill the roots, apply it when the weeds are growing vigorously, so they will do a better job of sending the herbicide down to the roots. Look for several inches of tender new growth at the tip of each stem or branch.

Shaker containers make herbicide applications easy.
Toby Bost

Never apply liquid herbicides on a windy day. Most herbicides are safe on some landscape plants but will damage others. It doesn't take much air movement for the spray to end up on the wrong plants.

When applied correctly, preemergent herbicides can prevent certain weeds from growing. These herbicides often have to be accompanied by rainfall or irrigation within a specified time after application. This disperses the herbicide so that it forms a barrier in the soil, where it kills weed seedlings as they start to germinate.

Few would deny that in the case of chocolate, more is better. But apply this line of thinking to herbicides and you may run into problems. The company that produced your herbicide spent several million dollars researching exactly how much is needed. Use too much and you may end up damaging your lawn, shrubs, or flowers. Even worse, you could contaminate lakes, streams, or groundwater.

If an herbicide fails to do the job, then you either misidentified the weed or applied the herbicide at the wrong time. Adding more herbicide is a waste of your time and money.

Take a sample to your county Cooperative Extension Center for identification. Once you have knowledge of the weed species and life cycle, you can make a good decision about which product will work best and when to apply it. As with all pesticides, be sure to read the label.

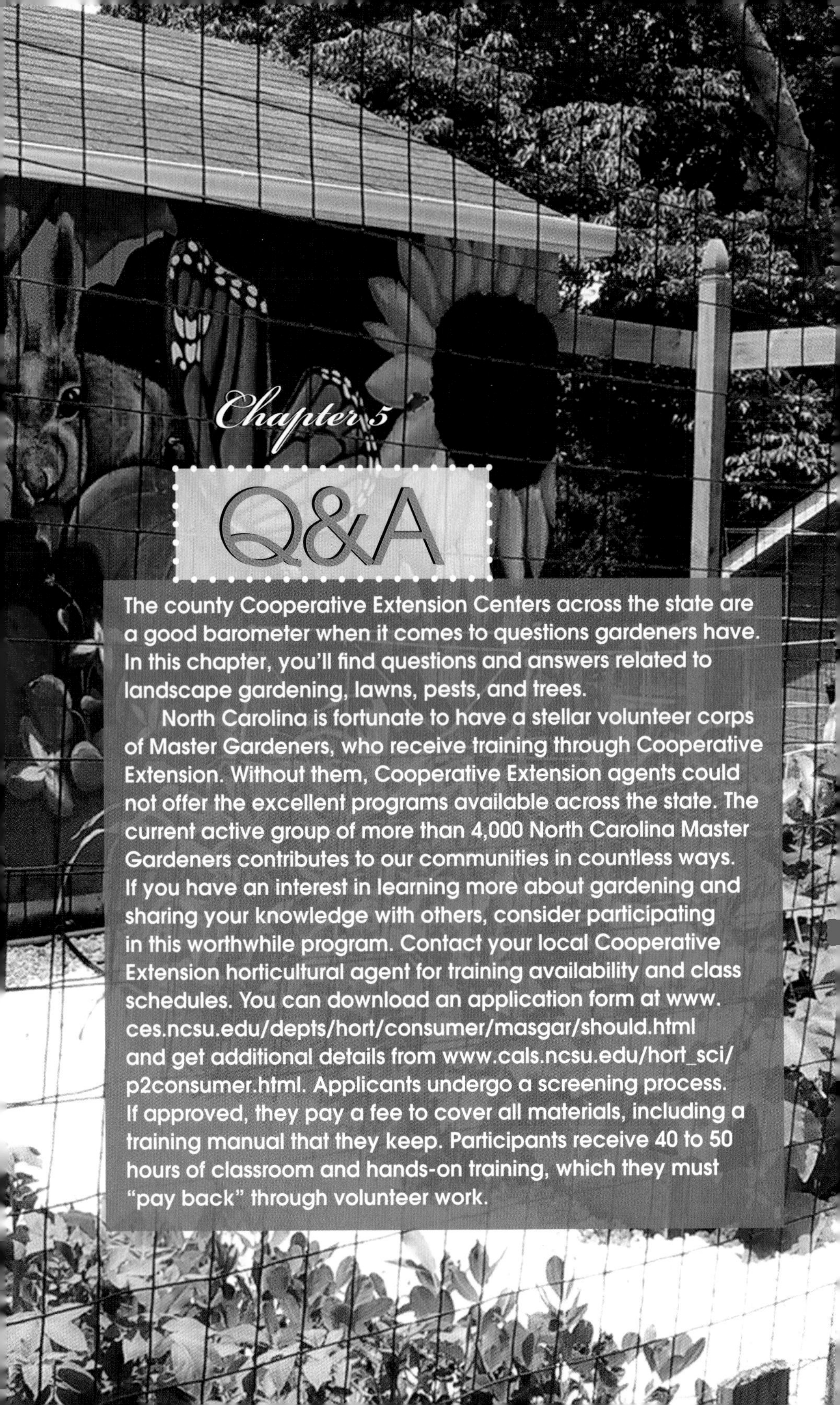

Chapter 5

Q&A

The county Cooperative Extension Centers across the state are a good barometer when it comes to questions gardeners have. In this chapter, you'll find questions and answers related to landscape gardening, lawns, pests, and trees.

North Carolina is fortunate to have a stellar volunteer corps of Master Gardeners, who receive training through Cooperative Extension. Without them, Cooperative Extension agents could not offer the excellent programs available across the state. The current active group of more than 4,000 North Carolina Master Gardeners contributes to our communities in countless ways. If you have an interest in learning more about gardening and sharing your knowledge with others, consider participating in this worthwhile program. Contact your local Cooperative Extension horticultural agent for training availability and class schedules. You can download an application form at www.ces.ncsu.edu/depts/hort/consumer/masgar/should.html and get additional details from www.cals.ncsu.edu/hort_sci/p2consumer.html. Applicants undergo a screening process. If approved, they pay a fee to cover all materials, including a training manual that they keep. Participants receive 40 to 50 hours of classroom and hands-on training, which they must "pay back" through volunteer work.

Gardentalk:

"Your first job is to prepare the soil. The best tool is your neighbor's garden tiller. If your neighbor does not own a garden tiller, suggest he buy one."
Dave Barry

Landscape Gardening

What number should I call before construction to prevent underground utility lines from being cut?

By Shauna Haslem, Cumberland County

North Carolina One Call (NCOC) is a program that puts homeowners, contractors, and anyone else dealing with excavations in touch with utility companies to prevent underground utility lines from being cut. If you plan to dig in your yard or to hire someone to do work that involves digging, call 811 to protect your utility lines.

When a call is placed, NCOC notifies its members, the utility companies, who send personnel out to locate underground utilities free of charge. You will be given a list of member companies that NCOC will contact. If you have an underground line with a utility company that is not listed, it is your responsibility to call that company to locate the line.

This service saves everyone money and time. The NCOC number is toll free. Locater requests are available Monday through Friday from 6 A.M. until 10 P.M. and Saturday from 8 A.M. until 4 P.M. (Emergency call-outs for special circumstances are available from 5 P.M. until 6 A.M. Monday through Friday and all day Saturday and Sunday.) To use this service, call 800-632-4949. Save precious time and money before any excavation project!

What is water-wise gardening?

By Emily Revels, Cumberland and Mecklenburg Counties

Water-wise gardening at its best occurs when landscapes are properly designed, installed, and maintained so that relatively small amounts of water are required. When water is used, it is done in an efficient and effective manner to make every drop count.

Water-wise gardening requires watering according to plants' needs. Established plants and lawns do not need to be watered every day. Deep, thorough, slow watering is better than frequent, light watering. Deep, thorough watering encourages deep root systems, while light, frequent watering encourages shallow root systems. The rule of thumb is one inch of water—including water from both rain and irrigation—once a week.

Use a two- to three-inch layer of mulch around trees, shrubs, flowers, and vegetables to hold in moisture. When water is scarce, avoid unnecessary plant stress; do not prune, fertilize, or use pesticides.

Water only the landscape, not the sidewalk, driveway, street, or house. Make sure all sprinklers, hoses, and irrigation systems are working properly.

Remember, plants don't waste water, people do.

What do I need to consider when hiring a landscaper?

By Emily Revels, Cumberland and Mecklenburg Counties

To make sure you hire the right landscaper for the job, do some research.

Ask your friends and neighbors or your local nursery or garden center for a recommendation. Word of mouth is usually dependable. Ask for references and look for experience. Reputable landscapers will be willing to have you visit previous job sites.

Visit sites and judge the quality of the jobs yourself. If possible, ask the homeowners what they think of the landscaper and if the landscaper completed the job on time.

Check to see if the landscaper has the proper equipment to do the job. This can be very important when you are trying to preserve part of an existing landscape.

Check for the proper licenses. Does the landscaper have a current pesticide license? Is he or she fully licensed and insured? Does he or she have any professional certifications? Ask for verification of these licenses and certifications. Do not sign anything until you see these licenses and verify they are current.

Ask for a written cost estimate. Make sure it specifies exactly what is to be included in the price. A contract is advisable. Include what work is to be performed, a completion date, and penalties for work not completed according to schedule.

Don't pay until the job is complete. In the case of large jobs, you may be asked to make a partial payment, but it should never be more than 20 percent of the total cost.

How can I dispose of yard debris in the most environmentally sound way?

By Toby Bost, Forsyth County

Until 1993, most yard waste ended up in sanitary landfills. It took a new law to force municipalities and homeowners to make more environmentally friendly choices.

In some municipalities, homeowners can place debris by the curb for pickup. In others, it may need to be hauled to a designated site such as a yard-waste facility. Leaves, branches, and grass clippings at yard-waste facilities are recycled into mulch and leaf compost that the public and landscapers can use.

Many gardeners routinely compost yard debris. It's best not to bag grass clippings, especially tall fescue and cool-season turfgrasses. Clippings decompose naturally when left on the yard, releasing organic fertilizer for a better lawn.

Instead of trashing your leaves, till them into the garden to enhance soil structure. Or cover your vegetable garden with leaves during the winter to prevent soil erosion. Invest in a composter if you want a ready supply of leaf compost. Use the compost as mulch in flower beds and to make potting soil. Don't ever burn leaves.

Rent or purchase a wood chipper to handle small branches. You can use the woodchips for a pathway or to create mulch rings under mature trees.

Why can't I reuse wash water in my garden?

By Toby Bost, Forsyth County

Although it may be ecologically sound to reuse non-toilet water—classified as "gray water"—in the home landscape, it may not be prudent. Gray water can make people ill and kill plants due to contaminants including salts, grease, bacteria, and disease-causing microbes.

The Environmental Protection Agency recommends that all household wastes in public-service areas go to municipal sewer treatment facilities to avoid public hazard. Some states allow untreated wastewater for irrigation, but not in beds of edible plants such as vegetable and herb gardens. Water used in showering and water captured from rinsing produce are examples of potential water sources for lawns and flower beds.

Check with your local environmental health department before using gray water for gardening activities.

Why aren't my plants blooming?

By David Barkley, Brunswick County

It's discouraging when a tree or shrub selected for its flowering habit fails to bloom or set fruit. It is often difficult to pinpoint the exact cause of a plant's failure to bloom, but here are some possibilities.

The plant may be in a location that is too shady. It may face excessive competition from adjacent shrubs or tree roots.

Planting too deep may prevent flower buds from setting. Pruning at the wrong time of year could be a factor. Spring-flowering shrubs such as lilacs, forsythias, azaleas, and rhododendrons produce their flower buds during the summer months; those buds open the following spring. If the plants are pruned in late summer, the flower buds will be removed. For late-summer-flowering shrubs such as *Buddleia davidii* or clethra, a midsummer pruning could remove their flower buds and thus prevent flowering.

Excessive growth of suckers (unwanted branches growing up from major limbs near the base of the trunk) might reduce or limit flowering.

Newly planted trees or shrubs may not flower for a year or two after transplanting. They may need sufficient time to develop their root systems before they again set flower buds.

Low winter temperatures or a late frost can kill flower buds.

Soil chemistry may be a factor. If nitrogen is not in balance with other nutrients, plants may produce an excessive amount of vegetative growth at the expense of flower development.

Why do plants' leaves turn yellow?

By Karen Neill, Guilford County

The leaves of deciduous plants occasionally lose their normal green color. The key reason that plants turn yellow is that they are not able to maintain adequate levels of chlorophyll, the green pigment. When this vital substance is absent, yellow pigments that are also present take over and the leaves fade. The yellowing of plant parts that are normally green is called chlorosis. Diseases, insects, and changes in a plant's environment cause leaves to become chlorotic. Determining which is to blame is not always easy.

Many environmental factors can cause a plant to yellow. The most basic is a lack of adequate light. When leaves become shaded by other plants or by branches higher on the same plant, the chlorophyll fades away and the leaves yellow.

Nutrient deficiencies also cause chlorosis. Nitrogen is a vital component of chlorophyll; inadequate levels of this element make leaves turn yellow. Too much or too little water can cause yellowing. Under water stress, plants shut down internally and cannot transport nutrients to the leaves.

Sucking insects such as aphids, mealybugs, and scales remove nutrient-laden sap from plants, restricting their ability to make more chlorophyll and leaving the leaves yellow. Fungal diseases and some viruses also cause the loss of chlorophyll in a mottled pattern on leaves and stems. Herbicides (weed killers) may cause yellowing. Some of these chemicals, including the widely used Roundup®, work by stopping photosynthesis in plants. Often, they do this by blocking the production of chlorophyll.

Is it possible to eradicate Bermuda grass from my tall fescue lawn without having to start over completely?

By Fred Miller, Catawba County

The answer is a qualified yes. Bermuda grass can be a difficult weed to control even when using herbicides containing glyphosate. These nonselective herbicides are generally considered to be the most effective measures against Bermuda grass but may require as many as three applications before control is achieved under ideal circumstances. Even then, there is a risk Bermuda grass may reestablish from seed or creep back in from neighboring properties. And since these herbicides are nonselective, they also kill the desirable turf, necessitating replanting of the treated areas.

Selectively removing Bermuda grass is even more difficult. Multiple years of repeated treatments will likely be necessary before you can achieve reasonable control. Current research indicates that repeated applications of fenoxaprop (Acclaim Extra) at four-week intervals throughout the summer provide the best results. Monitor

Ornamental grass garden
Connie Little

the treated grass the following summer. In the likely event that the Bermuda grass recovers and comes back, resume the above treatments.

As you might expect, multiple applications of herbicides can become expensive. Many home gardeners subscribe to the old adage, "If you can't lick 'em, join 'em." When grown properly, Bermuda grass can provide excellent turf. It is utilized at most golf courses east of the North Carolina mountains.

Why doesn't my holly tree have any berries?
By David Goforth, Cabarrus County

Holly trees are either completely male or completely female. Only the females have berries. Female trees have to be mature, which takes only a few years. Plus, they have to be healthy and energetic, which means they are getting adequate sunshine and proper nutrition. In partial shade, hollies will occasionally have a few berries, but not every year. In the long run, nutrition is seldom a problem. Too much nitrogen may make plants vegetative for a few years, but they will grow out of it.

Holly bushes occasionally get into an alternate bearing mode in which a heavy crop one year uses so much nutrition that the plants don't set berries the following year. While the plants have no berries, their nutritional status builds back up. The following year, they again set a heavy load, and the cycle is repeated. Although some hollies can set a partial crop without cross-pollination, most female hollies need a nearby male tree and some type of insect to go back and forth. Be careful not to spray insecticides during the blooming period. If no male plants are within 400 yards, consider planting some. One male plant per five female hollies is a fairly good ratio.

Why do I need lime?
By Amy-Lynn Albertson, Davidson County

Lime is needed when the soil pH is low. Soil pH is the level of acidity present. A soil that has a pH of less than 7.0 is considered acidic. High levels of acidity can reduce root growth or cause nutrient deficiency. Low pH (high acidity) can also reduce a plant's ability to protect itself from disease and insect damage. Most landscape and garden plants grow best in a pH range of 6.0 to 6.5. Lime neutralizes the acidity of the soil, improves the availability of certain nutrients, and can supply essential calcium and magnesium, depending on the type of lime used.

Two types of lime are used for agricultural purposes: calcitic and dolomitic. Calcitic limestone contains calcium carbonate but little or no magnesium. Dolomitic limestone contains both calcium and magnesium carbonates. It is important to take a soil sample and apply lime based on current soil test recommendations. Overliming can reduce the availability of certain micronutrients. This problem is common in sandy coastal-plain soils.

What kind of mulch should I use on my ornamental shrubs?
By David Goforth, Cabarrus County

Your choice depends on your personal preference, but avoid solid plastic film. Solid plastic mulches can harm plants because they do not allow water or air exchange. Nonwoven landscape fabrics are available, but they may allow weeds to germinate in the fabric. Woven plastic landscape fabrics do a better job of weed control while allowing water and air exchange. Most gardeners prefer to cover landscape fabrics with another mulch to reduce heat and improve looks. Pine bark, hardwood bark, and pine needles are the premier landscape mulches readily available in North Carolina. Rock, gravel, or brick nugget mulches look good and keep down weeds, although removing fallen leaves from them can be troublesome. Chipped tires and rubber mulches haven't been evaluated properly.

Tree-care professionals sometimes provide free woodchips. This mulch works okay when used on top of the ground, but care should be taken to keep it away from plants. Fresh woodchips tie up nitrogen as they decompose. If they are applied too thickly, the heat generated during decomposition can injure plants, particularly herbaceous plants.

Use mulch after planting ornamentals, and replenish as needed. A good time to replenish mulch is in autumn after the leaves fall. Pine needles can be piled five inches thick. Most gardeners use no more than three inches of pine bark and even less right next to the bark of large trees. Deeper mulch may cause problems; research has produced varied results.

When should I prune?
By Jeff Rieves, Union County

Many people prune when plants get in their way or become too big for their

Pruning tools
Connie Little

space. But most plants will give more satisfying results if you prune to encourage their growth habits.

Plants that bloom in the spring form next year's flower buds on this year's growth. They should be pruned just after they bloom. This gives them time to put on new growth and form new flower buds. Azaleas and camellias are two examples.

Plants that bloom in the summer form their flower buds on new growth. Prune them in the spring. They will put on new growth, form flower buds on it, and then bloom the same year. Often, they can be lightly pruned to encourage more flowers late in the same season. Crape myrtles, buddleias, and most roses are among this group.

Not all plants are grown for their blooms. Broadleaf evergreens such as boxwoods and aucubas can be pruned as needed. But heavy pruning is best done in winter or early spring. Be careful when pruning near the first fall frost date. Late flushes of new growth can be burned by cold temperatures.

Deciduous plants benefit from pruning while dormant. Their shapes are more clearly visible when the plants are free of leaf cover. Shade trees can benefit from pruning in late summer.

Find out more about pruning at your county Cooperative Extension Center, or visit www.ces.ncsu.edu. May your pruners always be sharp!

Lawns

When should I fertilize my lawn, and how much fertilizer do I need?

By Mary Helen Ferguson, Randolph County

It depends on what type of turfgrass you have. For tall fescue, apply 1 pound of nitrogen per 1,000 square feet of turf in February, September, and November. Use a complete N-P-K fertilizer with a 3-1-2 or 4-1-2 ratio (for example, 12-4-8 or 16-4-8). The actual amount of fertilizer will depend on its percentage of nitrogen. To calculate how much fertilizer to apply, use this formula: The pounds of nitrogen desired divided by the percentage of nitrogen in the product equals the pounds of product needed. If you use 16-4-8, the product is 16 percent nitrogen, so you will need 6¼ pounds of fertilizer to get 1 pound of nitrogen per 1,000 square feet. Putting additional nitrogen fertilizer on tall fescue will also discourage it from going dormant for the summer. Dormancy helps to conserve water.

Tall fescue is a cool-season grass, meaning that its active growth occurs in the cool seasons. Bermuda, zoysia, St. Augustine, and centipede are warm-season grasses. For Bermuda grass, apply 1 pound of nitrogen per 1,000 square feet in April, May, June, and July. For zoysia grass, apply 1 pound of nitrogen per 1,000 square feet in April and ½ pound in June and August. For St. Augustine grass, use ½ pound in May, June, and August and 1 pound in July. Centipede needs the least nitrogen—just ½ pound per 1,000 square feet in June.

Ideally, you should determine potassium and phosphorus needs through a soil test. They are often applied with nitrogen in fertilizers that contains two or all three of the nutrients.

For more information, see "Carolina Lawns: A Guide to Maintaining Quality Turf in the Landscape" at www.turffiles.ncsu.edu. Type "Carolina Lawns" in the search box.

When should I put out preemergent herbicides?

By Donna Teasley, Burke County

Because preemergent herbicides work by preventing weed seeds from germinating, it is necessary to apply them before weeds germinate.

The most common annual weed that requires preemergent products is crabgrass, which germinates when air temperatures reach 65° to 70° for four consecutive days. On average, this happens around March 1 for the coast and March 15 to 30 for the Piedmont and the mountains.

When applying preemergent herbicides to annual weeds that germinate in the fall, wait until night temperatures fall to around 55° to 60° for four consecutive nights. This will occur around September 15 to October 1 for the coast and September 1 to 15 for the Piedmont and the mountains.

These herbicides are effective for six to 12 weeks, depending on the product. When season-long control is needed, make a second application about nine weeks after the first.

Some herbicides can be very damaging to newly sown lawns. Before applying to a new lawn, read the product label to see if the active ingredient will be safe for young plants. As always, read the directions carefully before using any pesticide.

Will a preemergent herbicide kill all my weeds?

By Ben Dungan, Gaston County

When it comes to successful gardening, there are no easy answers to yes-or-no questions. Many factors must be taken into account.

It is true that the job of preemergent herbicides is to control weeds. However, they

Turfgrass and shade
Toby Bost

only control weeds that have not yet germinated. Any weed that is already established will not be affected by a preemergent herbicide application. (A postemergent herbicide can kill existing weeds if used according to instructions.)

Preemergent herbicides kill certain weeds such as crabgrass, henbit, and chickweed. It is important to know the life cycles of weeds before applying herbicides. Make sure you apply before you expect these weeds to germinate.

When successfully applied to a landscape planting, a perennial or annual flower bed, or a lawn, the product makes its way into the upper portions of the soil. It does not move into the root zones of plants. It serves as a barrier, keeping unwanted weeds from germinating and surviving past the seedling stage.

Make sure you identify which weeds you are trying to control. Then read the label to verify that you can safely apply the product to the chosen area. Contact your Cooperative Extension Center for more details.

What do the three numbers on a fertilizer bag mean?
By Carl Matyac, Orange and Wake Counties

As easy as one, two, three, the numbers on the bag tell the percentage of nutrients in the fertilizer by weight. Each is important to basic plant nutrition.

Both processed organic fertilizers such as bone or fish meal and synthetic fertilizers such as 10-10-10 are identified by their "analysis"—that is, the three numbers on the container. The numbers refer to the percentages of nitrogen, phosphorus, and potassium, respectively, in the fertilizer. For example, a bag of 10-10-10 contains 10 percent nitrogen, 10 percent phosphorus, and 10 percent potassium.

Nitrogen (N) is essential for green growth such as leaves and shoots. It provides proteins needed for plant growth and development. It also is part of the green pigment, chlorophyll, that is necessary for the process of photosynthesis, which uses energy from light to make the compounds required for plant growth.

Phosphorus (P) is essential for root development but is really needed for any process in the plant that requires energy, such as bud formation and shoot growth.

Along with phosphorus, potassium (K) is essential for flower and fruit formation and is important to the overall well-being of the plant. Potassium is particularly important in helping plants withstand and recover from stress such as that caused by pests and cold temperatures.

Can I manage my lawn naturally?
By Donna Teasley, Burke County

Many natural fertilizers are readily available to homeowners who prefer the organic approach to lawn care. Products such as alfalfa pellets, blood meal, and composted chicken or cow manure can be applied with good results to the home lawn. As with any proposed fertilizer application, a soil test is recommended to determine the fertilizer needs of the lawn. Soil test kits are available at your local Cooperative Extension Center.

Weed control is a large part of most lawn-care regimens. Some products are touted as ways to control weeds without the use of synthetic pesticides. One such product is corn gluten. It controls weeds by preventing sprouting seeds from developing normal root systems, making them more susceptible to dehydration, as the new roots don't have sufficient means to search for water.

While research shows that corn gluten does a good job preventing weeds, it also reveals that its weed-control abilities are short lived in the soil. Because corn gluten is also a good source of nitrogen fertilizer, lawns treated with it may actually produce more crabgrass during midsummer.

Pests—Animals, Insects, Diseases, Weeds

Does anything kill nutsedge?
By Mary Helen Ferguson, Randolph County

The most cost-efficient options for killing nutsedge may be hand-weeding or using a hoe or shovel. Nutsedge grows from tubers in the ground after it dies back during cool weather. One way to get rid of it is to remove the tubers, which can be as deep as 14 inches but are often less than half that. Dig up the tubers with a hoe or shovel while the plants are young or during the dormant season, if you can remember where the infestation is. Plants produce new tubers when they have five to six leaves, so remove the old tubers before that stage. If you remove only the leaves, do so every two to three weeks, so the plants never reach the five- to six-leaf stage. Tilling nutsedge-infested areas can spread the tubers. But if you till frequently enough that the plants never reach the five- to six-leaf stage, tuber formation can be prevented.

A common herbicide that kills nutsedge is glyphosate (available in Roundup® and other brands). Among selective herbicides (ones that kill only certain plants), halosulfuron-methyl is probably the most versatile. It is contained in products for vegetables (Sandea®) and for turf and ornamentals (Sedgehammer™). Other options are products containing bentazon (for yellow nutsedge), EPTC, imazaquin (for purple nutsedge), MSMA, pelargonic acid, sufentrazone, and sulfosulfuron. Read the label before buying any product containing these ingredients to make sure it is compatible with other plants growing where it will be used. Most of these chemicals can be safely and legally used only on certain plants. The labels explain how to use them effectively.

How can I control fire ants?
By David Goforth, Cabarrus County

First, determine if you are in the quarantine area. To see a map on the North Carolina Department of Agriculture and Consumer Services website, visit http://www.ncagr.com/plantindustry/Plant/entomology/IFA/pdfs/FireantMap2008.pdf. If you are outside the quarantine area, contact your local Cooperative Extension Center for advice. Within the quarantine area, controlling fire ants is your responsibility. You will not be able to totally rid the world of fire ants, but it is possible to treat areas with high potential for human contact.

When fire ants first show up, only one or two mounds may appear. You can treat the individual mounds. Use a pesticide drench that gets the chemicals down to the queen. Be sure the pesticide is labeled for the area in which you plan to use it. If the queen gets away, a new mound will pop up several feet away, so recheck the area and treat again.

Between queens occasionally getting away and new queens migrating into the area, many homeowners are not happy with the results of mound treatments. The other option is to broadcast a bait. Several baits are available. Put the bait out on a dry day when the ants are actively foraging. If the bait gets wet and turns rancid, the ants will not take it into their mounds.

Plan on a treatment once the weather warms in April or May, plus a treatment during the last warm spell in the fall.

For more information about suitable control methods for fire ants, visit www.ces.ncsu.edu/depts/ent/notes/Urban/ifa.htm#chemical.

How can I manage moss?
By Mike Wilder, Nash County

Would you like to get rid of it or make it thrive? Moss is a wonderful evergreen groundcover to some and a nasty weed to others. The answer to either option is to provide the proper environment. In most situations, moss depends on low fertility, acidic soil, high moisture, compaction, cool temperatures, and shade. The absence or presence of all these conditions is necessary for successful elimination or enhancement, respectively.

To eliminate moss, remove excessive moisture by grading, installing a drainpipe, or both. Take a soil sample to evaluate soil pH and fertility levels. Adjust with lime and fertilizer according to the requirements of your desired plant species. Provide at least four hours of direct sunlight by removing vegetation, low limbs, or even entire trees. Alleviate compaction by plowing, tilling, or deep aerification. Physically removing moss or applying chemicals are short-term solutions. If the previous steps are not taken, moss will return very quickly.

Getting moss started in a place it has not previously grown can be just as challenging. Take a soil sample test, adjust the pH to 5 or lower (no higher than 6), and provide the conditions above that your anti-moss friends just eliminated.

Is it possible to control fire blight without chemicals?

By Diane Turner, Henderson County

Apples and pears are commonly plagued by fire blight, a bacterial disease that can severely damage blossoms, fruit, fruit spurs, twigs, and branches. Gardeners sometimes face this disease in home orchards and occasionally on other ornamental plants when humidity levels are high and temperatures are above 60 degrees.

If you suspect your plants may have this disease, look first for water-soaked, wilted, or brown to black blossoms. This normally is the first sign that appears early in the season. Eventually, twigs and water sprouts will become wilted at their tips and resemble a shepherd's crook in appearance. Limb and trunk blight will also occur when the bacteria move down into larger branches or the trunk.

This bacterium, *Erwinia amylovora*, overwinters in diseased tissue within the tree. In the spring, bacteria are carried by wind, rain, and insects to natural openings in the flowers, stomata in the leaves, and wounds. Although control of this disease may be difficult for homeowners, many practices help reduce the severity of fire blight. Look for resistant varieties at planting time and prune out all blighted twigs before growth starts in the spring. Be sure to disinfect your pruners with a diluted bleach-and-water mixture (one part bleach to 10 parts water) after each cut.

What are the caterpillars that show up in my landscape in early fall?

By Karen Neill, Guilford County

There are a few possibilities.

One caterpillar, the fall cankerworm, plagues maple and oak trees in the Charlotte area. Control strategies for fall cankerworms involve trunk banding to trap female moths in the fall and possibly applying pesticide sprays containing *Bacillus thuringiensis* (Bt) or other foliage protectors in the spring. You can see a banding photo at www.forestryimages.org/images/768x512/4723057.jpg.

Another caterpillar that affects oaks is the orange-striped oakworm. It starts as a tiny green caterpillar and eventually grows into a black caterpillar with yellow or orange stripes running lengthwise along its body. These caterpillars have a prominent pair of spines or slender horns sticking up behind the head. They sometimes defoliate small trees completely by midsummer. Control is complicated by the size of many of the infested trees. Fortunately, late-summer defoliations are much less damaging to the health of trees than early-spring defoliations. In most cases, it is probably better to rely on birds, diseases, and parasites to lower the population next year.

The fall webworm is yet another caterpillar that shows up in landscape trees. It starts building its web at the branch tip and enlarges it to encompass fresh, green leaves until the web may be two to three feet long. Fall webworms are best managed by pulling down the webs and destroying the caterpillars if the webs are within reach of a pole. If they are within reach of a sprayer, use a Bt product when the caterpillars are small.

What's the best way to discourage snakes from taking up residence around my home?

By Peggy Drechsler, Gaston County

The best way to discourage them is to control rodents, the diet of choice for snakes. Trim the lower branches of shrubs, mow your grass regularly to keep it short, and remove brush, leaf piles, logs, boards, and other hiding places that attract both rodents and snakes. Place all rodent food sources such as grass seed, bird food, flower bulbs, and pet food in secure metal containers. Clean up pet feeding areas after each meal.

Cooperative Extension Centers often receive calls from citizens about repelling snakes. It turns out that many of the control methods some people believe will work are simply myths or old wives' tales.

Mothballs or flakes (composed of naphthalene or paradichlorobenzene) will not deter a snake hunting mice or seeking a cool hiding place. Mothballs are a potential poisoning hazard to small children and pets.

Sulfur will not repel snakes. If a snake crosses a sulfur barrier, sulfur will become embedded under the scales and cause irritation, potentially making an otherwise harmless snake ill tempered and aggressive.

Lime has never proven effective at repelling snakes. When hydrated lime, also called quicklime, encounters moisture, it can cause severe skin burns to wildlife, pets, and people.

How can I get rid of English ivy?

By Diane Turner, Henderson County

English ivy can be an unruly evergreen climbing vine that attaches to the bark of trees, brickwork, and other surfaces around homes. Although it is now considered to be invasive throughout North Carolina and the United States, it is still a popular landscape plant choice. In trying to control English ivy, standard glyphosate products sold at home improvement stores will likely be too diluted to be effective. Look for stronger glyphosate products sold under the brand names Accord, Rodeo, and Roundup® PRO Concentrate.

One of the options is applying the chemical to freshly cut stems. The vines will eventually die with time. If the remaining vines are climbing into trees, they must be removed or they will look quite unsightly.

Another method is foliar application of glyphosate with a nonionic surfactant added at the rate of 0.5 to 1.0 percent. It's best to use this technique in the spring when new leaves emerge.

The final removal option is for those with strong backs and lots of patience. Manual removal involves repeatedly cutting off the vines at ground level until all energy from the root system is exhausted. Keep in mind that this option will likely result in vigorous regrowth. Dedication is required to ensure long-term control.

What's the best way to control scales on shrubs?

By Donald Breedlove, Iredell County

If your landscape includes camellias, hollies, or euonymus shrubs, chances are scale insects will be a problem from time to time. The adults often attach to leaves and branches, where they suck plant sap and reproduce, meaning many small, immature insects will soon join them. Their cover is also a good shield against predators and insecticides. Scales are not highly visible because they prefer shady areas such as the inside of a plant's canopy and the undersides of leaves. On hollies, for example, gardeners may overlook these insects but see evidence such as a black coating on the leaves. This is called sooty mold, which can grow on the honeydew that some scales secrete.

Horticultural oil is recommended throughout the year except when the foliage is new and tender. When plants are under drought stress, it's best to avoid spraying. The best way to tackle the problem is to apply the oil multiple times to smother or suffocate the pests. It is advisable to wait 10 to 14 days between applications in cool weather and seven to 10 days when it is warm. Pruning heavily infested branches before treatments will reduce the population and allow for better contact. The best control will be obtained with a good coating of oil over the scale-infested portion of the plant. Avoid overapplication, as it will kill the natural predators of scales.

How can I keep voles from eating my bulbs?

By Mike Wilder, Nash County

Missing or partially eaten bulbs indicate the culprits are below ground. This, along with evidence of tunnels 1½ inches in diameter, indicates pine voles have invaded your yard. Not only do pine voles eat bulbs, they feed on the roots of shrubs and trees, either killing or subjecting them to disease and insect injury. Pine voles may spend their entire lives below ground within a 1,000-square-foot area. They also are known to come above ground to feed at night. Since they have a gestation period of 24 days, an average litter size of three, and a production of four to six litters per year, control is challenging. But it is not impossible.

Before taking control measures, use the "apple sign test" to confirm their presence and location. This requires establishing bait stations consisting of shingles or boards placed over vole holes or runways at 15-foot intervals. Five days later, place a ½-inch cube of apple under each board or shingle. If the cubes have been chewed or disappear within 24 hours, you'll know where in the landscape to set mousetraps or apply poison bait.

To trap pine voles, excavate enough of the runway to allow placing a mousetrap crosswise to the run. Cover the trap with a bent shingle and bait it with a small bit of apple. The alternative to trapping is using chlorophacinone pellets (Rozol). Place two tablespoons of pellets under the runway covers and repeat in 21 days. Another 21 days later, check for remaining voles with another apple sign test. Be patient and vigilant. These virtues and the procedures described above will prove a successful combination.

How can I keep deer from eating my plants?
By Ben Dungan, Gaston County

Deer invasions continue to be a problem for home gardeners. There are more deer today than ever, and they adapt very well to suburban living. Control measures include fencing, repellents, and plants that are deer resistant.

When considering fencing as an option, the size of the fence is crucial. If you choose a woven fence, nine feet is considered adequate. However, a six-foot solid fence will also deter deer, as it prevents them from seeing where they are jumping. A two-strand fence or a single-strand electric fence will work well if the deer population in the area is light.

Repellents also may work well. Spray these chemical products on the plants you don't want deer to eat. Reapply them after big rains and on new plant growth. Hanging bars of scented soap from tree branches or distributing human hair or other items containing human smells also serve as deterrents if the deer population is small. However, just as with repellents, you must reapply or replace the materials after rainfall and new growth for them to be effective.

For a list of deer-resistant plants, contact your county Cooperative Extension Center or visit www.ces.ncsu.edu/depts/hort/hil/pdf/hil-575.pdf.

How can I get rid of slugs in my flower beds?
By Darrell Blackwelder, Rowan County

One of the most successful ways to control slugs is to remove their habitat. Their favorite locations are usually in moist, shady areas of the garden. Remove any debris that provides a hiding place. Alternately, trapping slugs under boards or overturned flowerpots is an effective control method. Keep the traps in the garden several days to allow slugs to find them. Handpicking is another alternative, especially during the evening and early-morning hours.

Add mulch that slugs don't like. Cedar chips, pine needles, and rinsed, crushed eggshells often repel slugs due to either odor, resin, or sharp edges. Many hosta growers report remarkable success with pine needles that are applied two to three inches thick.

Another control method is to use beer as bait. Use margarine tubs with plastic lids. Cut holes into the sides and bury the tubs up to the holes. This prevents animals from discovering the beer and draining the bait. Slugs are attracted to the yeast smell. They drown when they crawl into the containers.

Slug baits are available at garden centers and other retail outlets. Most of the products contain metaldehyde or methiocarb, which are either pelletized or powdered. Pelletized baits tend to provide longer residual than powdered forms. Most baits need to be moist in order to attract slugs. Baits may be attractive to some pets, so use them with caution. Make sure you read and follow all instructions.

Are old pesticides still usable?
By Diane Turner, Henderson County

Gardeners who have pesticides from a few seasons back often wonder if they are still usable. The biological efficacy of pesticides gradually decreases with time, regardless of how the products are stored. Although nearly all chemicals have a limited shelf life, proper storage will increase the amount of time pesticides can be used. If they are stored under dry, cool conditions, out of direct sunlight, and with the containers properly closed, they should retain their effectiveness for several years. Extreme heat or freezing temperatures will reduce the effectiveness of pesticides.

The best way to dispose of pesticides is to use them while they are still good, always following the label instructions. Never use chemicals that have undergone physical changes such as forming lumps, discoloring, or separating. Never use a chemical that has been suspended or canceled or does not have a label. If you are unsure of the name of a pesticide, contact your local Cooperative Extension Center for help in identifying the product. Your Cooperative Extension Center also can advise you on where to take old pesticides for disposal.

What are those little white flying insects underneath my petunia leaves?
By Amy-Lynn Albertson, Davidson County

Whiteflies are one of the most common greenhouse pests on bedding plants and other potted flowering crops. Whiteflies are in the same order as aphids, mealybugs, and scales. They have sucking mouth parts. Many are carriers of plant pathogens. They often are present in great numbers on the undersides of leaves and may be abundant on greenhouse plants and houseplants.

They lay their eggs on the undersides of leaves. In four to 12 days, the eggs hatch into active, six-legged crawlers. The crawlers insert their beaks into plant leaves and start sucking sap. After the first molt, they look like small scales. After the second molt, the insects become pupae. Finally, the four-winged adults leave the pupal skins.

Whiteflies secrete honeydew, which supports the sooty-mold fungus. They may be controlled with insecticidal soaps and horticultural oils.

Trees

How can I protect my trees during construction?
By David Barkley, Brunswick County

Trees damaged by construction don't always show the effects until after the builders have moved on. Significant damage to the roots often results in structural failure that may show up 10 to 20 years later. Other construction injuries are quite noticeable and may affect the trees for years to come.

Grading equipment and weedeaters injure trees, resulting in wood decay.
Toby Bost

It is important to protect trees throughout the entire construction phase. Obvious injuries include broken limbs, stripped bark, and split trunks. But other, more indirect injuries are not so easily noticed. They include soil compaction, changes in soil drainage or soil fertility (or both), and deposits of fill materials that affect future growth.

Homeowners need to manage construction impact. They should consult a professional to assess their trees prior to the beginning of the job. Plans should include accurate and precise locations for the trunks, crowns, and major soil areas colonized by the roots. Construction danger zones and tree protection zones should be defined. Adequate space should be provided for these areas. A rule of thumb is to allow one foot from the base of the trunk for every inch of trunk diameter; the larger the space, the better.

During construction, strive to minimize damage and eliminate potential problems. Limit construction machine access, material storage, the rinsing of potential contaminates, vehicle parking, and site-office location. It may be necessary to create barriers by placing fences or retaining walls to protect root zones. You can ensure your trees' future by limiting access, mulching high-traffic areas, and minimizing soil disturbance.

How can I protect tender plants from winter injury?

By Mike Wilder, Nash County

November often brings sudden drops in temperature and frosts that can be deadly to tender plants. Sunscald, frost heaving, and desiccation are other concerns. Tender plants are those that are incapable of resisting these factors. Most houseplants, annuals, many herbs, and some landscape plants are considered tender.

The "easy" solution is to bring plants indoors or into a greenhouse before temperatures fall below 40° F. Remember to inspect and treat for pests before bringing them in. A root drench of mild insecticide solution or warm water will prevent indoor surprises.

If your indoor space is limited or you have no greenhouse, place containerized plants in protected areas, bury them in the ground, or heavily mulch them to avoid injury. Place a barrier of burlap over or around containers and in-ground plants to protect them from winter wind and sun damage.

Plants that are properly watered during dry periods are better equipped to withstand injury than those that are not. Thoroughly water the soil around plants once every two weeks if necessary. Inspect soil moisture after freezes as well. Proper mulching around the bases and over the root zones of plants helps protect the soil from the freezing and thawing that are responsible for heaving. Replant and quickly remulch heaved plants. Wait until spring to determine the extent of injury and the need for replacement.

Should I fertilize my landscape trees?

By David Barkley, Brunswick County

Trees require certain elements to function and grow. For trees growing in forest sites, these elements are usually present in sufficient quantities in the soil. Landscape or urban trees, however, may grow in soils that do not contain sufficient elements for satisfactory growth.

Trees that are not showing symptoms of nutrient deficiency may not require fertilization. Those growing in turf that is fertilized routinely or where grass clippings are left may not require supplemental fertilization. Excess fertilizer can lead to an unnecessary increase in growth; it also may leach into lakes and streams, adversely affecting water quality.

The rate at which to apply fertilizer depends on the age, health, and species of the tree, the form of the fertilizer, and the site conditions. Young trees will benefit, but be careful not to apply too much fertilizer, since it may damage their roots. Older, more established trees may get by without additional fertilizer because of their extensive root systems. Fertilize mature trees after testing the soil; follow report recommendations.

One general recommendation for homeowners is to use a slow-release fertilizer in late spring that will carry the plant through the summer. Avoid late-summer fertilization, since it can promote late growth, which is undesirable before winter.

You can learn more by visiting www.ncstate-plants.net. Click on "Consumer Hort Leaflets."

Whom should I hire to do some tree work?

By David Goforth, Cabarrus County

If you intend to keep the tree, hire an arborist certified by the International Society of Arboriculture (ISA). Ask to see the arborist's card or check his or her name on the ISA website, www.isa–arbor.com. Certification isn't a legal requirement, but it proves an arborist is professional and knowledgeable. This knowledge extends to pruning, fertilization, planting, cabling, bracing, and lightning protection. Arborists also can evaluate a tree to see if it is dangerous. They may prune a tree for various reasons, including raising the crown, reducing danger, shaping the canopy, or reducing conflicts with driveways or houses. Certified arborists use proper pruning techniques to avoid creating hazards.

If you just want to take down a tree, a number of companies can do that. Go to the phone book and get several bids. Make sure the companies have insurance, including workers' compensation, on their employees. Check a few references. Make sure the company you choose has safety equipment and provides training for its employees.

How should I deal with storm-damaged trees?

By Carl Matyac, Orange and Wake Counties

Giving trees "first aid" after a storm can make the difference between helping them survive and losing them. Here are a few simple rules.

Don't do it all yourself. If large limbs are broken or hanging or if high climbing or overhead chain-saw work is needed, it's a job for a professional arborist.

Take safety precautions. Be alert for power lines and hanging branches that look like they're ready to fall.

Remove any broken branches attached to the tree. Prune small branches where

Japanese maple in winter
Todd Lasseigne

they join large ones. Large broken branches should be cut back to the trunk or a main limb. Make clean cuts just outside the branch collar to quicken recovery. Flush cuts are not recommended. Large branches can tear loose during pruning, stripping the bark. That won't happen if you take the following steps.

- Make a partial cut from beneath, several inches away from the trunk.
- Make a second cut from above, several inches out from the first cut, to allow the limb to fall safely.
- Complete the job with a final cut just outside the branch collar, the raised area that surrounds the branch where it joins the trunk.

Repair torn bark. Use a sharp knife to smooth the ragged edges of wounds.

Resist the urge to overprune. Missing branches may cause the tree to look unbalanced or naked. The tree will quickly grow new foliage and return to its natural beauty.

Don't top the tree! Topping (cutting main branches back to stubs) is one of the worst things you can do to a tree.

Chapter 6

Tried-and-True and Hot New Plants for Carolina Gardens

North Carolina State University has several plant breeders on its faculty who are introducing new plants to the market on a regular basis. When their efforts are paired with those of our excellent nursery industry, gardeners in this state may as well be in plant heaven. In this chapter, you will no doubt find a new plant you'll want in your garden.

Gardentalk:

"The love of gardening is a seed that once sown never dies."

Gertrude Jekyll

The availability and staying power of newly introduced landscape plants are a bit of an enigma. Nurserymen continually discover new selections of old staples. Many of them are on display at the annual "Green & Growin'" trade shows. Unfortunately, the excitement of the day can be short lived following a visit to your local garden center.

New cultivars, also known in the trade as "hot plants," can take years to reach the market in significant enough quantities to justify the publicity they frequently receive from garden writers. It is expensive—sometimes even cost prohibitive—for nurseries to produce patented plants. On occasion, large wholesale nurseries use sophisticated micropropagation to ramp up production, then make a big media blitz with the goods in inventory. A few examples are the recent introductions of the sensational Knock Out® roses, Encore® azaleas, and Endless Summer™ hydrangeas.

The gardening public's insatiable thirst for new ornamentals drives the industry. People have warmed up to the notion of finding something colorful and intriguing with every foray to large garden centers. Customers can become enamored of the convenience of purchasing specialty herbaceous perennial collections known by names like Stepables®, Proven Winners®, and Fall Magic®.

Indeed, the garden marketplace is both diverse and dynamic. New plants of exotic parentage arrive in America yearly from around the globe. Many introductions have great utility in factors such as drought or shade tolerance. Thanks to research and enhanced breeding technology, more and more compact cultivars serve urban gardeners who have limited space.

Most new cultivars found in our state or promoted in gardening books and magazines may have lesser-known selections of equal or better quality available. The Internet is a good tool for locating new plants, as many nurseries have websites that list new cultivars. In addition, the horticultural industry has numerous trade directories known as locator guides that are quite helpful. Nursery associations also are willing to assist in finding new plant introductions.

'Lo & Behold'™ dwarf butterfly bush
Toby Bost

North Carolina Cooperative Extension, in cooperation with the North Carolina Nursery and Landscape Association, provides annual updates of superior plant releases via the "Showstopper Plants" marketing program. Cooperative Extension agents cooperate with nurserymen to ensure that their featured plants are available in sufficient quantities in time for the annual home-and-garden shows. Look for Successful Gardener Learning Centers or other booths hosted by Cooperative Extension horticulture agents and Master Gardeners at these shows for a copy of the latest "Showstopper Plants" list.

Cooperative Extension, the North Carolina Division of Forest Resources, and myriad arboreta and botanical gardens across the state post plant lists on their websites. Visit these sites and talk with horticulturists before buying any "hot plant" to confirm that the introduction is adapted to your county's climate and soil conditions. Ask generic questions, too. Is the plant pest prone, invasive, susceptible to deer browsing, self-sowing, or high maintenance? Even if your space is limited, you can choose most any dwarf variety for a container garden.

Contrary to popular belief, native plants cannot be planted throughout all our geographic regions, so do a bit of homework before purchasing and installing new plants. Choose the plant for the site. That's sage advice to keep in mind for any plant purchase.

While it is impossible to provide an exhaustive list of all the great new plants found across the South, we have attempted, with the help of a few plantsmen, to ferret out an offering of interesting taxa including promising upstarts and not-so-cutting-edge mainstays. We thank the staffs at Frank's Perennial Borders, Hawksridge Farms, Inc., L. A. Reynolds Garden Showcase, the North Carolina Nursery and Landscape Association, Old Courthouse Nursery, Piedmont Carolina Nursery, and Tinga Nursery for their assistance.

"Hot Plants" List

Flowering Deciduous Shrubs

Abelia × *grandiflora* 'Kaleidoscope' PP#16988 and *A.* 'Mardi Gras' PP#15203 (variegated abelia)
Buddleia × 'Blue Chip' PP#19991 (Lo & Behold™) and *B.* 'Miss Ruby' PPAF (dwarf buddleia)*
Chaenomeles × 'Scarlet Storm' (hybrid flowering quince)*
Edgeworthia chrysantha (paperbush)
Heptacodium miconioides (seven-sons flower)
Hydrangea arborescens 'Annabelle' (white mountain hydrangea)
Hydrangea arborescens 'NCHA1' Invincibelle Spirit® PPAF (pink mountain hydrangea)*
Hydrangea macrophylla 'Endless Summer' PP#15298 and 'Penny Mac' (bigleaf hydrangea)
Hydrangea paniculata 'Limelight' and *H.* 'Tardiva' (panicle hydrangea)
Rosa × 'Radrazz' and 'Sunny' Knock Out® PPAF; 'Rainbow' PP#17436; and 'Double' Knock Out® PP#16202 (Knock Out® landscape roses)
Viburnum × *carlcephalum* (fragrant sterile snowball)

Flowering Evergreen Shrubs

Rhododendron × *hybrida* Encore® (Encore® azaleas)
Camellia sasanqua 'Yuletide' (sasanqua camellia)
Gardenia 'Crown Jewel' PP#19896, 'Kleim's Hardy', and 'Frost Proof'
Loropetalum chinense 'Ever Red Sunset'™, 'Carolina Moonlight' PP#18977, and 'Baruma' (Chinese fringe-flower)

Gardenia 'Crown Jewel'
Piedmont Carolina Nursery

Abelia 'Kaleidoscope'
Piedmont Carolina Nursery

Evergreen Shrubs

Buxus microphylla 'Faulkner'; *Buxus* × 'Green Velvet'; *Buxus* × 'Green Beauty' (boxwood)
Cephalotaxus drupacea 'Prostrata' (Japanese plum yew)
Ilex crenata 'Sky Pencil' (Japanese holly)
Ilex × 'Conaf' Oakleaf™ PP#9487 and *Ilex* × 'Conive' Festive™ PP9498 (red holly)
Ligustrum japonicum 'East Bay' (compact privet)
Nandina domestica 'Gulf Stream' (nandina)
Pittosporum tobira 'Wheeler's Dwarf' and 'Louisiana Dwarf' (dwarf pittosporum)
Prunus laurocerasus 'Majestic Jade' (cherry laurel)
Rhaphiolepis umbellata 'Minor' Gulf Green ™ (dwarf yeddo hawthorn)
Rhododendron hybrida 'Chionoides' (hybrid rhododendron)

Screening Shrubs

Thuja × 'Steeplechase' PP#16094 (western red cedar)
Viburnum awabuki 'Chindo' (viburnum)

Shade Shrubs

Aucuba japonica 'Rozannie' (dwarf green aucuba)
Leucothoe populifolia (Florida leucothoe)
Pieris japonica 'Katsura'® PP#15452 (pieris)

Pieris 'Katsura'®
Piedmont Carolina Nursery

Flowering Vines

Campsis × 'Mme. Galen' (Chinese trumpetvine)
Wisteria 'Amethyst Falls' (native wisteria)

Herbaceous Perennials

Sun Perennials

Agastache foeniculum 'Tutti Frutti' (anise hyssop)
Heuchera villosa 'Caramel' (coralbell)
Nepeta cataria 'Walker's Low' (catmint)
Phlox paniculata 'Nora Leigh' (variegated garden phlox)
Sedum cauticola 'Lidakense' and 'Angelina' (spreading sedum)

Shade Perennials

Helleborus × *hybridus* 'Ivory Prince' (hellebore/Lenten rose)
Pulmonaria longifolia 'Diana Clare' (longleaf lungwort)

Grasses

Lomandra longifolia 'Breeze'™ PPN#15420 (breeze grass)

Specimen Flowering Trees

Amelanchier × *grandiflora* 'Autumn Brilliance'® (serviceberry)
Betula nigra 'Summer Cascade' PP#15105 (weeping river birch)
Cercis canadensis 'Hearts of Gold' PP#17740 (eastern redbud)
Cercis 'Ruby Falls' PPAF (weeping redbud)*
Cercis texensis 'Traveller' PP#8640 (Texas redbud)
Cornus × *hybrida* 'Appalachian Spring' (hybrid flowering dogwood)
Magnolia 'Katy-O' (pink sweetbay magnolia)
Styrax japonicus 'Emerald Pagoda' (snowbell)

* New cultivars from North Carolina State University

New Cultivars from North Carolina State University

Researchers and plant breeders from North Carolina State University have introduced some lovely plants that have garnered widespread acclaim in the plant world. Here are some recent introductions worth considering for your garden.

- A new variety of hydrangea developed by North Carolina State horticulturist Dr. Thomas G. Ranney has gardeners thinking pink. *Hydrangea arborescens* 'HCHA1' Invincibelle Spirit® PPAF is the first pink mountain hydrangea to be made available to the public. The plant is a hybrid of the white-flowered *Hydrangea arborescens* mountain hydrangea known as 'Annabelle'. Invincibelle® holds its pink color. This native species is tough, adaptable, impervious to cold, and heat tolerant. It can be grown in full sun to partial shade and is adaptable to many soil types, producing months of beautiful pink flowers regardless of soil pH. It has been praised as the "most exciting development in hydrangeas since 1988." Another pink-colored plus is that the flowering-shrubs brand Proven Winners® Color Choice® will donate a dollar from each purchase of Invincibelle® Spirit hydrangea to the Breast Cancer Research Foundation.

- New redbud trees developed by North Carolina State horticulturist Dr. Dennis J. Werner will be available for the first time in the spring of 2011. *Cercis* 'Ruby Falls' is the first redbud with purple leaves and a weeping form. *C.* 'Merlot' has purple leaves similar to 'Forest Pansy', but its form is vase shaped and the trees tend to be shorter and more compact with denser branches. 'Merlot' is a hybrid of two wild redbuds—the eastern redbud and the Texas redbud. Texas redbuds tend to be heat and drought tolerant. Werner expects 'Merlot' to have these characteristics and hold up well during hot summers. A third redbud, 'Whitewater', has a weeping habit

Variegated sweetgum
Toby Bost

Chocolate mimosa
Toby Bost

and unusual variegated leaves. It should follow the other two in propagation by about a year. Look for it beginning in the spring of 2012.

- Dr. Werner has also developed and introduced a dwarf butterfly bush, or buddleia. Lo & Behold™ 'Blue Chip' was named the best new plant for 2009 and received a gold medal at the Salon du Vegetal Nursery Show in France. It has a dense, compact growth habit. It is typically two to three feet in height and width, which is quite different from the large, gangly plants that often need at least six feet of space in the landscape. 'Blue Chip' is unlikely to produce unwanted seedlings; this also differentiates it from typical buddleias, which can be somewhat invasive. 'Blue Chip' is the first of a number of butterfly bushes that are being developed in a trademarked series known as Lo & Behold and released to retailers by Proven Winners® ColorChoice®. *Buddleia* 'Miss Ruby' has extremely bright pink flowers. More vigorous than 'Blue Chip', it was also released by Proven Winners® ColorChoice®.

Top 10 Performers from the North Carolina Urban Tree Evaluation Study*

Cornus mas 'Spring Glow' (corneliancherry dogwood)
Chionanthus retusus (Chinese fringe)
Acer truncatum × *platanoides* 'Norwegian Sunset' (red maple)
Acer truncatum × *platanoides* 'Pacific Sunset' (red maple)
Acer × *freemanii* 'Jeffersred' Autumn Blaze® (red maple)
Liquidambar styraciflua 'Rotundiloba' (fruitless sweetgum)
Magnolia × 'Wada's Memory' (deciduous or tulip tree magnolia)
Ulmus parvifolia (lacebark elm)
Prunus × *bliriana* (bliriana plum)
Prunus serrulata 'Royal Burgundy' (Japanese flowering cherry)

* The availability of these tree varieties is limited.

North Carolina Cooperative Extension County Centers

For links to all the Cooperative Extension County Centers, visit www.ces.ncsu.edu. Address all faxes to Cooperative Extension Service.

Alamance County Center
209-C N. Graham-Hopedale Rd.
Burlington, N.C. 27217
336-570-6740
336-570-6689 (fax)

Alexander County Center
376 First Ave. S.W.
Taylorsville, N.C. 28681
828-632-4451
828-632-7533 (fax)

Alleghany County Center
90 South Main St.
Sparta, N.C. 28675
336-372-5597
336-372-2279 (fax)

Anson County Center
501 McLaurin St., Box 633
Wadesboro, N.C. 28170
704-694-2915
704-694-2248 (fax)

Ashe County Center
134 Government Circle, Suite 202
Jefferson, N.C. 28640
336-846-5850
336-846-5882 (fax)

Avery County Center
805 Cranberry St.
Newland, N.C. 28657
828-733-8270
828-733-8293 (fax)

Beaufort County Center
155A Airport Rd.
Washington, N.C. 27889
252-946-0111
252-975-5887 (fax)

Bertie County Center
106 Dundee St.
Windsor, N.C. 27983
252-794-5317
252-794-5375 (fax)

Bladen County Center
450 Smith Circle Dr.
Elizabethtown, N.C. 28337
910-862-4591
910-862-6939 (fax)

Brunswick County Center
25 Referendum Dr.
Bolivia, N.C. 28422
910-253-2610
910-253-2612 (fax)

Buncombe County Center
94 Coxe Ave.
Asheville, N.C. 28801
828-255-5522
828-255-5202 (fax)

Burke County Center
130 Ammons Dr., Suite 2
Morganton, N.C. 28655
828-439-4460
828-439-4468 (fax)

Cabarrus County Center
715 Cabarrus Ave. W., Box 387
Concord, N.C. 28027
704-920-3310
704-920-3323 (fax)

Caldwell County Center
120 Hospital Ave. N.E., Suite 1
Lenoir, N.C. 28645
828-757-1290
828-757-1251 (fax)

Camden County Center
120 N.C. 343 N.
Camden, N.C. 27921
252-338-1919
252-338-0277 (fax)

Carteret County Center
303 College Circle
Morehead City, N.C. 28557
252-222-6352
252-222-6361 (fax)

Caswell County Center
Agricultural Building, 126 Court Sq.
Yanceyville, N.C. 27379
336-694-4158
336-694-5930 (fax)

Catawba County Center
1175 S. Brady Ave., Box 389
Newton, N.C. 28658
828-465-8240
828-465-8428 (fax)

Chatham County Center
45 South St., Box 279
Pittsboro, N.C. 27312
919-542-8202
919-542-8246 (fax)

Cherokee County Center
39 Peachtree St., Suite 103
Murphy, N.C. 28906
828-837-2917
828-837-2172 (fax)

Cherokee Reservation Center
876 Acquoni Rd.
Cherokee, N.C. 28719
828-554-6931
828-497-6811 (fax)

Chowan County Center
730 N. Granville St., Suite A
Edenton, N.C. 27932
252-482-6585
252-482-6590 (fax)

Clay County Center
36 Davis Loop, Suite 1
Hayesville, N.C. 28904
828-389-6305
828-389-8872 (fax)

Cleveland County Center
130 S. Post Rd., Suite 1
Shelby, N.C. 28152
704-482-4365
704-480-6484 (fax)

Columbus County Center
45 Government Complex Rd., Suite A.
Whiteville, N.C. 28472
910-640-6605
910-642-6315 (fax)

Craven County Center
300 Industrial Dr.
New Bern, N.C. 28562
252-633-1477
252-633-2120 (fax)

Cumberland County Center
301 E. Mountain Dr.
Fayetteville, N.C. 28306-3422
910-321-6860
910-321-6883 (fax)

Currituck County Center
120 Community Way
Barco, N.C. 27917
252-232-2261
252-453-2782 (fax)

Dare County Center
517 Budleigh St.
Manteo, N.C. 27954
252-473-4290
252-473-3106 (fax)

Davidson County Center
301 E. Center St.
Lexington, N.C. 27292
336-242-2080
336-249-7300 (fax)

Davie County Center
180 S. Main St.
Mocksville, N.C. 27028
336-753-6100
336-751-1184 (fax)

Duplin County Center
165 Agriculture Dr.
Kenansville, N.C. 28349
910-296-2143
910-296-2191 (fax)

Durham County Center
721 Foster Rd.
Durham, N.C. 27701
919-560-0525
919-560-0530 (fax)

Edgecombe County Center
201 Saint Andrews St.
Tarboro, N.C. 27886
252-641-7827
252-641-7831 (fax)

Forsyth County Center
1450 Fairchild Rd.
Winston-Salem, N.C. 27105
336-703-2850
336-767-3557 (fax)

Franklin County Center
103 S. Bickett Blvd.
Louisburg, N.C. 27549
919-496-3344
919-496-0222 (fax)

Gaston County Center
1303 Dallas-Cherryville Hwy.
Dallas, N.C. 28034
704-922-0301
704-922-2140 (fax)

Gates County Center
112 Court St.
Gatesville, N.C. 27938
252-357-1400
252-357-1167 (fax)

Graham County Center
39 S. Main St.
Robbinsville, N.C. 28771
828-479-7979
828-479-2000 (fax)

Granville County Center
208 Wall St.
Oxford, N.C. 27565
919-603-1350
919-603-0268 (fax)

Greene County Center
229 Kingold Blvd., Suite E
Snow Hill, N.C. 28580
252-747-5831
252-747-3884 (fax)

Guilford County Center
3309 Burlington Rd.
Greensboro, N.C. 27405
336-375-5876
336-375-2295 (fax)

Halifax County Center
359 Ferrell Ln.
Halifax, N.C. 27839
252-583-5161
252-583-1683 (fax)

Harnett County Center
126 Alexander Dr.
Lillington, N.C. 27546
910-893-7530
910-893-7539 (fax)

Haywood County Center
589 Raccoon Rd., Suite 118
Waynesville, N.C. 28786
828-456-3575
828-452-0289 (fax)

Henderson County Center
740 Glover St.
Hendersonville, N.C. 28792
828-697-4891
828-697-4581 (fax)

Hertford County Center
301 W. Tryon St., Box 188
Winton, N.C. 27986
252-358-7822
252-358-7880 (fax)

Hoke County Center
116 W. Prospect Ave.
Raeford, N.C. 28376
910-875-3461
910-875-9044 (fax)

Hyde County Center
30 Oyster Creek Rd.
Swan Quarter, N.C. 27885
252-926-4486
252-926-4490 (fax)

Iredell County Center
444 Bristol Dr.
Statesville, N.C. 28677
704-873-0507
704-878-3164 (fax)

Jackson County Center
538 Scotts Creek Rd., Suite 205
Sylva, N.C. 28779
828-586-4009
828-586-5509 (fax)

Johnston County Center
2736 N.C. 210
Smithfield, N.C. 27577
919-989-5380
919-934-2698 (fax)

Jones County Center
110 S. Market St.
Trenton, N.C. 28585
252-448-9621
252-448-1243 (fax)

Lee County Center
2420 Tramway Rd.
Sanford, N.C. 27332
919-775-5624
919-775-1302 (fax)

Lenoir County Center
1791 Hwy. 11/55
Kinston, N.C. 28504
252-527-2191
252-527-1290 (fax)

Lincoln County Center
115 W. Main St.
Lincolnton, N.C. 28092
704-736-8452
704-736-8828 (fax)

Macon County Center
193 Thomas Heights Rd.
Franklin, N.C. 28734
828-349-2046
828-349-2405 (fax)

Madison County Center
258 Carolina Ln.
Marshall, N.C. 28753
828-649-2411
828-649-2020 (fax)

Martin County Center
104 Kehukee Park Rd.
Williamston, N.C. 27892
252-789-4370
252-789-4389 (fax)

McDowell County Center
60 E. Court St.
Marion, N.C. 28752
828-652-7874
828-652-8104 (fax)

Mecklenburg County Center
1418 Armory Dr.
Charlotte, N.C. 28204
704-336-2082
704-336-6876 (fax)

Mitchell County Center
10 S. Mitchell Ave., Box 366
Bakersville, N.C. 28705
828-688-4811
828-688-2051 (fax)

Montgomery County Center
203 W. Main St.
Troy, N.C. 27371
910-576-6011
910-576-2635 (fax)

Moore County Center
707 Pinehurst Ave.
Carthage, N.C. 28327
910-947-3188
910-947-1494 (fax)

Nash County Center
1006 Eastern Ave., Room 102
Nashville, N.C. 27856
252-459-9810
252-459-9850 (fax)

New Hanover County Center
6206 Oleander Dr.
Wilmington, N.C. 28403-3822
910-798-7660
910-798-7678 (fax)

Northampton County Center
9495 N.C. 305
Jackson, N.C. 27845
252-534-2831
252-534-1827 (fax)

Onslow County Center
4024 Richlands Hwy.
Jacksonville, N.C. 28540
910-455-5873
910-455-0977 (fax)

Orange County Center
306 E. Revere Rd.
Hillsborough, N.C. 27278
919-245-2050
919-644-3067 (fax)

Pamlico County Center
13451 N.C. 55
Alliance, N.C. 28509
252-745-4121
252-745-5082 (fax)

Pasquotank County Center
1209 McPherson St.
Elizabeth City, N.C. 27909
252-338-3954
252-338-6442 (fax)

Pender County Center
801 S. Walker St.
Burgaw, N.C. 28425
910-259-1235
910-259-1291 (fax)

Perquimans County Center
601-A S. Edenton Rd.
Hertford, N.C. 27944
252-426-5428
252-426-1646 (fax)

Person County Center
304 S. Morgan St., Room 123
Roxboro, N.C. 27573
336-599-1195
336-598-0272 (fax)

Pitt County Center
403 Government Circle, Suite 2
Greenville, N.C. 27834
252-902-1700
252-757-1456 (fax)

Polk County Center
60 Gibson St.
Columbus, N.C. 28722
828-894-8218
828-894-5693 (fax)

Randolph County Center
112 W. Walker Ave.
Asheboro, N.C. 27203
336-318-6000
336-318-6011 (fax)

Richmond County Center
123 Caroline St., Suite 100
Rockingham, N.C. 28379
910-997-8255
910-997-8257 (fax)

Robeson County Center
O. P. Owens Agriculture Center
455 Caton Rd., Box 2280
Lumberton, N.C. 28360
910-671-3276
910-671-6278 (fax)

Rockingham County Center
525 N.C. 65, Suite 200
Reidsville, N.C. 27320-8861
336-342-8230
336-342-8242 (fax)

Rowan County Center
2727-A Old Concord Rd.
Salisbury, N.C. 28146
704-216-8970
704-216-8995 (fax)

Rutherford County Center
193 Callahan-Koon Rd., Suite 164
Spindale, N.C. 28160
828-287-6011
828-288-4036 (fax)

Sampson County Center
55 Agriculture Pl.
Clinton, N.C. 28328
910-592-7161
910-592-9513 (fax)

Scotland County Center
231 E. Cronly St., Suite 800
Laurinburg, N.C. 28352
910-277-2422
910-277-2426 (fax)

Stanly County Center
26032-E Newt Rd.
Albemarle, N.C. 28001
704-983-3987
704-983-3303 (fax)

Stokes County Center
700 N. Main St.
Danbury, N.C. 27016-0460
336-593-8179
336-593-8790 (fax)

Surry County Center
210 N. Main St.
Dobson, N.C. 27017
336-401-8025
336-401-8048 (fax)

Swain County Center
60 Almond School Rd.
Bryson City, N.C. 28713
828-488-3848
828-488-3575 (fax)

Transylvania County Center
98 E. Morgan St.
Brevard, N.C. 28712
828-884-3109
828-884-3142 (fax)

Tyrrell County Center
407 Martha St.
Columbia, N.C. 27925
252-796-1581
252-796-2881 (fax)

Union County Center
3230-D Presson Rd.
Monroe, N.C. 28112
704-283-3801
704-283-3734 (fax)

Vance County Center
305 Young St.
Henderson, N.C. 27536
252-438-8188
252-492-3830 (fax)

Wake County Center
4001-E Carya Dr.
Raleigh, N.C. 27610
919-250-1100
919-250-1097 (fax)

Warren County Center
158 Rafters Ln.
Warrenton, N.C. 27589
252-257-3640
252-257-5616 (fax)

Washington County Center
128 E. Water St.
Plymouth, N.C. 27962
252-793-2163
252-793-1562 (fax)

Watauga County Center
971 W. King St.
Boone, N.C. 28607
828-264-3061
828-264-3067 (fax)

Wayne County Center
208 W. Chestnut St.
Goldsboro, N.C. 27533
919-731-1521
919-731-1511 (fax)

Wilkes County Center
201 Curtis Bridge Rd., Suite A
Wilkesboro, N.C. 28697
336-651-7331
336-651-7516 (fax)

Wilson County Center
1806 S.W. Goldsboro St.
Wilson, N.C. 27893
252-237-0111
252-237-0114 (fax)

Yadkin County Center
209 E. Elm St.
Yadkinville, N.C. 27055
336-679-2061
336-679-3088 (fax)

Yancey County Center
10 Orchard Dr.
Burnsville, N.C. 28714
828-682-6186
828-682-7680 (fax)

Plant Index

Index